# Man in the Modern Novel

# Man in the Modern Novel

*John Edward Hardy*

Seattle and London: *University of Washington Press*

A substitute for all the gods:
This self, not that gold self aloft,

Alone, one's shadow magnified,
Lord of the body, looking down . . .

*The Man with the Blue Guitar,* Wallace Stevens

# Author's Note

This book has been many times begun, and twice finished. It is difficult to date its actual completion. For the most part the essays are the result of a series of lectures I gave during the academic year 1959–60 at the American Institute of the University of Munich—where the situation in the German Hörsaal obliged me somewhat to formalize the kind of barely audible musings over a text with which in the years before I had entertained my smaller, more indulgent classes at the University of Notre Dame.

To the Fulbright Commission, therefore, and to both the universities, my thanks are due for the Munich sojourn. I would especially acknowledge the generous renewal of my grant, and leave of absence from Notre Dame for a second year, during which time, at a convenient aesthetic distance from the linguistic community of the novels themselves, and over long weekends in the incomparable quiet and beauty of a Bavarian village, I was able to reshape the lecture materials into the chapters of this book.

Those of my students, both at Munich and at Notre Dame, who have been especially helpful in the classroom testing of my ideas, know who they are.

The originality of the essays is in their total statement. Wherever I have been conscious of indebtedness to other critics for specific insights—or aware, simply, of having been anticipated in print—I have tried adequately to acknowledge it. If there are oversights in this regard, they are not intentional.

The essays are placed here in the approximate chronological order of publication of the novels with which they are principally concerned. The essay on *Delta Wedding*, although not a product of the series of lectures mentioned, I have included on the strength of its obvious connection with the central theme of the volume. I am grateful to the *Sewanee Review* for permission to use this essay, and to the *Virginia Quarterly Review* for allowing me to reprint the essay on Robert Penn Warren.

J. E. H.

# Contents

# Man in the Modern Novel

# Introduction

My title for this volume of essays may prove troublesome. Why, or in what sense, *modern?* I mean, making a slight exception for *Heart of Darkness* (of one year, to be exact), the twentieth century. But that is now more than half gone. A good many of my novelists—some of them long since dead—may appear to younger readers already old-fashioned. So that I cannot pretend to a strictly *contemporary* concern.

Nor do I want to. I have wanted to bring the study just nearly up-to-date at one end, and to carry it back at the other just nearly out-of-date. For such is the best one can ever do in defining, chronologically, a literary era. Perhaps especially if it is one's own; but the contemporary of any period, present or past, is quite indefinable.

But I do think there is such a thing as a modern era of the novel in English, that it begins, roughly, at the start of the present century, and that it is characterized by certain recurrent thematic concerns. I may be let off from answering the question of when it is to end; for we are accustomed to excusing even the critic's timidity about assuming the office of prophet. But I shall hardly be able to evade responsibility for the pretensions of my hindsight.

What, then, is the special significance of the theme of the self and the effort to know it, the quest for identity, in the literature of the twentieth century? Assuredly, it is our great preoccupation, in and out of literary studies—the subject, in some aspect, of every other book one picks up these days, by theologian, metaphysician, cultural historian, psychologist, sociologist, *and* literary critic. I claim it, as the integrating theme of my volume, simply as inevitable, in no sense original. The only, I think, unusual thing I have attempted to do in the essays is to insist upon the primary relevance of the theme to certain problems of *form* in the modern novel—thus to resist the abstractionist tendency of most critics who have occupied themselves with it, as if the work of literary art were merely the indifferent vehicle of theme, i.e., document, of psychology, cultural history, or whatever. That is, I have insisted that the formal processes of the novel yield a distinct vision of the human being, available nowhere else. But before turning to consideration of the specifically novelistic, specifically modern, formal problems, it would be well to review, at least briefly, the general historical context.

The theme, indeed, is as old as literature—which is to say, as old as reflective man. Not only the question, crudely, "Who is that man?", that other, the one who did it, what are his lineaments, his name and habitation, even, more subtly, his motives—but the far more perilous "Who am I?", not to be answered by identification of himself as "the one who did it," is Oedipus' question. And before that it was the question of Odysseus, and afterwards of Aeneas. And of Narcissus, and of Io abandoned by Jove. And (anticipated by Job, and the Hero of the New Testament, as well as by the heathen ancients) of the "I" of Augustine, and of Dante.

But we can fairly easily define certain turning points in the history of its formulation. The same theme, in different ages, presents different problems—of artistic expression, of the relationship between expression (or expressive form) and belief. I have spoken of the "heathen ancients." But we can hardly suppose, for example, that there are no significant differences between Homer's and Virgil's ways of putting the question, as well as between either of theirs, let us say, and Dante's. Nor, clearly, could we make very much sense of the Christian Ego if we failed to distinguish between Augustine's version of that, and Dante's. (There is, if nothing else to be reckoned with in the interim, Aquinas.) All of this, not to speak of the subtle dangers of confusing Oedipus Rex with Oedipus at Colonus, or the narrator of the *Vita Nuova* with him, after his great experience, of the *Divina Commedia*. Fortunately, such is not our concern. And we can content ourselves here with remarking only the coming of Christ as one of the major, most obvious crises.

If Jove himself, pursuing the earthling nymph, may not be supposed to have been gnawed by self-doubt (he is, in Ovid's account, ready and eager to identify himself to Io, if not the latter to Juno), Jesus of Nazareth certainly was. The question *is* His Godhead.

The end of the first great age of Christian civilization, approximately at the time of Dante, brings us just as obviously to another turning. We do not currently, as in the recent romantic period of scholarship, hold with unquestioning awe the notion of the medieval artist's anonymity. (Cf. Henry Adams, Gaston Paris, Emile Mâle, Julius Schlosser, etc.—and then, for example, in *European Literature and the Latin Middle Ages*, the skepticism of Ernst Curtius in his excursuses on the problem of whether the medieval writers meant to "sign" their works.) But to whatever extent this humility of purpose, the surrender of the individual intent and design to the cosmic vision, was characteristic of the medieval, creative mind—it works pretty well with architecture, if not with poetry; and surely the fact that modern scholarship felt compelled to "invent" the attitude, whether or not it can be objectively "proved" to have existed, is significant—the self-effacement was the concomitant of a profound self-assurance. Self-identity, in and of the eternally individual soul, the constant and unflagging care and sorrow of God and the Antagonist alike, was so firmly assured that it did not need to be asserted or advertised. If there is one thing that is certain about the difference between the medieval and the modern mind, it is that the former was entirely ignorant of anything resembling our concept of the personality—and, therefore, of the distinction we take for granted, between the soul and the person.

The distinction began to be made, or realized anyway, before it was defined, in the Renaissance. And, for the English-speaking world, its first significant literary embodiment is in the Elizabethan tragedy: especially in Shakespeare. I mean simply that Shakespeare—although his mind was still burdened, of course, by a full freight of medieval ideas, the theology, the ethics, the faculty psychology—was centrally fascinated, in his heroes and villains alike, by the irreducible uniqueness of the person. Here was Shakespeare's essential newness; here, the new mystery and the new mystery play. There was something in the individual, here and now, in this life, in the unique complex of his motivations and sensibilities, that remained forever obscure, unreadable, not to be adequately explained under any of the old categories, ethical and psychological, deriving from the notion of his immortal destiny. We think first of the tragedies: of Lear and Hamlet and Othello, and Iago. But is not the mystery equally there in the histories, in the characters of Henry and Falstaff and Richard? (This common element seems to me, indeed, the principal difficulty in the way of making any really satisfactory distinction between the histories and the tragedies.) Most of the comedies, perhaps, fall outside the pattern and represent a reversion to older modes of thinking. But the "divine comedy" of *The Tempest* is precisely the allegory of this new tragic hero in triumph and prosperity.

But, we begin queasily to recognize Shakespeare's form of the question as very like ours, the problem of our own times. I have already spoken of the medieval as distinguished from the modern mind, and used Shakespeare as illustrative of the latter. And this commonplace division of the ages (medieval history and modern history, Middle English and Modern English) seems to me quite valid, as far as it goes. I am obliged to recognize this larger sense of "modern" as comprehending, or lurking behind, any special adaptation of the term to the problems of the twentieth century; to feel, if the qualifying phrase "as far as it goes" is to have any meaning, if we actually are to go farther than the medieval-modern opposition, that it is time now to start making more refined distinctions; and it is hard to know where to begin. One of the difficulties is simply that with Shakespeare we have well entered the era of printing—the Gutenberg Era, as Marshall McLuhan calls it. There is so much more, well-preserved evidence to deal with; so much mere *text*, primary and secondary, all too well established. More than any other technological achievement, the printing press has threatened (and, Mr. McLuhan's auguries notwithstanding, to my mind still does threaten) to flatten out the cycles of history. And, besides the poems and stories and plays, in print, so much speculative thought—whole new disciplines emerging and multiplying themselves.

We are concerned primarily with the literary art, with poetry in all its forms. The work of art has, at all times, a way of breaking free of the patterns of the discursive thought of its period. And this is especially true in the modern (i.e., post-medieval) age. But, without becoming hopelessly lost in the complex currents of the modern history of ideas, either with repetition of clichés or a specious attempt at originality—above all, taking care to avoid the familiar fallacy of talking as if man's metaphysical plight itself were at any given time determined by changing modes of systematic thought—perhaps we can risk one more generalization toward defining the cultural starting point of my concern in these essays, the beginning of the specifically modern consciousness of the problem of identity.

After Immanuel Kant had written an end to the rationalism of the Enlightenment—specifically, to the hope of reconciling the ambiguity of Descartes' famous declaration, and finding a satisfactory formula for identification of man's being with his reason—the turmoil of nineteenth-century European thought produced two movements which have become the dominant, "official" philosophies of the twentieth century, determining the new concept of man's identity. These are: positivism and dialectical materialism.

There are, of course, many occasions of opposition between them. Their rivalry in the political and economic sphere is the most important phenomenon of contemporary history. But this is in more senses than one a "cold war." For they have a common philosophical origin; to borrow (no doubt mistakenly) a favorite term of Eric Voegelin's, it is only that the "gnosticism" of the Communists has been exercised, paradoxically, with greater positiveness (as the methodology of political tyranny) than ours. Both serve the ideal of technological progress as the supreme good, and from the point of view of our concern here the effects are much the same:

To reduce the man to a "unit" of history, or of biology— "responding" to "stimuli," "communicating" without concern for what is being communicated; to deny him any sense of the value of his feeling and suffering part except as it may be manipulated to someone's economic advantage (whether his own or another's hardly mattering in the government of unself);

in other words, to cut off that part altogether from his sense of
effective order, and to commit him to the service of a practical
rationality that he dare not suppose is Reason. In short, to deny
that he has a self—any right to expect other than the experience
of Forster's "panic and emptiness" when he finds himself
alone.

Nothing deriving from the splinter systems of nineteenth-
century thought, transcendentalist and intuitional theories, the
romantic notion of a logic of the imagination, has been very
effective in our time to combat that denial. In aesthetic theory,
for example, the new intuitionalism of Henri Bergson, still a
dominant influence, has usually been accepted in a way calculated only to widen all the gaps between "poetry" and "belief,"
"art" and "life"—to confirm, if not to contribute to, the
dehumanization of art. Beyond aesthetics, the prospect for
establishment of a firm counterfaith is even dimmer. We have
taken up residence, it might seem permanently, in the region of
unhope; and, whenever we have a moment's leisure from the
all-prevailing commitment to positivistic programs of doing
without meaning, seek out, some of us, doctrines designed
merely to console us in our despair.

Catholic philosophers, by and large, have continued at once
to maintain a more manful surliness than others and to seek
possible alliances. But, with a few significant exceptions, they
are still bogged down with one foot in historical argument—the
effort merely to prove that everything new came from St.
Thomas (Maritain)—and, all too "modernly," if still somehow
Thomistically, with the other in the reduction of metaphysics to
logic (Bocheński). Whatever the validity of the Church's
claims to possession of the theological truth of the self, its
thinkers have found no way adequately to accommodate the
experiential fact of man's loss of identity.

The Freudian psychology—although it may ultimately have,
as some have hoped, genuinely "humanistic" (read "Christian,"
if you like) implications in its emphasis on the history of the
individual—has not yet been successfully divorced from determinism. At least as popularly practiced (both as a healing craft
and as a method of art criticism), it continues to suggest that
the personality is less real than the psychological states that

compose it, reducing the quest for self-knowledge to a search merely for the means of "integration." Ultimately, in common with the practice of the anthropologists and the sociologists, it deals with identity only as a phenomenon of relationship—with what might be called, in general, status identity, the identity of the individual as product of age, sex, family, profession, social class, nationality, etc. It affords no concept of absolute identity. (With regard to the last point, I make bold, moreover, to make light of the dispute between the Freudians and the Jungians. In either case, the identity of consciousness is lost in analysis of its components.)

Again, there are a few partial exceptions—e.g., Reinhold Niebuhr and Paul Tillich. But the best of liberal Protestant thought—which is very often all but indistinguishable from liberal Jewish—seems largely a kind of mystical anthropology, bent on making religion as comparative as possible, and giving up the Ego (and therefore, I think, the *te*) as a bad job . . . "after such knowledge, what absolution," anyway, if not forgiveness? The non-Christian existentialists (Jean-Paul Sartre) offer existence simply in place of being, the heroism of pure will, of "selling one's life dear" as Edmund Wilson put it, without questioning whether there is actually any market for such a commodity.

Nowhere is there a fully coherent suggestion for putting man back together; nowhere anything better than Hamlet's advice to his mother concerning her broken heart, that she learn to live with the better half (and take your choice as to which *is* the better); nowhere, particularly, a method for reconciling the word and the deed, not to speak of the Logos. I mention only one example: that the nausea following the stench of Dachau and Buchenwald—that, one might have hoped, ultimate, nightmare triumph of the "unit" idea of man—seems to have awakened the Germans (and, if we are honest, the rest of us) to no more profound reflection than that they might better have put their unfaith in purely economic rather than biological or ethnological determinism. Had we hoped for the purgation of the bloodbath, salvation by catastrophe? Alas, this crack-up was not the Grand Canyon either, but only a magnified version of Fitzgerald's old plate. The Herrenvolk too, by and large, and with American approval, have retired quietly if sullenly to the tidy backyard of their Wirtschaftswunder, there to cultivate the bourgeois virtues with only a little more cynical self-satisfaction than before, and no greater uneasiness of conscience than might be indicated by the universal sign on the gate of Vorsicht vor dem Hunde. For, of course, when you do not believe in man in the first place, it really does not matter how many of him you annihilate; the corpse is scarcely likely to impress you as any more real than the body.

Nowhere, then, philosophic implementation of the will to being—that is, again, to unity of self—nowhere, a means of defining the connection between one's inward experience of being, one's wish, one's private *desire* to be, and the strange, compulsive, meaningless *duty* merely to maintain existence in the community of material need. It is not, as I have observed, that there is any lack of concern with the problem. The European phenomenologists—Martin Heidegger, Gabriel Marcel, *et al*—have been most eloquent in describing the predicament. But, in the attempt to push beyond the descriptive phase, their energies have been dissipated, paradoxically in imitation of that vice of systematic philosophy which they so deplore, in the anxieties of a search for exact terminology. We are like those terrifying "shell" sculptures of Henry Moore's; where the little foetus self, the person, crouches inside the great, empty, grotesque body, all full of holes and yet offering no avenue of communication.

But (I speak of one of them) the artists, meanwhile, those eternal dogs of discontent, have continued more effectively than anyone else to keep us awake to the fact that there *is* a problem—and with a variety of voices that defy philosophic oversimplification. If not always the hope, for indeed we grow fond of our despair, then at least the fear, that there may be a significance in our existence, we are still privileged to entertain in our art.

In our part of the world we are also still permitted to talk about it critically. And that fear, or hope, is the large subject of this book. In John Keats's anxiety that he might "cease to be," there was already some ambivalence of emotion; although he called it fear, it was hope, too. I start, however, from the point at which the issue itself, as well as the emotional attitude, became ambivalent—when it became a question for the poet whether he meant "might never have been" or "might always be."

It began in England somewhat later than on the Continent; it is impossible to say exactly when, or with whom. Perhaps it was later than in America, too. Nathaniel Hawthorne, Herman Melville, Mark Twain even, were "modern" in a way that practically nothing in the writing of their English contemporaries approaches. But there is, in the twentieth century, a line of *technical* influence of the British novel on the American that cuts across the pattern of our native development of thematic concerns, justifying my exclusion of the earlier American novels. I might have included something of Henry James's later work. *The Sacred Fount*, say, would have been essentially as much to my purpose as *Heart of Darkness*; simply as expatriate, in himself unselfed, the one author as pertinent an example as the other. But I have everywhere consulted first of all my own convenience; and, for many reasons, Conrad seemed easier to handle.

For one thing, I think it not unlikely that the pre-eminent success of British imperialism in the nineteenth century, somewhat offsetting the dehumanizing effects of the industrial revolution, for a time insulated the English against the more radical self-doubts suffered by Europeans and Americans. And this particular problem—in clear connection with almost all the other themes of my concern—a profound questioning, precisely, of the imperialist value assumptions, is the starting problem of *Heart of Darkness*.

Now, no doubt this or any other historical argument will seem specious to some readers. One must recognize exceptions to every rule in dealing with literary and cultural history. Even in England, there were earlier novelists—Laurence Sterne as far back as the eighteenth century, and Samuel Butler in the nineteenth—who anticipated something of the twentieth-century preoccupation with the theme of identity. But it would be difficult, on the other hand, to argue that there are no significant differences in treatment of the theme attributable to differences of cultural era.

In any event, whatever the precise limits of its "modernity," I would make it clear that I did not begin with the theme as such, and then select novels to illustrate it. Rather, I was interested first in the novels themselves, separately, and in no particular sequence, and the theme only very gradually emerged over a considerable length of time as the burden of my preoccupations in reading and talking about the books. I chose at last eleven authors whose work I thought I understood. Moreover, though the method varies considerably from essay to essay, I have for the most part concentrated in each upon a single novel.

This same, close concern with the works as artistic wholes also dictated my decision to limit the volume to essays on the novel in English. Obviously, from the point of view of theme, there was much to be tempted by on the Continent. Thomas Mann, Marcel Proust, André Gide, Georges Bernanos, Franz Kafka, Albert Camus, Ivo Andrić. But one has only to start the list to realize how *too* rich it is. Besides, there was some arguable unity of tradition in the one language. But, finally, I had to face the inevitable and never quite answerable question, about the foreign authors, whether to try to deal with the texts in the original or in translation. Neither I nor my probable audience, I felt, could make a very convincing pretense at the former; and if I was to keep any consistency of method, in close reading, the latter choice seemed even more questionable. (Andrić, for example, who would offer some of the most interesting thematic problems, I happen to know only in a *German* translation. One has merely to consider such a misty situation as this to sense how perilous literary criticism is at even one linguistic remove from home.)

And yet, the theme is there, throughout. I have been happy enough to let it be obscured wherever possible; and in some essays there will be little explicit discussion of it. Most of the time—"luckily," as Charles Marlow says—there are the surface realities to be attended to. But in every one of the books, by whatever devious ways, we are led eventually back to the heart of darkness that is the self.

To repeat what I said at the beginning, I am interested in the theme primarily as a key to problems of novelistic form. But this is in no way meant to minimize its importance. Even if the situation had been the reverse of that I have described, and the theme had come first to mind, I believe I might anyway have chosen to limit this volume to studies in the novel, and to exclude the materials of possible thematic interest that modern poetry would have provided—simply because the novel has more of the self in it still, in tangible form, is more *anthropomorphic*, so to say, and thus more immediately available to my purpose.

This is the one thing I want finally to stress, the character of the novel as the form that presents to us, more effectively than any other, what D. H. Lawrence called "the whole man alive." It is my contention that all questions of formal design in the novel are radically related to this, its unique expressive purpose. I contend that the novel, so conceived, provides us not an opportunity, merely, but the best possible opportunity for understanding of the problem, or mystery, of the human self—an opportunity that formal philosophical discourse, by the very nature of its characteristic use of language, is barred from offering.

I have indicated my impression that most of the contemporary philosophers who pretend to address themselves to the problem—there is no more popular subject—are, whether they know it or not, actually seeking ways to evade the central issue. One of the exceptions to this general tendency, I briefly noted, is Gabriel Marcel. Marcel, I think, really does try to look at the problem squarely. By professional philosophers, he would be regarded, I suppose, as a relatively minor figure in the history of the phenomenological movement. But no one has described with greater clarity and greater compassion than his the predicament of modern man, who "as a result of deep historical causes, which can as yet be understood only in part, . . . has been led to see himself more and more as a mere assemblage of functions" ("On the Ontological Mystery"); and few have been so convincing in their attempts to point a way out of the predicament. His distinctive strength in the effort to construct an adequate notion of the self and self-consciousness—based on the phenomenological principle that "before it is anything else, consciousness is above all consciousness *of* something which is other than itself" ("The Need for Transcendence")—is his unbending awareness that man lives, and must define himself, in a community of selves. His whole doctrine of the I-Thou relationship, the doctrine of "intersubjectivity" which in his version contains one of the most cogent examinations of man's ontological character attempted in our time, is grounded in that awareness.

But there is throughout Marcel's writings a significant, recurrent uneasiness about the use of metaphor in philosophical discourse. (The lecture from which I have just quoted, in a passage immediately following the quotation, provides a good example.) Like Bergson, from whom he takes so many of his basic attitudes, Marcel himself is fond of metaphors. But he repeatedly warns himself and his audience against overindulging the fondness, and his efforts to draw clearly the line between the kind of metaphor that advances and the kind that hinders the process of metaphysical thinking are never quite satisfactory. The idea that language itself, all language, is fundamentally, perhaps essentially, metaphorical—the suspicion that one simply cannot use words without using metaphor—is at once a constant fascination and a constant anxiety for him.

It is the same uneasiness that compels him to apologize for his career as a dramatist, for, of course, the play is a large metaphor. In common with a number of other modern French thinkers, he seems never to be quite sure whether he is a dramatist who writes philosophical essays to explain his plays or a philosopher who writes plays to explain his philosophizing.

Now, the whole issue here—I have written on it at greater length in *The Curious Frame*—is one of ancient complexity. We must be wary of oversimplification. But, especially with regard to the truth of the self, I believe a remark of Marcel's on the drama—in "Truth as a Value: The Intelligible Background"—is instructive beyond his intention at the moment. "The role of the drama," he says, "at a certain level, seems to be to place us at a point of vantage at which truth is made concrete to us, far above any level of abstract definitions."

If I may take leave to apply this specifically to the truth of the self, the question it suggests to me is whether this context of dramatic concreteness may not be, indeed, the *only* one in which we can apprehend the self—the only one with reference to which the problems of the self can be adequately formulated. For the concreteness of the drama is simply its representation of that situation of the self in what I have called the community of selves. And I am inclined to doubt that the self can be in any way realized apart from that community, outside a context of active involvement with other selves, or some metaphor of such involvement. In other words, I wonder whether, as soon as we do what must be done in any formal philosophical discourse, as soon as we form an abstract concept or definition of the self, attempt to isolate it for consideration, we have not already lost its essence.

Moreover, it seems to me that, in providing the necessary metaphor of involvement, the novel, being a form both dramatic and reflective, has a certain advantage over the drama proper. The stage drama is likely to flourish as the highest form of verbal art only in an age in which there is a relatively stable body of belief—belief that, in a certain sense, does not have to be reflected upon, but only celebrated. Our own, manifestly, is not such an age. For us, the novel has the advantage, in its superior capacity for presenting the act of reflection simultaneously with and as a part of the act of dramatic involvement.

Finally, then, and even with regard to the specific character of the volume's guiding theme, I have chosen to write about novels—because they are novels.

Not every one is a novel I especially like. Nor, liked or disliked, are they all of equal stature. In some instances—notably the books which are the focal points of my chapters on Joseph Conrad and James Joyce—they are minor works of the authors concerned. But I make, in any event, no pretense to having had my final say on the entire career of any of the writers. There is, in every case, a measure of despair even in contemplation of the effort to grasp the single work within the space of twenty-or-so pages. And the situation would have become quite impossible if—besides two of the major novels of William Faulkner, who is even more difficult than Joyce to read in any one book without taking all the others into account, thereby defying the kind of unity aimed at in the other essays—I had tried to "include" such a thing as *Ulysses*.

In keeping with the desire to concentrate attention upon the works themselves, I have also avoided any overt effort to define my theoretical position as a critic among the rival, contemporary schools or movements. Such a definition is, I trust, implicit in the essays, but I hope never more than implicit. This is a book of responses, of appreciations if you will, and of judgments—not a book of demonstrations.

# 1 *Heart of Darkness:*

# The Russian in Motley

In talking about Charles Marlow in *Heart of Darkness*, we have to deal with two problems: that of his identity as hero of a story in which he himself, helpfully enough, is primarily engaged upon a quest for self-knowledge—and that of his identity as narrator of the story. In Marlow's eyes, it is apparent from the first, the two roles are radically related— the whole importance of the tale he tells is, for him, in the "kind of light" it throws upon everything that has happened to him before and since his journey to the Congo. Like the Ancient Mariner, he feels strangely compelled to tell the story, and that compulsion to tell is an inseparable part of *what* he tells, of his character as hero. The journey is continued in the telling.

But we have to try to distinguish the identities, although we cannot separate them. And, to this end, we must distinguish— with respect to the narrator's role, between Charles Marlow and Joseph Conrad—and, with respect to the part of the hero, between Marlow and Kurtz.

Marlow tells. To some extent he explicates as he tells, and incidentally he moralizes. Ultimately, we may say, abstractly, the distinction between his voice, as that of storyteller, and the voice of Kurtz, the spurious prophet—"the man presented himself as a voice"—is clear enough, and essential. It is as clear, and as essential, as the distinction between the voice of Marlow and the voice of Conrad.

Yet, the possibility of the voices' becoming confused, Marlow's and Kurtz's, as well as Marlow's and Conrad's, is one of the dramatic problems of the story. And the critical danger lies in making the distinctions too abstractly, specifically in a radical separation of the two relationships. The narrative frame-structure—the "we" situation established at the beginning and end of the novel, with the scene on the deck of the *Nellie*, and the two or three reminders in between, when Marlow interrupts himself—provides only a superficial safeguard against what would be most prejudicial to a reading of the story as fiction: the supposition that Marlow, moralizing and all, is Conrad. To consider the Marlow-Conrad relationship as tightly bound up with that of Marlow and Kurtz takes us in, where we have to go, a little deeper.

It is a commonplace observation that Marlow, not Kurtz, is the hero of the story. What we know about Kurtz is hardly enough, even by implication, to make up a coherent story with him as its central figure. Kurtz is important to this story precisely to the extent that he is important to Marlow. This, to be sure, is a very great extent. The shadowy Kurtz is the object of the expedition, if it has an object; certainly he is Marlow's constant preoccupation, if not throughout the events of his tale, then forever after those events, and while he tells the story. "The foundations of our intimacy were being laid—to endure—to endure—even to the end—even beyond." For Marlow's part, the expedition has no object at the outset. The object becomes Kurtz, very gradually, but so decisively that Marlow can say that before the crawling steamboat reaches the inner station, "for me it crawled toward Kurtz—exclusively." What he seems to be struggling to say is that *he* became, or almost became, Kurtz.

And yet, this matter must be kept straight: it is not a fatalistic discovery he makes, that Kurtz is the object of his search. He makes Kurtz his object, abandons himself in the preoccupation with Kurtz, by a deliberate act of the will. The act is negative, perhaps, is a revulsion against the lie that is the company and its purposes, a rejection that at least at first results in the acceptance of the idea, the fable, of Kurtz only as something that happens to be ready to hand. But it is nonetheless deliberate; and this, the act of will, of moral choice, is made clear in the end—"Ah! but it was something to have at least a choice of nightmares," and again, "It is strange how I accepted this unforeseen partnership, this choice of nightmares forced upon me in the tenebrous land invaded by these mean and greedy phantoms." "Strange," and "forced upon me"—the moral situation, that is—but, emphatically, a choice. And the reason he gives for remaining loyal to Kurtz is that Kurtz too made a "choice."

If there is any fusion of selves—and the point is, of course, that such fusion is finally avoided (cf., for example, *The Secret Sharer*)—it might better be said that Kurtz becomes Marlow, rather than Marlow, Kurtz. Marlow retains moral control; and he retains control as storyteller. If he had gone quite all the way with Kurtz, clearly there would be no story—for that would have been for him too to be "lost—utterly lost"; literally, he would not have "lived to tell the tale." And this too is one of the central themes of the story, the temptation to a kind of pride in the *power* of the word, such pride as Kurtz had, which is fatal to the artist. It is by narrowly avoiding participation in such pride, in the symbolic action by bringing Kurtz—which is at this point to say himself, Kurtz being already "irretrievably lost"—back to the boat when he had tried a last time to slip away into the jungle, that Marlow is able to control his narrative and the influence of Kurtz. It is thus that he is able to perform the duty of the artist and give his words a substance, a reference to some reality, that the rhetoric of Kurtz does not have, that has in fact the advantage of a marked contrast to the vagueness of Kurtz's talk. And it is thus that he can give his hearers just as much as, and no more than, he wants them to have in the way of knowledge of Kurtz, no more than the story as story requires.

But we must think of the artist now as Conrad rather than as Marlow. Marlow is in control as he tells the story; but the question is how he got that way.

If the reasons are clear for keeping back all but a few scattered facts of Kurtz's person and career, still, something has to be told. It has been observed by several critics that the education of Marlow and the tragedy of Kurtz merge. This means, what is implicit in the remarks already made here, that the vague legend of Kurtz has to be pursued to some kind of actuality. Marlow must finally meet a Kurtz real enough to justify the feeling he has of the man's necessity to him, without at the same time losing his own identity, his ability to *judge* Kurtz, and to establish his intimacy with him as a matter of choice. Further, there is a simple problem of standard, narrative technique. A Kurtz has to be presented who is actual enough finally to satisfy the suspense of the search which is the story's plot, without at the same time shifting the center of interest away from Marlow himself. Actually, the two problems coalesce, because Marlow is to some extent both hero and artist. Their coalescence is a central nexus of the fiction's structure. And the essential agent of the connection, *Conrad's* special agent, is the "improbable," the "inexplicable," figure of the young Russian.

It is the Russian who provides the essential minimum of information about Kurtz without which the story as story would collapse. Moreover, without his intervention, or prevention, Marlow's meeting with Kurtz must have resulted either in complete frustration for Marlow, in his revulsion both from the company and from the legend of Kurtz as unmitigated lies, or else in his yielding without reservation to the temptation, losing himself wholly in the nightmare that Kurtz represents.

As offering a solution to a problem, the Russian at first glance does not look very promising. The first sign of him, the book in the shack where he had left wood for the steamboat, the outdated manual of seamanship, with its notes in Russian that Marlow took for cipher, Marlow describes as "an extravagant mystery." And the man, when Marlow first sees him, is himself "an insoluble problem."

But all this, of course, has to be taken in context. In the first place, something of the original mystery is cleared up as the story goes on. The Russian cherished the old, practically useless book simply because it was his last book—which is, after all, understandable enough under the circumstances. Marlow does find out that the notes are not in cipher, but in Russian. And so on.

Further, in terms of Conrad's consistent usage in the story, there is no real contradiction between the Russian's being inexplicable, improbable, fantastic, a "mystery," and his furnishing a key to the "truth" of Kurtz, the truth of Marlow's relationship to Kurtz. What Marlow wants to find in knowing Kurtz is, without question, truth, to set against the lie, which he loathes, which has the "taint of death" about it for him, in the behavior and purposes of the "pilgrims." But if anything is certain about the way Conrad is using words in the novel, it is that mystery is not opposed to truth. The defense of illusion in the melodramatic post-climax of the tale, Marlow's "lie" to Kurtz's Intended—and, incidentally, what a beautiful irony there is in this man-of-all-good-intention's so referring to his fiancé!—is finally only a way of saying that truth, or the love of truth, is a matter of a certain, right attitude toward mystery. It is respect for the reality and integrity of mystery—in short, intellectual humility. And untruth, lying and the love of lying, is deliberate ignorance of mystery, a contempt for it; it is the divorcing, say, of all moral problems from metaphysical questions and reducing them to problems of mere "method" (Kurtz's "methods were unsound," says the manager to Marlow, wagging his head)—in other words, intellectual pride.

Simply as a matter of narrative technique, again, Kurtz can never be fully revealed. But, beyond that, the Russian is mysterious because the truth to which he provides a key also partakes of mystery; and no mystery, by definition, is a "problem," simply, to be "solved"; a mystery is explicable solely in terms of other mysteries.

Marlow, therefore, leaves the Russian still half-unbelieving in him. "Sometimes I ask myself . . . whether it was possible to meet such a phenomenon!"

But a plausible account of his role, his function if not his identity, can be made out. If the inquiry takes an indirect course, in pursuit primarily of a symbolic or metaphorical or allegorical significance in the details of his appearance and behavior—that, I think, is in the nature of the case. For his career in the story is erratic, oblique; the very self-effacing quality characteristic of all his references to himself is symbolic of his role. He has no significance, no identity, except in his function, in relation to Kurtz and Marlow and the savages. And yet that function is all-important for the story.

Marlow's "explication" of his story is limited, of course, by the fact of his own involvement in the fiction—a fact I have already insisted upon. In every instance, Conrad has taken care to temper the finality of any interpretation Marlow puts upon the incidents of his adventure; the repeated pattern of Marlow's commentary is that of a never quite successful groping for a definition, of a broken series of insights brilliant but too brief for complete illumination at any point. To put it another way, Marlow never entirely succeeds in extricating his heroic role— that determined quest for his own absolute identity, the ardor of which distinguishes him among the other, contented half-men of the tale—from the accidents of his mere workaday vanities, his opinions and attitudinizing: as Englishman against the Continentals, apologist for the relative sanity of *British* imperialism in the general madness, as honest workman, seaman, against the capitalists and their sycophants, as man of common sense (again, so terribly British) against the worshipers of "method." Yet, if one does have to go beyond Marlow, the direction the inquiry might take is often clearly indicated, especially by his characteristic play of variations on a motif of image or association. Thus, Marlow's references to the Russian, repeatedly, from the first, insist upon a quality of the unreal, or the extrareal, the symbolic, but specifically upon the mimetic, the aspect of the clown.

The young man had met the boat at the bank before Kurtz's station, and Marlow recalls how:

*His aspect reminded me of something I had seen—something funny I had seen somewhere. As I maneuvered to get alongside, I was asking myself, "What does this fellow look like?" Suddenly I got it. He looked like a harlequin. His clothes had been made of some stuff that was brown holland probably, but it was covered with patches all over, with bright patches, blue, red, and yellow,—patches on the back, patches on the front, patches on elbows, on knees; colored binding around his jacket, scarlet edging at the bottom of his trousers. . . .*

And later: "There he was before me, in motley, as though he had absconded from a troupe of mimes, enthusiastic, fabulous." Marlow takes precise note of the patches once more just as the man is leaving him: "One of his pockets (bright red) was bulging with cartridges, from the other (dark blue) peeped 'Towson's Inquiry,' etc., etc."

This is whimsy, of course; but Marlow is constantly so whimsical a fellow that there is little about him to be taken seriously that can be entirely separated from the whimsy. And, actually, the Russian's character of clown makes a good deal of sense if one takes it as a part of his office as representative of Kurtz. Kurtz has made himself a godling-emperor in the jungle; we learn of his court, of the "ceremonies used when approaching Mr. Kurtz," as Marlow with a shudder of revulsion puts it, from the Russian himself. And much of what the Russian tells of his own relationship with Kurtz, his attitude toward him, curiously qualifies him as something very like the court fool.

He is not the fool simply of jests and capers. The young man is too serious, takes Kurtz too seriously, for one to imagine his ever having consciously performed stunts for Kurtz's amusement. The hyperseriousness is one of the more obvious ironies of the clown characterization. But he is the fool of unquestioning and unambitious loyalty, cheerful, unembittered, endlessly grateful for whatever brief favor of Kurtz's company is granted him, the willing butt of his moody abuse and neglect. It is not difficult to make out, from the hints he gives about the course of their relationship, a probable pattern of Kurtz's feelings toward him. And the pattern resembles pretty clearly the conventional one of the tyrant-fool relationship.

One must suppose that Kurtz has, or had, as the case may be, enough of Marlow's kind of intelligence to be amused by the Russian somewhat in the way Marlow is. Further, even in Marlow there is a trace of contempt in such amusement; in Kurtz, with his brooding vanity, that element would have been much stronger. Given the circumstances of Kurtz's position, his evident need for the sympathy of his own kind, of a civilized man, the kind of understanding, at least partial, at the level of idea and articulate emotion that only a white man could furnish; given the evidence of his having succumbed to the charm of the Russian's admiration to the extent of taking him into his intellectual confidence, reciting his poetry to him, "enlarging his mind"; and given, again, the probable amusement at the man's wide-eyed, glamour-struck absurdity—it is not difficult to imagine what would have happened. Kurtz would have realized, suddenly, that the intellectual sympathy was hardly very deep, or very complimentary to himself, that he had allowed himself to take seriously the companionship of this absurd fellow, a man more "simple" than the savages themselves;

the amusement would have turned wholly to contempt, and the Russian would be once more threatened, kicked out, or brutally ignored. In short, Kurtz would have come perilously close to allowing the fool to perform his highest service, that of showing him his own absurdity.

And this is Kurtz's tragedy: either he, or the Russian, or both, lack some essential quality of mind—the ironic sense, perhaps, that Marlow has, and that is surely a good part of what he is talking about when he says Kurtz had no "restraint." Kurtz would have come perilously close to a saving self-contempt. But the clear evidence of the Russian's story is that any such promptings in Kurtz were always turned against him, the Russian, according to the familiar pattern of the attempt to destroy the mirror that shows the hated self. And the quality of the Russian that Marlow dwells upon, his innocence, his selflessness, if Kurtz had detected it at all, would only have exaggerated the projected self-reproach. It could not have been flattering to Kurtz to realize, as Marlow does, that only the Russian's insulation of innocence made his hero worship possible, that a more knowing man would have done what this "simple" man could not do, would have "judged" Kurtz, and to devastating effect. Or, it might be suggested, the very realization that such innocence could exist, persist under the most pressing occasions of evil, that there was in the Russian something incorruptible even by the subtlest influence of his hero's personality, would have rankled deep in Kurtz.

But what the Russian failed to do for Kurtz, he does for Marlow. Because Marlow has the ironic sense, but also because the Russian shows up at precisely the right moment to appeal to that sense, the fool finally performs his highest function, providing a measure of the absurdity that there is in all word and action of high seriousness and that, if seen, prevents its overreaching itself.

His good sense and steady good humor, the calm ironies of his talk, his doctrine of the value of work, its at least provisional reality, might seem most stably characteristic of Marlow from the first. I imagine, therefore, it is one of the least convincingly presented of all the story's effects for some readers—but the possibility has to be somehow entertained that Marlow actually could, as he is tempted to do at one point, jump overboard and join the savages on the bank. It has to be supposed even that he could under slightly different circumstances have joined Kurtz, in his knowledge "of gratified and monstrous passions." This is one of the extremes of action, one that might almost have been justified, as an expression of Marlow's revulsion from the depravity of the "pilgrims," that is prevented by the Russian's appearance.

For Marlow, despite his incredulousness, does see him, sees him as the fool—as a vision of youth and innocence and incorruptible selflessness. He sees him, that is, as the one thing that, caught between the pilgrims and the terrible evidence of Kurtz's ruin, he must otherwise have ceased to believe was possible—the truly "simple" spirit, the man who wants nothing, "nothing from the wilderness but space to breathe in and to push on through . . . with a maximum of privation." Explaining his confidence that he can make his way again in the jungle after he has left Marlow and the traders, the Russian says of the savages, and with the manner of one who is merely stating a fact, "They are simple people—and I want nothing, you know."

Marlow is reassured, in effect, by the apparition of the Russian, that the moral universe is not, after all, entirely reducible to the opposition of Kurtz and the pilgrims. In good time, before he has to make his "choice of nightmares," he is permitted to take the measure of Kurtz's absurdity in this man's infatuate admiration. The heads on the poles around Kurtz's stockade, says the Russian, "were the heads of rebels." "I shocked him excessively by laughing," Marlow says. "Rebels! What would be the next definition I was to hear? There had been enemies, criminals, workers—and these were rebels." Marlow's laughter is bitter enough, to be sure.

" 'We talked of everything,' [the Russian] said, quite transported at the recollection. 'I forgot there was such a thing as sleep. The night did not seem to last an hour. Everything! Everything! . . . Of love, too.' 'Ah, he talked to you of love!' I said, much amused. 'It wasn't what you think,' he cried, almost passionately. 'It was in general. He made me see things—things.'

*He threw up his arms.* . . . *I looked around, and I don't know why, but I assure you that never, never before, did this land, this river, this jungle, the very arch of this blazing sky, appear to me so hopeless and so dark, so impenetrable to human thought, so pitiless to human weakness."*

And later:

"*I suppose it did not occur to him that Mr. Kurtz was no idol of mine. He forgot I hadn't heard any of these splendid monologues on, what was it? on love, justice, conduct of life—or what not. If it had come to crawling before Mr. Kurtz, he crawled as much as the veriest savage of them all."*

But bitterly or not, perhaps the more effectively because it is bitterly, Marlow does laugh; and the laughter provides him with the essential perspective he requires for his meeting with Kurtz.

Yet, Marlow admires the Russian too. "I was seduced into something like admiration—like envy. . . . If the absolutely pure, uncalculating, unpractical spirit of adventure had ever ruled a human being, it ruled this be-patched youth. I almost envied him the possession of this modest and clear flame." The essential qualification, of course, immediately follows: "I did not envy him his devotion to Kurtz, though. He had not meditated over it. It came to him and he accepted it with a sort of eager fatalism. I must say that to me it appeared about the most dangerous thing in every way he had come upon so far." But unquestionably the admiration Marlow has for the Russian extends itself somewhat into a new respect for Kurtz. If Kurtz's relationship with the Russian, as Marlow learns of it from the youth, provides an insight into Kurtz's shame and the absurdity of his pride, it also must put the true power of his personality in a new and more favorable light—the realization that the man who could seduce such a spirit as the Russian's, however fatalistically, must indeed be what Marlow finally pronounces him, "nevertheless . . . a remarkable man."

The words that bear the stress of the rather subtle point of distinction here are: "He had not meditated over it"—his devotion to Kurtz. "It came to him and he accepted it with a sort of eager fatalism."

Marlow himself does not reject Kurtz, of course. The other extreme of reaction he finally avoids, opposite to that of joining Kurtz, and again I think prevented largely by his meeting the Russian, is that of a complete and profound revulsion from the whole business, lumping Kurtz and his self-betrayed idealism with the hypocritical pilgrims as indeed the worst of the lot, refusing in utter despair to make even the "choice of nightmares." He is close enough to this at times. The passage about the rebels already quoted expresses momentarily the same bitter contempt for Kurtz that Marlow has earlier for the masters of the "grove of death," for the "lugubrious drollery" of the French man-of-war's firing at invisible enemies in the coastal brush. And something perhaps even stronger in the way of such a reaction as this he might have had on his own, without the intervention of the Russian, and his stories of additional horrors, at the sight of Kurtz's decorated stockade. Yet, in the end, he does not so react. And the reason he does not, the reason he can have his own admiration for Kurtz, while not envying the Russian his, is simply that Marlow's devotion is qualified precisely in the way that he has pointed out the Russian's was not qualified.

Marlow does not "accept it with an eager fatalism." He forms his loyalty to Kurtz as a matter of choice. There is a great deal of talk in the book of the adventure as a "dream." Marlow several times makes the explicit comparison; and, indeed, Conrad has succeeded admirably in evoking the real atmosphere of dream as reality. (Excepting Kafka, he has no rival in this ability.) But by the time Marlow's choice is determined, the "choice of nightmares," he has waked up from both of them. Not forgotten them; for, short of death, there is no awakening in this sense; the dream is an inseparable part of reality. But by the time the choice is made he has, unlike the Russian, waked up and "meditated over it." This is all the difference; and it is essential.

By seeing first what is the flaw, the only flaw, in the admirable Russian's moral equipment—the equipment of this man who has, following the voice of Kurtz's eloquence, wandered alone in the jungle, and who again "vanishes in the night" as he leaves him, even as Marlow himself might have done—Marlow is prepared to avoid the deficiency in equipping himself. He is prepared to insist upon his right to a choice. Thus, the Russian completes his office of fool in his service to Marlow. For the perfection of the fool's function, in its traditionally highest, dramatic development, is not simply, of course, to expose the absurdity of the heroic, the high-serious action, but by so doing to provide a final and accurate measure of what is truly, irreducibly heroic in such action. And this is what we get in Kurtz's summing up, and in Marlow's comment on it, that those words, solely, attested that Kurtz was "a remarkable man."

Marlow receives his commission of loyalty to Kurtz from the Russian. It is to him that he makes the promise: "Mr. Kurtz's reputation is safe with me." And the comment that immediately follows—"I did not know how truly I spoke"—sufficiently affirms at once the importance of the Russian as Kurtz's "agent" in extracting this promise, and also the element of unconsciousness in Marlow's susceptibility to the Russian's influence. In other words, the Russian is confirmed also as Conrad's agent, beyond the consciousness of either Marlow or Kurtz.

Morton Zabel remarks somewhere that the crisis in Conrad's stories occurs typically in a situation in which a man is committed suddenly to his destiny. The situation, further, often involves a peculiarly sympathetic relationship of the hero to another man, a feeling of kinship which he never fully understands but which is so close that it amounts almost to an identification—this being, I think, one of the most significant points of the simplified "formula" for interpretation of all the rest of his fiction that Conrad provides in the little story, *The Secret Sharer.* In *Heart of Darkness*, the commitment to his destiny involves for Marlow principally his feeling of identification with Kurtz. It is for Kurtz that he goes "far enough." But neither the identification nor the essential release of the two men from each other is complete here, not so complete as with the captain and Leggatt; and the missing element in the relationship might very well be defined as innocence.

Kurtz is, to say the least, experienced, knowing. And Marlow, in a sense, has to continue living his "lie" for Kurtz; the experience has touched him at the core of his mind, and he will never be released from brooding upon it.

Marlow does keep his freedom to choose this burden; he keeps his moral independence, in which there is always, necessarily, a measure of innocence. (Signs of his independence are, for example, the fact that he does bring Kurtz back to the boat, and that he does not, after all, quite die of the pretty obviously symbolic fever which presumably he has caught from Kurtz.) But it is only by first paying his respects to Kurtz's disciple, the Russian, that he acquits himself of full possession of Kurtz's knowledge, retains this certain measure of his own innocence. Kurtz himself can provide no example or counterpart for it. Thus, in *Heart of Darkness*, the hero's commitments to the other man are interestingly divided between Kurtz and the Russian. Marlow's preservation of Kurtz's reputation, keeping his secrets, is comparable to the captain's service to Leggatt. But between Marlow and Kurtz there can be no exchange such as that between the captain and Leggatt when each frees the other to seek alone his further destiny. Because Kurtz is not innocent, has knowledge "of gratified and monstrous passions," and suffers the consequences of such knowledge, death, there can be no question of Marlow's making to him gifts which are the talisman of protection for his continued career. The captain bestows upon Leggatt, who is innocent, the gold and the floppy white hat. Here, the talismanic gifts—the Martini-Henry cartridges, the handful of tobacco, the pair of shoes (this latter, of course, strikingly reminiscent of the shoes that Marlow earlier pulled off and flung overboard when another of his soul-brothers, the native steersman, filled them with his blood)—must be presented to the Russian.

The matters I have been discussing here are, clearly, moral matters. But the point might be recalled that the effect of his acquaintance with the Russian is only partly realized, or understood, consciously by Marlow. And from this it would be well to go back to a previous observation: that all Marlow's insights, moral and otherwise, are partial, provisional, expressed usually in terms of a pattern of recurrent imagery or verbal association which, we may say, is to be seen as merely "compulsive" for him, and consciously controlled only by Conrad; that his "moralizing," if this is what it should be called, is by no means to be identified with Conrad's voice in the story. Marlow, to repeat, is involved in the fiction. The matters under discussion are matters of morality, but of morality in fiction. And to put the emphasis where I should prefer to have it, upon form, a term I had occasion to use in an essay on Ellen Glasgow might serve the turn here. The whole problem might be spoken of as a problem of "moral probability"—which *is* a problem of form, and in a rather basic and simple sense, that of tying up Marlow's state of mind, Marlow himself, as we see him at the beginning, with the Marlow and his state of mind of the ending, by way of something that happens in the meantime. The thing that happens, the essential link of action, is the appearance of the Russian.

Nor is the introduction of the Russian left by Conrad to be justified formally on these grounds alone: that he exercises an essential influence in developing the pattern of complex and subtle shifts of attitude that make up the plot of Marlow's moral adventure. Other matters of form in *Heart of Darkness*, of narrative structure, of the structure of imagery and symbolism, of the interrelationship between these and the development of the character of Marlow, etc., etc., have already received much critical attention. And if there is still more that needs to be said on these questions, it is the subject of an essay other than this one. But one or two observations may illustrate the point that the Russian is not, after all, so "incomprehensible," so "inexplicable," so "altogether bewildering," if one has detected anything of a pattern in the imagery, the recurrent themes, and the set of the diction already well established in the novel before his appearance.

Marlow's descriptive adjectives for him, it has been previously suggested, are themselves part of a flowing verbal pattern in which the reader must, by the time the Russian appears, have got something of a drift of significance. The French man-of-war too, one remembers, was "incomprehensible." The law of the white man had come to the Negroes of the chain gang "an insoluble mystery from the sea." The elegant clerk, who trained the native woman to do his shirts, Marlow at first took "for a sort of vision." He too was "amazing." About the pilgrims, when it first occurred to him to name them so, "bewitched inside the rotten fence," Marlow remarks—"By Jove! I've never seen anything so unreal in my life." And so on. By the time we get to the Russian, mystery has become quite familiar. And we have some idea what Marlow means by it. At the risk of over-generalizing, but without danger of going basically far wrong, we may say that he finds something unreal, absurd and incomprehensible about anything that figures, or shows the effect of, or is analogous to, the traders' own clinging to official and casuistical formulas in their manners and their talk about what seems to him actually purposeless activity. Marlow's reaction to this unreality may be at times one of disgust (the pilgrims), at other times one of a kind of admiration (the clerk and his starched shirts), according to the form the particular sign takes. At the extreme depth of this state of dubiety, what is most fantastic may seem most real. But, at any rate, we become familiar with it, and we understand the connection between the uncertainty of values and the sense of unreality.

We see first that the Russian is part of an extended pattern of absurdities, of unrealities, and thus are prepared to understand what makes him finally unique. His fool's role—the effect of his folly as divine simplicity, innocence, restoring sanity, a grasp of reality, to Marlow just as he approaches that depth of dubiety—finally opposes him directly to the "flabby, pretending, weak-eyed devil of a rapacious and pitiless folly" that rules the world of the pilgrims. But in order to see the difference between the two kinds of folly, the divine and the diabolical, and to understand the importance of the distinction—the importance of the fact that Marlow does not use the word "folly" except in the diabolical sense—we have to see first that a great many other words are deliberately being used in both senses, that the distinction, and Marlow's escape, in the event, are hairbreadth.

Further, the Russian's book—Towson's, or Tower's, *Inquiry into some Points of Seamanship*—has its place in the thematic pattern of Marlow's admiration for work and good workmanship. His remarks on the book—"dreary reading enough," but showing the author's "honest concern for the right way of going to work," and in the way the notes were made in the margins, and the back "lovingly stitched afresh" where the cover had fallen off, revealing a similar concern on the part of the Russian—recall Marlow's praise of the clerk, who in spite of the hardships of his situation kept his account books "in apple-pie order," and Marlow's own satisfaction in the work of repairing the steamboat. Again, later, Marlow takes note of the extreme neatness with which the Russian has done the fantastic patching on his clothes. This theme itself, of course, is tied in with that of the mystery, of reality and unreality; and the connection is emphasized in the passage describing the Russian's book. Despite the "extravagant mystery" of its appearance, Marlow had, holding the book, "a delicious sensation of having come upon something unmistakably real."

Finally, the description of the Russian is tied in closely with the basic pattern of the novel's title-symbolism, already established in the opening scene on the deck of the *Nellie* before Marlow takes over. The Russian appears in the sunshine, and disappears in the darkness. There is a corresponding fluctuation in his moods, usually described in terms evocative of the light-dark opposition. As Marlow comes close to him for the first time, looking at him over the side of the boat, there were "smiles and frowns chasing each other over that open countenance like sunshine and shadow on a wind-swept plain." The simile adumbrates the development of his role, the self-effacing, totally receptive function of his innocence, the field of his mind that takes all impressions, the light and the dark of Kurtz's influence, countenances all, we may say, but judges nothing—"I am a simple man; I do not attempt to judge him"—and is, finally, affected by nothing. Marlow has to judge at last, to hazard an answer to the question he has formulated about Kurtz's voice, his gift of expression—whether it is "the pulsating stream of light, or the deceitful flow from the heart of an impenetrable darkness." His judgment preserves, even finally, much of the paradox. But it is a judgment, to which he commits himself without reservation. To the Russian, the question never so much as occurs.

Conrad, invisible, judging and not judging, stands somewhere between them.

If F. R. Leavis had bothered to make the fundamental

distinction between author and hero, and to try defining the theme of the novel before starting to criticize its style, his judgments might have been imposed more accurately and with a more becoming modesty. It is true, of course, that like most writers Conrad has a certain fund of merely habitual rhetoric, which he sometimes uses rather desperately to fill the gaps between moments of real intensity of thought. But we need to discriminate, much more finely than Leavis is capable of doing, between instances of this in *Heart of Darkness* and those passages where Marlow's difficulty in expressing himself is "in character" and the uncertainty is part of Conrad's consciously controlled thematic concern. Leavis' critique is hardly more useful than the self-indulgent nonsense of E. M. Forster's attack on the Conradian "obscurity," which it proposed to correct and redefine. (The kind of obscurity Forster attributes to Conrad is actually more characteristic of his own *A Passage to India*.)

*Heart of Darkness* remains a mystery, as Conrad himself always said it was to him, for whatever an author's opinion is worth. It is the basic mystery of human existence; indeed, this question embodied in Marlow's judgment of Kurtz, of what is left of a man to make him "remarkable" beyond the destruction of all his talents and the fallacy of his reasoning. But it is a mystery for the understanding of which the author has provided a good deal of ritual and basic theology. Except in a very limited, though important, sense, one might be disinclined to think of Conrad as a "*simple* old sailor." In truth, we need a kind of cipher for taking notes on his work. But Conrad, indeed like Tower or Towson, has "an honest concern for the right way of going to work" that makes the pages of this book, too, "luminous with another than a professional light." Mysterious it assuredly is—but not obscure.

# 2 *Howards End:*

## The Sacred Center

*Howards End* is a novel of integrity. No other term will serve at once to indicate its structural unity and to define its theme—thus to suggest the peculiar interdependence of structure and theme that is realized, or achieved, here as in few works of modern fiction.

First, the novel is in a very obvious way concerned with the problems of personal integrity. This is one of the many rather old-fashioned aspects of E. M. Forster's thought: he does not take the view of the human person suggested by the other, currently more acceptable, derivatively technical term, "integration"—as in "integration of personality," "social integration." He does not regard the person as simply the product of his experiences. The persons to be encountered in this book are not so much personalities, in the usual modern sense of the word, as they are, precisely, characters. They are conceived as beings whose actions are something which not only can be accounted for, but for which they are accountable. The quest for the wisdom of self-knowledge—Margaret Schlegel's development is the most instructive example—is emphatically a quest for responsibility. The person is defined, defines himself, in and by his responsibilities.

And this conception of character, this notion of integrity, what we mean when we say that a person is or is not a man *of* character, or that he *has* character or hasn't, is also the source of Forster's emphasis, so unusual in the novel of the twentieth century, on plot. There is a thoroughly modern, a rich and complex system of symbolic motif in the book. But this has a secondary, supporting function. The essential order is the order of action, intelligible as consequence of human intention—and, where it turns on coincidence, as in the embarrassing reappearance of Jacky at Evie's wedding, suggesting only, further, that intention need not be always conscious and specific, that the limits of man's foreknowledge do not excuse him from the responsibility of moral foresight. The coincidences of this novel are quaintly conspicuous, perhaps because it is one in which the action is not, as in most modern fiction, all coincidence.

But it is not so easy to define the active principle of the integrity. The motto "Only connect . . . ," its provocative incompleteness, clearly indicates the problematical character of the work. Connect what, we are to ask, with what? And how? The novel pictures a civilization in which everything is disconnected—past from present, country from city, culture from economic reality, morality from manners, institutions from human need, purpose from technique, reason from impulse, the unseen from the seen, masculine from feminine, man from nature, man from man. How, if at all, are the rifts to be healed? Lionel Trilling wants to refer everything to the "class war" and the battle of the sexes. But these concepts are hardly comprehensive, although both are, in a sense, central. With due allowance for the ironic fact, which Mr. Trilling notes, but fails to make very much of, that all the major characters really belong to different ranks of the middle class, the concept of class struggle will serve well enough to define the conflict between the Wilcoxes and Leonard Bast. But that is finally to be resolved by the combined influences of the Schlegel sisters' personalism and the nature mysticism which is embodied (or, perhaps it would be more accurate to say, disembodied) in the first Mrs. Wilcox. Nor will it do simply to interpret Margaret's humbling of Henry Wilcox as the triumph of the feminine over the masculine. No formula of this kind, socioeconomic or sociopsychological, will cover the whole range of issues raised by the novel.

With sly casualness—"One may as well begin with Helen's letters to her sister"—Forster goes to work at once on the theme of disconnection. There are the letters, communications which do not communicate, that in their very style, however charmingly self-ironic the air of distraction, discover Helen's own despair of getting through, even before we see their effect on Margaret and Mrs. Munt. The correspondence, then, is abruptly terminated in the "anti-letter" of the telegram—which belatedly confesses at once the folly both of love and of writing. Both, we get the impression, love and letters, are simply out of date; in the age of "telegrams and anger," it is no good trying to cultivate those antique arts. There is Margaret's and Aunt Juley's talk of the "engagement" of Helen and Paul. The word is richly and variously ironic in the situation. Not only are these two not engaged in any specific and formal sense—Margaret, against her better judgment, allows herself to be carried along by Aunt Juley's meddling excitement—and are not going to be; but by the time Mrs. Munt appears on the scene at Howards End, if not before, it is fairly apparent that the only kind of engagement likely to occur between the two families, the two worlds, of Schlegel and Wilcox, is a battle engagement, not a betrothal.

Now, of course, at the same time that he is showing us the conditions of conflict, Forster is carefully planting hints as to the nature and means of possible resolution. The opening sentence of Helen's first letter—"It isn't going to be what we expected"—applies not only to Howards End, the house and place, but to the whole situation of the novel. It is fair warning against any kind of oversimplification. Even at first glance it is apparent, for example, that Mrs. Wilcox may be an unpredictable element, that in her case the so easily reversible attitudes of the volatile Helen toward "Wilcoxes" in general are probably irrelevant. And on a second reading, when we have seen the promised engagement and marriage after all fulfilled, the Wilcox and Schlegel worlds after all joined, although not in the persons of Paul and Helen but of Henry and Margaret, we will detect how this was foreshadowed in the opening pages. The surprise development was really inevitable. It is through Mrs. Wilcox's mysterious agency that Henry and Margaret are brought together, as in a sense it was also by her that Paul and Helen were separated. And the final episode of the novel, with the cutting of the hayfield and Mr. Wilcox's revelation concerning the destroyed will of his first wife, returns us smoothly to the characterization of her in Helen's first letter. There, her chief distinguishing feature is her immunity from the hayfever that afflicts all the other members of the family.

But the dominant impression in the first four chapters, to be redeemed but slowly and with frequent reversals thereafter, is one of disorder and division, of a profound uncertainty of motives and values which can only be overcome by the Schlegels as well as by the Wilcoxes, after this first skirmish, by retreating from the issues of conflict, behind hastily re-erected and already patently inadequate barriers of moralistic formulae. The Wilcoxes have their strident slogans of "soundness" and "progress." But hardly less spurious, hardly less a slogan, if not so pompously asserted, is the central article of the Schlegels' faith—that belief in the supremacy of "personal relations" to which they return with all the greater fervor after the brief period of doubt created by the first "Wilcox episode." "I know that personal relations are the real life, for ever and ever," says Helen upon her return to Wickham Place; and "Amen!" echoes Margaret; and the overtones of self-mockery do not conceal the pietism of the avowal.

On the far horizon is the threat of international conflict. The time of the novel's main action is one in which old Ernst Schlegel's hope for a re-emergence in Germany of the "mild intellectual light" of pre-Bismarckian idealism, about which we are told at the end of Chapter IV in the sketch of the sisters' childhood, has been long since abandoned. The stereotypes of national character are hardening, the rival, imperialistic chauvinisms of Germany and Great Britain—the book appeared only four years before the beginning of World War I—more and more loudly, intransigently defining themselves. Closer to the center is the opposition of the families, the Schlegel and Wilcox worlds of idea and attitude—a conflict whose theme extends itself into the area of the German-English opposition on the one hand, and, on the other, with the introduction of Leonard Bast, into that of the "class war." Still deeper are the frictions between the sisters, between Henry Wilcox and his son, between Mrs. Wilcox and her husband and children, which are discovered and exacerbated in the trials of the two families' encounters. And, finally, at dead center, the source of all the rest it is suggested, is the disturbance within the individuals, the sickening uncertainty or ambiguity of purpose, pull of the idea against the passion—in short, the disunity of the self.

When they set out on their successive projects, as they might be called—to "connect" first with the Wilcoxes, then, briefly failing that, with Leonard Bast, and finally to connect the connections, bring Wilcoxes and Basts together—what the Schlegel sisters are really seeking is self-justification. Suspended, so to speak, as they are, above or beyond common life and common loyalties, with their mixed German and English heritage, the two elements of which tend simply to neutralize each other, economically classless, a species of charming drones who live effortlessly on the income from obscurely defined, for the most part "foreign" investments, they are in a sense compelled to seek perfection of the inner life, the life of private sensibility. There is, literally, nothing else for them to do. But they are beset by anxieties about the isolation to which they are thus condemned.

The question is not whether the inner life is worth sustaining—they are never in any doubt on that point—but whether it can be entirely self-nourishing. They suspect, from the rather compelling evidence of Tibby's case, that the life of pure self-containment is not very easily distinguishable from one of simple self-indulgence. Again, the insistent repetition of the word "engagement" in the opening chapters suggests the theme. Helen may quickly have to abandon, as an obvious absurdity, the idea of becoming engaged to Paul, but both she and Margaret very definitely retain the need to be *engagé*. In other words (they are in more ways than one comparable to Ursula and Gudrun Brangwen at the beginning of Lawrence's *Women in Love*), they suspect that the person, the truest, inner person, is somehow able to know or discover himself only in his relations with other persons, in the discovery of other inner lives.

"Personal relations, for ever and ever." But the trouble is that they find very few others, if any, who are either willing or able to enter into such relations—i.e., which according to the implicit definition of the terms are truly relations, and at the same time truly personal. And when it appears, thus, as with the Wilcoxes, that one's concept of "person" must exclude a considerable number of "people," exclude them from all possibility of the establishment of personal relationships, then the reiteration of the formula begins to take on a note of desperation. It risks becoming, as we have observed, mere slogan—as impersonal, despite the words, as any other slogan. Schlegels risk becoming as insincere, as self-deceptive, as Wilcoxes.

The irony is most readily apparent in Helen's case. She is ready, at first, to abandon all the most cherished Schlegel convictions in order to admire the Wilcoxes. And this quixotic youthfulness, the quick, affectionate changeability, is in the beginning more than charming. It has the look of an innate wisdom, the capacity to cut through ideas, categories, to tear off the labels that she and Margaret had prematurely attached to the Wilcoxes, and to get at the real persons. But, at second glance, we can see even from the letters the dangerous tendency in it. She is still, actually, confusing the person with the ideas. She cannot yield her own position, in the arguments with Mr. Wilcox, without feeling that she must go over to his. And once, then, her pride has been badly injured in the affair with Paul, and she has, in defense of herself, to reattach the labels, which in truth she had never discarded, this time they are on to stay. The engaging changeability, based as it is on a really profound insecurity—Helen, we should not forget, is the pretty one, the one who from childhood has the more readily attracted "new acquaintances," and who "did enjoy a little homage very much," who, in brief, has always felt herself inferior to her clever, quieter sister—is revealed as the early symptom of fanaticism.

It is the same quality that shows itself, its true dangers at least partially detected at the time by Margaret, in Helen's "ramshackly" behavior at the concert where they meet Leonard Bast. Quite enough, probably, has been written about that concert, and Mr. Bast's umbrella. Certainly, there is no need further to indulge either ourselves or Mr. Forster on the subject of Beethoven's Fifth Symphony. But the essential point is the ironic contrast between the formal unity of the music itself and the disunity that it inspires among the listeners. It is an irony several times reversed, wrung, turned upside-down and inside-out. But the final, tragicomic effect is to show us a group of people who are most earnestly at, but as far as possible from being in, concert. And the central figure of the episode, in whose reactions this effect is chiefly revealed, is Helen.

It is more than the necessary limitations of words that prevents our getting at the symphony itself. The allegorical tale of heroes and goblins into which Helen translates the music is a deliberately distorted interpretation, something we are meant to see as being, in its way, as arbitrary as Tibby's purely technical appreciation, his demand that the others prepare themselves for "the transitional passage on the drum." That "symphony itself," the music as it really is, probably exists somewhere between the Helen and Tibby accounts of it, between her impressionism and his jejune expertness of response. If anyone is capable of hearing that, we are probably to assume it is Margaret, who at least wants to, as she tries to explain later to Leonard Bast, "treat music as music." But the matter of essential interest, for us, for the purposes of the novel as a whole, is not that Helen's interpretation is specifically wrong—nor even, as Margaret would have it, no doubt as spokesman at this point for Forster, that the wrongness is attributable to a generally false critical doctrine, of the "interchangeability" of the arts, "Wagnerism"—but, rather, it is just the desperately self-concerned eagerness with which she clings to her "reading" of the work, right or wrong.

"She desired to be alone. . . . The notes meant this and that to her, and they could have no other meaning, and life could have no other meaning." And, snatching up that meaning, along with Mr. Bast's umbrella, clutching it to her in entire indifference to social amenities, the party, the programme, the possible feelings or opinions of anyone else whatsoever, she pushes her way out of the hall and goes home.

Helen's carelessness about the umbrella foretells the pattern of her entire relationship with Mr. Bast. All that Leonard Bast wants—and he is representative of the majority of mankind in this respect, not just of a certain economic and social class—is security, secure possession of the attributes of status, an umbrella, an epistolary style, an authentic manner for after-concert conversation. Of identity, in the deepest personal sense, he is incapable. Perhaps not essentially incapable: there is a certain absurd heroism in the very incongruity of his seekings, that he should have hit on Ruskin as an escape from the bedtime blandishments of Jacky; and once, if only once, he is able for a few minutes to talk honestly and unaffectedly to the Schlegel sisters about a personal experience, his all-night walk through the city into the country. But he is incapacitated by circumstances. The oblivious voice of Jacky, calling from the bedroom, out of her "degraded deafness," will in the end drown all others, all strains of a higher mood, whether that of his very soul's prompting, or merely the voice of Ruskin. And it is Helen's prideful refusal to accept this, her insistence on making him, in her battle with the Wilcoxes, more of a person than he can be—on electing him, despite her own exasperated awareness that he does not and cannot understand, to the company of those who say "I"—that leads her in the end to destroy the little he is. It is the cruelest irony that Helen should use Leonard to prove her doctrine of responsibility in "personal relations." For, from the umbrella episode, to the discussion of the "I" and the *Übermensch* in the hotel room after Evie's wedding, to his seduction and death, what she really proves in all her relations with him is her total indifference to him as person.

She does, precisely, use him. She sacrifices the person to the idea. Obviously, as a person she could never have chosen him for a lover; it is only the embodiment of the idea that she sleeps with. And if, in so doing, she has violated him, no less has she violated herself.

The doctrine, then, on the evidence of Helen's experience, stands self-refuted. And yet, it is somehow still the doctrine of the novel, Forster's own doctrine. And perhaps we are meant simply to see Margaret, by contrast to Helen, as exponent of it in a truer form—truer, by virtue precisely of being less rigorous. She it is who, after Helen's return from her visit to Howards End and the Paul episode, tends to retain the doubts her sister had first formulated and then so fervently repudiated. Of the life of the Wilcox world, the world of "telegrams and anger," of marriage settlements and death duties, Margaret says— "This outer life, though obviously horrid, often seems the real one—there's grit in it. It does breed character. Do personal relations lead to sloppiness in the end?" And, although Margaret follows this in a moment with her "Amen!" to Helen's reaffirmation of faith, we are conscious still of a reservation, a measure of irony on her part of which Helen is not conscious. Moreover, we suspect that this faculty of irony, of self-doubt, of continuing reluctance to commit herself too rigorously to the doctrine *qua* doctrine, is what will make her the more effective champion of it in the end.

Margaret, in other words, although the idiom of such distinctions is superficially as much hers as Helen's, senses the danger of believing too ardently in the division of the "worlds"—the Wilcox world, the Schlegel world—and of uncompromisingly declaring one's solidarity with one or the other. It is this cautious good sense, not weakness or vacillation as it might at first appear, but a tolerance born of a greater, basic self-certainty than Helen's, which enables her to see Henry Wilcox as an individual. And it works the same way with Leonard Bast, actually.

She is capable, after Bast has come to grief through the advice they had solicited for him from Henry, of a rather callous-seeming indifference to his plight. But her attitude actually does greater justice to his human dignity than does the righteous anger of Helen, which casts him in the role of ideal victim.

Margaret knows that human beings seldom, if ever, achieve entire personal integrity in their actions. They act always, in part, as representatives of a class, social or other, on the basis of prejudices, received ideas, of what they believe they should feel rather than what they do feel. And she recognizes the practical value, the practical necessity even, of these stereotypes of attitude. She knows, for example, that whatever the differences between her own and her sister's way of life and that of the Wilcoxes, they are not so great as the differences between Schlegels and Basts. However distasteful the fact may be to Helen's idealism, she knows that the Wilcoxes are more "their sort" than the likes of Leonard and Jacky, and that it is extremely dangerous to pretend otherwise. But, on the other hand, this recognition does not blind her to the evasiveness and dishonesty of Henry's thinking when he is confronted with an issue of moral responsibility. On the contrary, the same candor is operative in both instances. And it is by virtue of her knowledge of and respect for the mechanism of convention in people's behavior that she is also not to be deceived by it, and can transcend it—at the truly crucial juncture, can both of herself and of others *demand* integrity.

But is Margaret Schlegel, then, the whole embodiment of truth in the novel, her way the way of hope for the final "connection"? Since Trilling's book on Forster, critics have generally recognized in Howards End, the house, a symbol of England itself, and in Margaret's coming into possession of it, thwarting after all the efforts of Charles Wilcox and his father to set aside the will of Ruth, a symbol of hope for England's future—for a future, that is, informed by the past, preserving tradition. It should also be apparent that Margaret's having the place is the reward of her willingness to give it up, her indifference to it merely as possession, as property, expressed when she throws the keys to the house on the ground before Henry. The clear implication is that true possession is of the spirit, that the "house" will survive so long, and only so long, as the pattern of integrity in personal relations among the inhabitants is maintained. The implication is that so long as this is done it will not matter if the building itself is obliterated by the tide of suburban development which Helen, in the final chapter, sees creeping inexorably toward them from London. But, does it matter?

K. W. Gransden has noted the significance of Ruth Wilcox's answer to Margaret's comment that a house "cannot stand by bricks and mortar alone." The first Mrs. Wilcox replies, "It cannot stand without them." There is, in fact, a persistent note of misgiving on Forster's part about this. It is more than nostalgia. The opening description of the house at Howards End begins the statement of a large and complex architectural metaphor which is extended throughout the novel. Buildings, and the design of them, the architectural character of a civilization, would seem to be in Forster's mind fundamentally related to its character of manners and morals. The question would seem to be raised whether, when an effective sense of this relationship is lost—when it really no longer shall matter that a city should "rise and fall in a continual flux," waves of building replacing one another as indifferently as the undulations of the sea—we shall not also have lost the essence of civilization.

Consistently opposed to the building symbol as expressive of the stability of tradition, and associated with the loss of that stability in modern society, is the symbol of the automobile.

"The city . . . rose and fell in a continual flux . . . this famous building had arisen, that was doomed. Today Whitehall had been transformed: it would be the turn of Regent Street tomorrow. And month by month the roads smelt more strongly of petrol. . . ." And again, concerning the spiritual impoverishment of the ground-landlord who had doomed the Schlegels' house in Wickham Place: "He has built flats on its site, his motor-cars grow swifter . . . but he has spilt the precious distillation of the years, and no chemistry of his can give it back to society again."

The motorcar, of course, is the chief attribute of Wilcox. In almost every picture we are given of Henry and Charles, either they are in the car, or it is somewhere in the near background. They are constantly talking of motor trips, of road conditions, of drivers' habits and the dangers of farm vehicles on the highways. They interrupt Margaret's last meeting with Ruth Wilcox, at the railway station when the two women had meant to go together to Howards End, with the story of an accident in which they have been involved—significantly, a collision with a horse cart. And twice, when Margaret herself is a passenger in the car, there are incidents of heavily symbolic import. On Margaret's first trip to Howards End with Henry, in the midst of a conversation about whether the automobile has "come to stay"—which, of course, he complacently assures her it has—he calls her attention to a "pretty church" they are passing. But she is "not sharp enough" to see it in time; and the episode, with its description of the landscape which "heaved and merged like porridge" before her eyes, ominously foreshadows that of the trip to Evie's wedding at Oniton, two chapters further on, when the car in which Margaret is riding runs over a little girl's cat. Once again, preceding the account of the accident and Margaret's indignant leap from the second car when Charles has tried to hustle the ladies away from the scene, there is a lengthy description of the landscape of Shropshire, "robbed of half its magic by swift movement," and of the architectural features of the town as they come in sight of Oniton. When they strike the cat and the driver throws on the brakes, he has just turned round hastily to call their attention to the prospect of Oniton Grange.

Thus, the loss of manners, of a humane moral perspective—the hateful, vulgar complacency of Charles Wilcox's kind who can make light of the little girl's anguish over the death of her pet on the grounds that it was not, after all, a dog as they had first supposed but "only a cat," and try to buy her off with money—all is clearly associated with the blurring of the aesthetic outlook, the effect of the preoccupation with speed and progress which is to render man insensitive and indifferent to the forms of his dwelling places. Margaret's heroic leap from the moving machine, her refusal to be bullied into silence by Charles, is a gesture in defense as much of the rights of Oniton and environs, simply to be seen, as of those of little girls and cats. At this point, she is still thinking that Oniton is to be her home when she and Henry are married; and behind her agitation over the accident is a whole day of exasperation at being brought to the place in the indecent hurry of the motorcade.

She leaps in defense of the principles of discrimination and proportion. The "porridge" to which the landscape is reduced for her by the speed of the car during the previous trip, to Howards End, is symbolic of the obliteration, in the new age, of all manner of distinctions—between people, institutions, classes, and orders of moral value. Margaret (we recall her objections to Helen's tendency to erase the differences among the arts, turning music into literature) is the constant champion of distinctions, of the fine sense of discrimination that is the only basis on which a really meaningful "connection" can be made. The essential paradox is perfectly symbolized in the leap from the car—awkward, embarrassingly painful, undignified, and yet an act in which she is somehow supremely ladylike.

But is it enough, that leap? Or, essentially the same question, is Margaret's marriage to Henry enough to save Howards End, let alone Oniton? One possible interpretation of the first Mrs. Wilcox's remark, that houses cannot stand without bricks and mortar, is simply that it lends support to Margaret's (her elected heir's) position in her later, protracted arguments with Helen over Henry's proposal. It is people like the Wilcoxes, Margaret argues, who ultimately assure the safety of the Schlegels on their little islands of money where they pursue the virtues of the inner life. (Another of the large, recurrent metaphors, inevitable perhaps in a book about the survival of an insular culture, is that of the sea-and-island.) Wilcoxes must not be despised; for, if they do not appreciate houses as do Schlegels, yet, unlike the latter, they are able to "get houses." They keep the essential bricks and mortar together. But there is much else in the novel to suggest that Margaret is involved here in a fatal fallacy—that keeping the bricks and mortar together is precisely what Wilcoxes do not do, that they "get" houses only in the long run for the fun of tearing them down.

Margaret may be right, to some extent, about Henry. He has, for all his habitual dishonesty of mind, some good stuff in him, a spark of fundamental decency. He is able to make a few rudimentary discriminations of his own. Over and over again, in the discussion of Ruth's will, in all the family arguments concerning the Schlegels, in his ability so improbably to fall in love with Margaret, we catch faint glimpses of a finer nature. Even regarding the car, he is sometimes rather engagingly impatient with his son's coarser, proprietary enthusiasms and anxieties. But Charles, precisely, that savage caricature of his father, is quite another matter. One may legitimately wonder whether, when he has the motorcade of progress firmly under his control, when his father is no longer there to put the slightest check upon his determined haste, he is to be prevented by the histrionics of bluestocking spinsters from running down every cat in Christendom—buying off every grief, blurring beyond recognition every landscape.

But, again then, where is the hope? For the book does have, essentially and finally, the look of comedy. The answer, I think, is to be found in re-examination of the proposition we had seemed obliged to abandon—i.e., that the house as such, the building, stands for something beyond itself; it is the house spiritual, not the house physical, that can and must be preserved.

What it stands for, to put the matter as succinctly as possible, is the value of the extrapersonal. The novel, it has been observed, is a novel much about death. Gransden has pointed out the importance of the Wilcoxes' fear of death. (The episode of the little girl and her cat, of Charles's flight from the scene, rather farcically dramatizes the theme which is more seriously elaborated elsewhere.) They are embarrassed and baffled by death, they flee it, try to hustle it out of sight. The whole anxiety of their kind to keep things moving, to keep the shape of the civilization constantly changing, can be interpreted just as this frenzy of flight from the intolerable fact of death. They strive, as it were, to bury death itself, under the life-appearance of change. But, it is implied, of course there is no possibly adequate understanding of life to be built upon a denial of death, no real acceptance of life without acceptance of death. And the continuing service of Ruth Wilcox to her husband after death, somewhat to redeem him from Wilcoxism, the effect of her refusal to "stay buried"—leaving the note that wills the house to Margaret, reincarnating herself as it were in the second wife, who with her bouquet of weeds is spookily mistaken for Ruth by old Miss Avery—is, in the final paradox, to keep Henry reminded that she *is* dead. Her presence, mysteriously identified with the house itself, survives to remind Henry, and Margaret and Helen too, that life continues and must be pursued beyond concern for any particular form, embodiment, of it; that there are values in life beyond the claim of, beyond our sympathy for, our responsibility to, any individual person; in brief, that the ultimate life values, as I have said, are extrapersonal.

This implicit, extrapersonalist doctrine is certainly not to be identified with the progressivist "realism" of Wilcox. That, and the moral blindness, blindness to self, which it engenders, stand unequivocally condemned in Margaret's climactic speech to Henry on his inability to see the connection between his own sin with Jacky and Helen's with Leonard—between his responsibilities to Margaret and hers to her sister. Henry, as "Wilcox," must be and is broken. (". . . to break him was [Margaret's] only hope.") But neither, then, is the extrapersonalism something which results, or is to be derived, from the marriage of Schlegelism to Wilcoxism—even from a marriage in which the former properly asserts its superior position. To see this, as many critics have done, as the essential "connection" proposed by the novel is the worst possible oversimplification. Here is the ultimate significance of the fact that the marriage of Margaret and Henry is in itself a sterile union. The final hope lies in something that transcends both the Wilcox progressivism and the Schlegel personalism, and also any compromise between these two opposed sets of values—anything like that mere "formula, both rational and patriotic, which should preserve the best qualities of each kind of outlook and condemn the worst," that Gransden sees Forster "trying to work out" in the novel.

The implication has been rather embarrassing to a number of readers, who want to see the novel as purely a novel of manners and of social morality, but there is no blinking the fact that what we are witnessing in the last chapter is a fertility ritual. The mower is "encompassing with narrowing circles the sacred centre of the field" as the chapter opens; at the end, Helen, with baby on arm, rushes into the house to hurrah the harvest—" 'The field's cut!' [she] cried excitedly. . . . 'we've seen to the very end, and it'll be such a crop of hay as never.' " Nothing could be plainer. "Circles," a "sacred centre," baby, bumper crop. The transcendent extrapersonalist principle to which Forster makes his final appeal is, purely and simply, the fertility principle.

There is no other way, than by taking very seriously the symbolism of her wisp of hay, to account for the mysterious power that Ruth Wilcox—herself so significantly devoid of personality, so nearly inarticulate, unintellectual, to the embarrassment of the Schlegel sisters' clever London friends—exercises over the lives of the others. It is the same power that redeems the merely impersonal fanaticism of Helen in her affair with Leonard Bast. Thereby, she had as we have seen violated both him and herself; but the rape produces a child, and in the end this is to make all the difference, to reconcile all three parties, Schlegel, Wilcox, and Bast, as they could not have been by any other means. His fatherhood redeems also the absurdity of Leonard himself. The merely satiric comedy of his murder—at the hands of a Wilcox wielding a Schlegel sword, the case of books, which had been his undoing in life, toppling over on him as he clutches at them in death—is raised, in the sequel, to high comedy. The son of farming people, Forster is careful to have told us, reduced to anonymity by the competitions of urban life, Leonard Bast unwittingly "comes home" at last to Howards End, and leaves his heir to repossess the land.

It is essential to the dignity of the proceedings, however, that

Leonard should die not knowing that he was to have become a father. For in the end, as embodiment of the extrapersonal values, the baby must be presented as no one's in particular—not Leonard's, not even, exclusively, Helen's. He is referred to, repeatedly, just as "baby." Helen does not want him, as she admonishes Tom, "cut into two or more pieces" by the mower. But this only ironically points up the theme of sharing, of the common, ritual participation that involves the whole group in the final scene at the farm. The baby, sent out with Tom to play in the hayfield, belongs like Howards End itself to everybody.

The fertility principle transcends even the particular, sexual shortcomings of the characters. Lionel Trilling complains that the ending of the novel is not an "entirely happy" one—"this rather contrived scene of busyness and content in the hayfield; the male is too thoroughly gelded, and of the two women, Helen confesses that she cannot love a man, Margaret that she cannot love a child." But, aside from the implicit, mere inaccuracy of the reference to Helen's "confession"—she does not say that she cannot love *a* man, in the sense of *any* man, but only that she finds herself forgetting Leonard—the criticism, it seems to me, fails to accommodate Forster's own obvious awareness of the incongruities in the situation. The triumphant, feminist liberalism of the Schlegels, for all the moral insight it yields, is openly acknowledged to be a sterile force in society. Especially as it is embodied in Margaret—with her meager figure, her face "all teeth and eyes," as Leonard Bast sees her during their first conversation—it is man-destroying, sex-destroying. Insofar as it is dedicated simply to "breaking" Wilcox, it can promise, ultimately, only its own extinction. It is pretty precisely Forster's point, I think, that the Schlegels have come very close to self-extinction. They have to be rescued by something beyond their rational view of themselves and their responsibilities, even beyond the power, still so dryly fastidious, of their moral intuition.

To come back once more to the question of Forster's attitude toward the house itself—how important is it that the place should, in physical fact, survive? The answer is implicit in this emphasis, in the final chapter, on what is going on in the field rather than in the house. It is a relatively simple answer.

The house is worth keeping intact, so long as it can be kept. Houses last, can and should be made to last, longer than individual human lives, longer even than families. That is their unquestionable value, to the defeat of Wilcox notions of property rights. But it would be worst folly to suppose that "as long as can be" is forever. (There is fair warning, at the very outset, of what happens when one attempts to deny altogether the fact of decay and change; it is what has happened to the cathedral at Speyer—"ruined, absolutely ruined, by restoration; not an inch left of the original structure," the thing destroyed by the very effort to preserve it. There is a telling appropriateness in the fact that the sisters should have met the Wilcoxes on this expedition. For the progressive conservatism of English Wilcox, at least with respect to the destruction of buildings if not otherwise, comes in the end to exactly the same thing as the work of the German restorers.) Howards End is the house; but it is also the wych elm, and the meadow. The house endures. But there is one thing still longer enduring—namely, the land itself. And it is there, in the field, that the drama of human survival finds its valid and final, "sacred centre."

I am not sure that it is altogether a convincing answer. *Cold Comfort Farm* may well, and maybe rightly, have prevented by now our taking this sort of thing—anti-intellectual antics of jaded intellectualism, Bloomsbury gone a-haying—with ultimate seriousness. Certainly, there are distressing lapses of psychological probability that perhaps account for the embarrassing effect of the conclusion and are not to be explained away by such an argument as I have brought against Trilling's complaint. The crucial sexual encounters, which prepare the way for the ritual of fertility, are put rather awkwardly offstage. Forster knows very well how to handle the rich comedy of Henry's courtship of Margaret. But the old affair with Jacky, absolutely essential to the moral argument of the book, is a rather unlikely contrivance. A man like Henry could, no doubt, have gone casually if guiltily to bed with such a woman, once or twice. But Forster unmistakably insists on its having been something more than this. And, if it is difficult to imagine these two repeating the act very often, it is all but impossible to think of Helen and Leonard at it even once. Again, they have to, for Forster's purposes; one understands that. But, as created personalities, persons, in the fumbling flesh, one must critically wonder how they could manage it.

But, entirely convincing, entirely satisfactory or not, I insist it is a clear answer. This novel, although not his most ambitious—that, obviously and rather painfully, is A *Passage to India*—is Forster's most careful performance. Anything that it fails to provide must simply be asked of another author.

# 3 *Sons and Lovers:*

# The Artist as Savior

D. H. Lawrence's *Sons and Lovers* is
something halfway between the autobio-
graphical life novel and a full-fledged
*Portrait of the Artist*. It is not an amorphous book, but it ex-
hibits what might be most accurately called a half-emergent
form—the portrait, the articulated figure of the hero, visibly
emerging, somewhat in the manner of certain Rodin sculptures,
from the still present and undifferentiated mass, stone, of the
life-experience. This character of the work, especially but not
exclusively from the viewpoint of my central theme in these
studies, constitutes its peculiar strength.

James Joyce's difficulty, in *A Portrait of the Artist as a Young
Man*, was with a rather cold-blooded impatience to abstract his
heroself from the flesh-and-blood encounters of existence too
quickly and merely intellectually. He had, it would seem, to
think his way back into a convincing representation of the
corporal sympathies and antipathies, of inarticulate feeling.
With Lawrence, the trouble was just the opposite. It was all too
easy for him to stay immersed in the vital, merely to recall and
to describe, rather than to construct in metaphor and dialectic,
to order and dispose; all too easy to identify art with the
procreative rather than the creative. He had, in contrast to
Joyce, to think his way out, from the fondness of his family
feelings, into the artist's isolation.

*Sons and Lovers* is the record of that struggle to emerge.
Simply as such, it is one of the tenderest and most moving, one
of the cruelest novels in English. But it is not merely a record.
For, to repeat, what is emerging is the artist-hero, not just the
man; and the consciousness of heroic purpose, the thrust *toward*
solitude, everywhere informs and shapes the basic human
struggle.

Joyce, perhaps in reflection of his greater certainty of control, of the achieved detachment from the image of his youth, made Stephen a writer. Lawrence makes Paul Morel a painter. It is, I think, significant in the first place, for differentiation of the two artistic characters, that Joyce's second art was music, and Lawrence's painting. Music, obviously, is the more abstract; painting, more tangible, fleshly, inarticulate. But Lawrence was clearly more anxious about the success of his effort to achieve remove from himself—and thus felt compelled to employ the mask of the secondary interest, thus ironically giving himself away the more patently than if he had taken no pains to conceal the identity.

We can start, then, with consideration of Lawrence's vitalism—or "organicism," as Mark Spilka calls it. The first embodiment of this in the novel is the opening passage describing the countryside of the mining district. It is a passage full of Lawrence's passion for the "world's body," and of nostalgia for the lost time of a supposed more intimate and simple, pure relationship of man's society to the earth. The nostalgia is conveyed in the "green" evocativeness of the place names— Greenhill Lane, Robin Hood's Well, Bestwood. Even the mining operations had been, for centuries, something relatively safe and natural, easily assimilated into the basically agricultural life of the country—"the brook . . . under the alder-trees, scarcely soiled by these small mines . . . some of which had been worked in the time of Charles II, the few colliers and the donkeys burrowing down like ants into the earth, making queer mounds and little black places among the corn-fields and the meadows." But with the demands of the industrial revolution, of course, all this had changed; the mines had become big business, the property of great, impersonal companies of financiers; and at the time of Mrs. Morel's marriage, the land has been for some sixty years literally in chains at the service of industrial progress. The six mines now in the valley are "like black studs on the countryside, linked by a loop of fine chain, the railway." This theme of solicitude for the enslaved and violated earth, the estrangement of human society from its natural environment, is concomitant throughout the novel with that of Lawrence's sorrow for man's self-enmity—the mutually ruinous antagonism of body and soul represented in the disintegrating marriage of Mr. and Mrs. Morel.

The equation of Walter Morel with the flesh, of Gertrude with the spirit, the psychological formula of the attraction-of-opposites that accounts for their union, is all but too explicitly stated in the passage describing their first meeting. The woman was "a puritan, like her father, high-minded, and really stern," and "*therefore* [Lawrence tells us] the dusky, golden softness of this man's sensuous flame of life, that flowed off his flesh like the flame from a candle, not baffled and gripped into incandescence by thought and spirit as her life was, seemed to her something wonderful, beyond her." She is married to what she cannot have—*because* she cannot have it, because it is beyond her. And he to her. All that Lawrence's explanation of the union does is to confirm its essential mystery. We can trace out the steps in the process of deterioration of the marriage, but ultimately it is not to be explained, because it is the essential mystery of our incarnate being—the intolerable yoking of body and soul, in yearning repulsion. The very intensity of Lawrence's preoccupation, throughout his career, with the unity of self, his search for a spirituality of blood, for "organicism," was of course the consequence of his experience of disunity.

The pattern of the novel's development may be seen as the statement and restatement of this conflict in three different, successive contexts: the relationship of husband and wife, of mother and son, and of the son with himself. Paul's love affairs, with Miriam and Clara, are but instrumental in the process of freeing him from the involvement with his mother to the task of the final self-confrontation.

The mother, of course, besides Paul himself, is the dominant personality of the book. She is the source and the end of life. The first victim of her destructive love is not Paul—nor the older brother, William, whose career in the novel serves as an immediate, partial foreshadowing, and incidental cause, of Paul's fate—but the father, Walter Morel.

What Gertrude does to her husband is to reduce *him* to a child, in refusal or inability to accept the only kind of maturity, simple and animal, of which he is capable—and thus, symbolically, to emasculate him. Two mysteries remain: that of moral self-responsibility, it being an essential part of Lawrence's own puritan high-mindedness that he never directly attributes Morel's unmanning to anyone but the man himself—"he had denied the God in him"; and that, concomitant, of the old miner's mere indestructibility—insulted, pathetic and contemptible, broken, his manhood and fatherhood denied, he is still there and still capable even, under his superficial, assumed sentimentality, of deep and genuine feeling when his wife dies, his weakness outliving her strength. But, if not at the level of the realistic life-story, in time, with its slow-yielding confusions and complexities, ceremonially at least the act is completed in the very first chapter.

The ceremonial occasion is the haircutting scene, with William. It is a familiar domestic crisis, when the mother must begin to yield the rights of her primary solicitude for the male child in his infant dependency—in which state, as symbolized by the long hair, he is essentially indistinguishable from the female—to the demands of the father that he be recognized as primarily, not child, but male, and begin to become a man. But, clearly, the crisis is already much more than usually severe for the Morels. The father's anxiety is evident enough in the fact that he undertakes the haircutting very early in the child's life, and that he does it without first consulting his wife. And the bitterness of her reaction, her venomous and undisguised hatred of him for what he has done, is beyond all bounds of normality. But further, Lawrence has exploited the situation with implicit reference to the ancient significance of the hair itself as potency symbol.

This might seem, at first glance, contradictory to the plain sense of the ceremony, which we have noted, with respect to the child. The child is to be recognized as male, beginning the process of maturation, toward potency, by the loss of the hair rather than its retention. But if we remember the other, opposite symbolism—and transfer its significance to the final emotional effect of the episode upon the father, rather than the child—then it does come into meaningful play, in a relationship not contradictory, but richly ironic, to the first.

Morel loses his own manhood—his rights and powers as husband and father—has his own "haircut," in and by the very act by which he had sought to secure his son's recognition. The point is unmistakable. But Lawrence, never one for economy in such matters, nails it down repeatedly. Morel "felt something final had happened." Mrs. Morel "knew, and Morel knew, that that act had caused something momentous to take place in her soul. She remembered the scene all her life . . . this act of masculine clumsiness was the spear through the side of her love for Morel . . . she ceased to fret for his love: he was an outsider for her."

And in case it should still be missed, the same chapter ends with the first of the famous flower passages of the novel. In the chronology of the life-story, much time has passed; the second child, Annie, the event all but unnoticed by Lawrence, has been born. But, in the account, it is no more than ten or twelve pages beyond the haircutting episode when Mrs. Morel, pregnant now with Paul, is pushed out of doors after a fight with her husband—and commits in the garden, with the flowers, an act of symbolic unfaithfulness that confirms even more strongly than her anger against him her rejection of Walter.

Her reaction to the touch and scent of the flowers—which "reel . . . and stretch in the moonlight" toward her—is almost literally orgasmic: more (and this is the terror of her situation all her life) in every sense more real, really sexual, than anything we can imagine of her experience with Morel. Dizzy with the scent, she "herself melted out like scent into the shiny, pale air . . . in a kind of swoon." Then, coming to herself finally, she looks "languidly" about her; and going inside, is described in the final scene exactly in the attitude of a woman returned from a meeting with her lover, in the delicious secretiveness of remembered passion noting the guilty stains still upon her person. Her husband, no longer important enough now even to look at—she "knew him too well to look at him"—is peevishly asleep; and "as she unfastened her brooch at the mirror, she smiled faintly to see her face all smeared with the yellow dust of lilies."

Paul remarks to Miriam, many years later, that his mother and father must once have had the complete relationship of married love, in body and soul. But, if so, this must be interpreted as an insight of his (or Lawrence's, into his own parents' psychological history?) beyond any material evidence available during his lifetime. For there is nothing left of the marriage, in this sense, by the time he is born. And unable to know and receive the man, capable in terms of real psychological experience only of the flower sexuality, the mother turns, even more desperately than to the first, to the second son—attempting, out of deepest spiritual necessity, to hold him permanently with her in that ecstasy of the garden, when she had felt him inside her "too, melt with her in the mixing pot of moonlight."

In the symbolic sequence, the scene of her holding Paul up to the sun (chap. ii) follows directly upon that of the garden. Child of the flowers or of the sun, the infant with its strange "clear, knowing eyes" is in any event no son of Walter Morel. Because "she no longer loved her husband, she had not wanted this child to come." And her reaction, then, to recognition of her guilt in "having brought it into the world unloved"—her impulse, as she herself interprets her act of holding the baby up to the sun, "to give him back again whence he came"—is one that only the more confirms the fatal incapacity of her love to detach itself from its object. She has "felt as if the navel string that had connected its frail little body with hers had not been broken." Her determination, thereupon, to "make up to it" for not having wanted it, "with all her force, with all her soul," to "love it all the more now it was here, carry it in her love"—the word "carry" is crucial—simply reiterates that feeling of the continuing, umbilical connection.

But the career to which Paul is thereby committed, the quest for the means to cut the cord, is not, at least overtly, the father search we might legitimately expect. He seeks his destiny, rather, the identity of his "divine" mission (as sun- or flower-child), primarily in relationships with women—attempting, as it were simply *in himself*, to make up for the inadequacy of his natural father. He plays the part, of "little husband," the son-lover, first to his mother herself—exploiting, actually, her own predisposition to accept him in this role—and then rather callously, with what he has learned in that relationship, to her rivals, Miriam and Clara.

But there is, after all, as I have previously insisted, a reality in this theme of the "divine," or at any rate more-than-human, mission of Paul's. And we can safely leave now for a time the merely sex-psychological ground of its origin—ground on which Lawrence, I think, is in any event comparatively shaky—and pursue this theme for its own sake. The mission, again, is the mission of the artist; specifically, what might be called "the artist-as-savior." The first major definition of this character in Paul is in the chapter called "Paul Launches into Life," describing his job in the surgical appliance factory. As always, from this point onward, the picture is of Paul-with-girls. But this is long before Clara's return to the factory, and his love affair with her; even before Miriam. And the workshop episodes give us, first, a more generalized, almost presexual, character of the artist.

He paints the girls of the workroom: Connie at her wheel, with her mane of long red hair; and Fanny the hunchback, with her hair of "bog-water" color. And the effect is, at least momentarily, to take them "out of themselves." They, in their dullness and dreariness, the rooms of the shop itself, are touched, elevated, by the wand of his brush. In the first scene with Connie, the point is reinforced with his childish literary allusion (ironically anticipating the "romantic" mentality of Miriam which he himself comes later so much to despise): "When you sit winding," he says to Connie, "it looks as if you were spinning at a spinning-wheel—it looks ever so nice. You remind me of Elaine in the 'Idyls of the King.' I'd draw you if I could." But the essential thing is that he does draw her: "later on, he had a sketch that he prized very much: Connie sitting on the stool . . . her flowing mane of red hair on her rusty black frock, her red mouth shut and serious, running the scarlet thread off the hank on to the reel." And the exact realism of the actual paintings is the more effectively "magical" than the romanticism of the words. It is he—as the girls themselves obscurely sense, though they jokingly chide him for the seemingly "uncomplimentary" coarseness of it—with his simple, direct, painterly eye, merely stating exactly what he sees, the "bog-water" color of Fanny's hair, who is able to make the hunchback "look just like anybody else." He heals, discovers to them their own capacity for joy and wonder, makes them "see," simply by the naïve directness of his own looking upon them.

And the same office is continued in his visits to the Leivers' farm—with his mother, and with Miriam and her mother. For in the beginning, and to some extent always, it is the family as a whole, the place itself, that Paul is in love with. And on the first visit he shares this love, completely, with his mother. There is, as they start out on the walk, the fatal premonition of her aging. Paul is all but angry with her, petulant, for her unyouthfulness. This in itself, of course, is loverly anger; if with any one person, at this point, it is with her that he is in love. But, most deeply now, it is simply the fully shared experience that they have. The ugly particularities of attachment, the jealous rivalry between Gertrude and Miriam, and between Paul and his father, Walter's justified accusations of abnormality against the mother and son ("At your mischief again?"), are to come later. At this stage, Paul does for his mother, only more intensely perhaps, nothing essentially different from what for some time later he does for the others. His mother, Miriam, and Mrs. Leivers, too, he makes to "see."

There are the man and the truck and the horse on the pit-hill—pointed out to him first by Gertrude—but for her *discovered* by him, when he sits down to sketch. And the legs of the heron flying. "He was constantly informing her, but she was interested." And, "He directed his mother, what she must see and what not. And she was quite content."

Later, when he first goes to the farm alone after his illness, it is the same on his walks with Miriam and Mrs. Leivers. "They looked for nests. There was a jenny wren's in the hedge by the orchard"; Paul puts his finger into the nest, and describes the feeling for them, "as if you were feeling inside the live body of the bird"; and "the nest seemed to start to life for the two women. After that, Miriam came to see it every day." Once again, as with his mother at the pit-hill, it is Mrs. Leivers who first merely shows him, points out to him, what to look for. "I *do* want you to see this," she has said of the nest. And Miriam too, "stimulated him into appreciating things thus." But following the stimulation, the essential insight, healing and redeeming, bringing the dead world of commonplace to life, is his, for their benefit. And essentially indifferent, at this point, to which of them in particular the touch is given. Regarding Miriam, we are told, "Personally, he was a long time before he realized her."

Even afterwards, when he has "realized her," he continues to serve primarily in the role of teacher to Miriam. Literally, he teaches her French and algebra, or tries to. But it is more than that. He would, in every sense, bring her to life, and the world for her. Gertrude, even in her jealousy, is perfectly right, that Miriam is the sort of woman who would "suck a man's soul out till he had none of his own left." But despite his own chafing resentment of it, he returns again and again, almost fatalistically, to the self-destroying, self-dividing agony of the effort to redeem her from *her* incompleteness—that suffocating "spirituality" of her shame in her body that makes earthly existence intolerable for her.

And equally for Clara, his love is sacrificial, redemptive. The final effect of his affair with her, almost as if from the first he had planned it so, indeed, is just to restore her to her husband. She has been dead to herself as woman—cf. Spilka's analysis of the flower passage in Part II, Chapter IX, when Paul first goes walking with Clara and Miriam in the fields—and he reawakens her, but only to give her back to the other man. The fight with Dawes is of obvious significance in this connection. Paul, as his subsequent behavior during Baxter's illness makes finally clear, wants to lose, must lose, in order to fulfill his redemptive purpose. He has, of course, to "make it good," for the benefit of his own as well as Baxter's conviction. He does not run, and he fights hard. But, beyond at the moment his own understanding, he does not press his advantage when he could have killed the man, and then quite consciously at the risk of his own life allows himself to be beaten, clearly and simply to the end of restoring Dawes's sense of self-esteem, of potency, so that he can reclaim Clara.

The contrast between Miriam and Clara, answering to two sides of Paul's personality, has been clear enough to most readers. Both, it is notable, are rather "heavy" women—slow, full-bodied, and a bit clumsy in movement. And the male-female opposition in Paul's relationship with them—his quickness and lightness, inspirited bodiness (we may note especially the swinging scene in chap. vii, Part II), against the earthbound heaviness of the female—is equally apparent in both cases. But in Miriam, as not in Clara, this corporeality is the ironic mockery of her soulfulness. She is, except in suffering passivity, permanently incapable of acknowledging her flesh. And Lawrence has carefully differentiated the novel's two seduction scenes. With Miriam, the colors of passion in the scene are all aboveground—the cherries that Paul, climbing the tree, throws down upon her, the fiery clouds at sunset. And when it is done, in the dark among the fir trees, all color is gone; and it begins to rain; and Paul feels dead, yearning for death and total impersonality, oblivion of being in "the great Being." With Clara, the redness is in the earth. They go *down*, on the path of bloody-colored clay, to the place on the bank of the rushing river. And when they stand up afterwards, the ground is covered with the scattered petals of the carnation she has worn in her blouse, "like splashed drops of blood"; and, after a momentary sadness in her, they are gay and gentle with one another, singing and laughing on the way into the village, and Paul speaking to her in the dialect.

And yet again, the likeness, the constant disposition of Paul in the two affairs, is perhaps more important ultimately than the differences. In both, to repeat, he at last sacrifices himself. The sacrifice is "successful," in some sense, with Clara. She is, it appears, "saved," restored, to realization of herself as woman, and to her husband. Miriam seems even in the end irredeemable. But Paul gets nothing, finally, from either.

For he is wasted by compassion. It is a suffering world that he sees, and he can never for long do more than suffer with it. What he does create is not so much the result of an active triumph over the suffering, as something rather squeezed out of it by its own, sheer, passive intensity. The invisible navel cord that still binds him, as a young man, to his mother—her fatal love that originates in self-guilt—entangles him also with the rest of the world, female and male alike. He is unable in any relationship to detach, to individuate himself.

The compassion is by no means always kindness. The other side of the coin is cruelty, not only to himself, but to others. The entire family, only especially Paul and his mother, "live off" each other's suffering in a manner that Lawrence was the first English domestic novelist to portray with quite such frightfully convincing honesty. The most obvious example is their delight in Walter's frequent mishaps; feeling never so happy and secure as when he is injured, and the sick payments from the workmen's compensation fund come in regularly, without anything going to the pubkeeper. They do, to be sure, "sigh with relief" when they learn that he will not, after all, die of the crushed leg. But this, clearly, is no more than a minimally enlightened self-interest; and the point is secured in the conclusion of the sentence. "They sighed with relief," . . . and then "proceeded to live happily"—i.e., for the rest of the time the father is sick.

Further, there is an irony beyond her intention in the aunt's complacent remark that Paul's illness following the death of William had "saved his mother." For if to be "saved" is to be bound all the more inextricably together, the mother's life now, as Lawrence puts it, "rooting itself in Paul"—then the death itself, which is a partial cause of the illness, is the "salvation" of them both.

There is, in fact, no joy for anyone except with its concomitant of pain, inflicted and received. And Paul's is simply the central, epitomal, the most intense experience of this universal situation. His angry detestation of Miriam's inability to enjoy anything except in suffering—her dumb, wounded, prostrate adorations of flowers, of poetry, of him—is the surest sign of his own sickness. The business in which he takes his first job, and where as we have noted he begins his career as savior-artist, provides the symbol of his whole existence. He redeems the squalor and pathos, to be sure, makes the hunchbacked girl beautiful. But the *need* for it is likely to make a more permanent impression than the redemption, the continuing ugliness than the momentary miracle of discovered beauty—in this place where profit is made of maiming. Nourished in such an atmosphere, Paul's art inevitably takes on something of the permanent character of his employer's grisly-merciful trade: of the artificial-limb maker's mocking ideal of "lifelikeness."

I overstate, perhaps, the painful side of the case. But the final point is, that in joy or pain, giving and receiving, Paul is never self-contained. He is torn, distributed. Some part of him, which threatens at any moment to become all, is always "outside of himself." His art, inspired by and dedicated to the women, the ones who would take him or keep him outside himself, is at once expression of and defense against the threat—defense, merely *by way of* expression.

Principally Miriam, and his mother—who in condemning the girl, for her desire to "suck the soul out" of Paul, of course condemns herself—are the vessels into which his being threatens to pour itself. And in the end he has nearly to destroy himself, since so much of him *is* already contained in them, in order to rid himself of them. Mrs. Morel, there is no blinking the fact, he does destroy.

It is a mercy killing, of course; merciful both to her and to himself. But Lawrence makes it perfectly plain that there is more to it than that. This is the one act of Paul's in which he does not merely suffer something to happen. He cannot, and does not, simply let her die, but must deliberately and wilfully kill her. And it would appear that he brings Annie into it, not for the comfort and protection of conspiracy, but primarily to provide a witness to the fact that it *is* murder.

An extreme and desperate measure; and one, as we have observed, that nearly defeats its purpose. But what the purpose is, is quite plain. Paul must kill his mother, before it is too late—that is, before the radical dependence of his will upon her, which he realizes, is irrevocably fixed by her death. Only, now, in the literal sense of the word, in preventing the natural death, in murdering her, can he assert his will; avail himself of the last chance to deny that his love for her has been self-destructive; and so preserve the idea of her goodness.

I am not sure that the ending is entirely successful. Let us note the emphasis in this last chapter on Paul the artist. He is, we are told repeatedly, unable to paint for some time after his mother's death. The recovery of artistic strength, presumably, in independence both of his mother and of Miriam (whose still soul-sucking, man-avoiding interest in his work figures prominently in the account of their last interview), will be both the sign and the principal object of his victory. And the final rejection of Miriam is clearly intended as a proof of his new disposition of self-assertiveness. He refuses to yield to the temptation of his loneliness to comfort himself with her, and thereby risk backsliding into another version of the same, incestuous, will-depriving relationship that he had with his mother. Miriam is, as she has been all along, too much like his mother. But it could also be interpreted as confirming his fatal attachment to Gertrude, a loyalty so secured by her death that he cannot think of betraying it in marriage to her rival.

Unquestionably, too, the very last scene—when Paul is tempted to suicide (wholly "spiritualized," of course, by means unspecified, but suicide), and turns away from it, "would not take that direction, to the darkness, to follow her" (his mother), but "walks toward the faintly humming, glowing town, quickly"—is meant to be decisive. He has recovered his will, and chosen, life not death. "Quickly," as Harry Moore has pointed out, means "quick," alive. But it is a little too quick in another sense, the "humming, glowing town" a little too pat a symbol for life-and-courage, pulled on us a bit too suddenly at the end, to be very convincing. One may legitimately feel that the preceding description of his experience of the darkness, the infinitude of space in which he discovers the near nothingness of himself, is altogether too convincing to be offset by the easy magic of the display of artificial lights; that his soul is already "abroad in the night . . . still with her"; that the suicide has already occurred. I remain unpersuaded by an argument such as Spilka's that Paul is thoroughly prepared for this decision by his "baptism of fire in passion" in the affair with Clara. The emphasis in the final passage of Chapter XIV seems to me too heavily upon the lapse of passion in Paul, upon Clara's vision of him as "shrinking together, getting smaller" in his preoccupation with his mother's death, to be so easily counterbalanced by the ending of the novel. The new life he had found in his relationship with Clara has died in him; the baptism has not "taken."

We know, of course, that Lawrence himself made that decision against death; he wrote a great many books—and dead men tell no tales. But where is the evidence, in the present fiction, for Paul's ability to make it?

The ending, then, the conclusion and solution, seems

something imposed on the work, after the fact of the evoked experience. It does not quite satisfactorily follow. But perhaps the ambiguity, or the effect of non sequitur, is inseparable from the achievement of the book. I remarked at the beginning that the novel's peculiar strength is in its half-emergent form; which is another way of saying that the hero is still intimately involved, struggling, with the author. We see them as it were in the act of the struggle to separate.

Paul asks himself in the next but final scene of the novel, in the process of his decision to reject Miriam: "Or was it a mate she wanted? or did she want a Christ in him?" And it is interesting that Lawrence did the rewriting of this novel during the period of his premarital love affair with Frieda von Richthofen, of whom he speaks in one of his letters at this time: "I feel I've got a mate and I'll fight tooth and claw to keep her." Then he adds, two lines further on—"I *loathe Paul Morel*." (The italics are Lawrence's.) That determination, to fight for his mate despite all the opposition of convention, to "come out wholesome and myself," as he puts it, to be "always common" (in a sense, to reassert the *Walter* Morel in himself!)—coming at the same time as his finishing this book which he was to speak of as the end of a phase for him ("I shall not write quite so violently . . . any more")—obviously contains the secret of his being able to finish it. It meant that *he* was through with playing Christ, the artist-as-savior, and with women who required him to take that role. And so he was able to impose the decision on the younger Paul, and to force the book to a conclusion.

But the point is that he had to force it, was still too close to the real pain of Paul's dilemma not to feel the personal, psychological need, the duty, of rescuing him. (Compare, again, Joyce's toughness with Stephen, his willingness to leave him in the lurch, incomplete, and still playing his version of the ersatz Jesus, in order that the book might be complete.) I am not sure, indeed, that Lawrence ever achieved the final detachment, that the phase of *Sons and Lovers* was ever quite so firmly closed as he wanted it to be. But this is not to say that he is only a kind of would-be Joyce. If there is much essentially of *Sons and Lovers* in the later novels, the continued wrestling of the artist with his created selves, they are none the worse for it. He is only a very different kind of person from Joyce, a different artist. Nor does this, in turn, mean that we have to choose between the two of them, as F. R. Leavis' recent book, *D. H. Lawrence, Novelist,* would suggest. We respond to them, rather, with different parts of the mind, and with a different critical vocabulary.

# 4 Joyce's *Portrait:*

## The Flight of the Serpent

The father search—the search for the giver and forgiver, for him to whom one may know himself responsible and answerable—is one aspect of the quest for identity. To find and know the father is to know, if not to define, oneself.

For Stephen Dedalus, hopeful of being fitted with a pair of the viewless wings, the father in question is the true keeper of the *word.* The power of words is Stephen's potency. Stephen is a type of the artist; and the artist is type, though heroic, simply of man. But his gift is special, although epitomal, and to some extent it is compensatory. Stephen is shy with girls, incompetent in games, "feeling his body small and weak" in the rush of the footballers upon him, and has very weak eyes.

The total complexity of the eye symbolism in the novel is beyond the scope of my purpose here. But that the eye is a prominent feature of the first father image presented—"his father looked at him [the infant Stephen] through a glass; he had a hairy face"—is of obvious importance. The enlarged, staring eye—notably *eye,* not *eyes;* we are to learn later that old Simon Dedalus wears a monocle—is in its association with the hairiness of the face, and in later contexts (as when Heron remarks to Stephen how Simon has ogled the girl, Stephen's love, at the college entertainment, "your governor . . . looking at her through that eyeglass of his"), clearly to be taken as a symbol of the powers of adult masculinity, and of the father's rivalry of the son.

I say, "father's rivalry of the son," rather than the reverse, because this is the way it shortly turns out—with Stephen's rejection of Simon, as utterly incompetent in the office of father, actually complete by the time of the visit to Cork, when

Stephen feels himself "infinitely older" than his parent and his cronies. The irony of the monocle as potency symbol is, of course, that it is an artificial aid, something to make the eye look bigger than it really is, a rather desperate boast on poor old Simon's part to cover the evidence of his failing powers. Stephen's search soon carries him quite out of Simon's sphere, beyond any concern whatever with the cause of reconciliation with his natural parent—one may say, with some ironic intent, his "efficient" parent. And the symbolism of Stephen's myopia is significant in metaphysical realms far beyond any suggestions of sex rivalry at the naturalistic level which might be put in terms of an opposition of the glasses (Stephen's) to the glass (Simon's). The monocle is pure sex symbol, always, pure bravado—having, as it does, little or no practical value in the correction of defects of vision—and Simon's powers are limited to this naturalistic range. Stephen, on the other hand, wears glasses because he needs them—his eyes are poor literally, *qua* eyes, quite apart from any symbolic reference to sexual inadequacy. And, further, the weakness of his vision has another range of symbolic significance, a cosmic range, in the pattern of his aspirations to demigodhead, in which his relationship with Simon is of no importance whatever except in the most remote and negative fashion.

James Joyce redirects attention from the contemporary, family situation almost immediately to the mythical. But we can start, anyway, at the naturalistic level, and have a look at the Oedipus allusion on the second page as complex rather than myth, so long as we keep in mind that it is, and thoroughly, myth also.

Superficially, the threat to Stephen—"the eagles will come and pull out his eyes"—might seem rather more to place him in the role of a Prometheus. And, of course, there is a great deal in his character and career to support such a reading. The smithy in which he will "forge the uncreated conscience of his race," rescuing it from its state of imaginative ignorance and poverty, is clearly to be heated with the stolen fire of the gods; etc. But Prometheus, in any event, obviously has a great deal in common with Oedipus, in his conflict with Father Zeus. And the substitution of "eyes" for "liver" (the latter itself an obvious euphemism on the order of the wounded "thigh" of Adonis, and the like) only, by reminding us specifically of the fate of Oedipus, whose self-blinding Freud interpreted as a symbolic castration, makes it the more plain that the threatened mutilation of Stephen has this ritual significance than it would have been if Dante had proposed an assault on some other part of his body. (Dante, it might be mentioned in passing, in addition to the other significances attaching to her name, is clearly an epicene figure, usurping many of the powers of the male elder. Stephen at one point, ironically in connection with a reference to the superior intellectual authority of the priests, whom he is later to despise precisely as half *men*, feels obliged to remind himself that his aunt is a woman. In the remembered episode of his childhood, the threat that if he does not "apologize" for some unspecified offense, in all probability an impudent or disrespectful remark to an elder, he will be blinded, Dante might be seen as assuming the role of a Tiresias—a character, again, in many other ways not out of keeping with that of her Italian namesake.)

That the infant Stephen prefers the smell of his mother, as "nicer" than his father's, might have little significance in itself. But his hiding under the table at the end of this overture passage, beginning as it does the development of an elaborate motif of retreat in the novel (compare, for example, the episode of his wrapping himself in the bedclothes in the agony of self-pity for his initial failure as poet), is clearly a womb retreat. Much later, in his university years, when his mother reproaches him for being such a baby that she has to wash him, Stephen replies "but it gives you pleasure"—an exchange which follows the incident of old Simon's shouting down the stairs to ask the sister if her "lazy bitch of a brother (Stephen) has gone out," and Stephen's sarcastically taking note of the implicit jealousy, the slur on his manhood, with the remark that his father "has a curious notion of gender if he thinks that a bitch is masculine."

Stephen has, moreover, in this period of their declining fortune, tried for a brief time to take over the functions of the father in holding the family together—running the loan bank with his prize money, painting the woodwork of the house, keeping the accounts. And, finally, to return to the motif of the "eye," when he breaks his glasses at school, and is punished by the sadistic Father Dolan as a "loafer" and a "liar," the episode ends, upon his subsequent appeal to Father Conmee, with his being hurrahed by his schoolfellows in a celebration that is plainly a type of preliminary male initiation ceremony—by which, in turn, both the pandying by Father Dolan (with all its overtones of perverse sexuality, the straightening of the fingers for the blow, the firm-soft feel of the priest's hands, etc.), a punishment, in effect, *for* having lost his glasses, and again, retrospectively, the threatened blinding by Dante, are established beyond any question as types of ritual castration. All causes of shame and humiliation, his feelings of inadequacy of whatever kind, his fears of being found wanting by the "fathers," first Simon and then the priests, and his resentment of their arbitrary power over him, are, at least in the early stages of Stephen's development, inevitably associated with, or transmuted into, the pattern of his anxiety about the most prominent of his congenital deficiencies, his poor eyesight. And, again inevitably, whether consciously or not on either his or his elders' part, it is for this deficiency, or the effects of it, that he is threatened and punished.

Summing up then: To some extent the development of Stephen follows the familiar pattern, of alienation from the father in rivalry over the mother, of growing anxiety and a feeling of inadequacy in the competitions of the world, of guilt, of the fear, in short, of "castration" that is the consequence of the father's rejection; and so finally, of the discovery of the need for reconciliation with the father or with whatever surrogate may be found, for forgiveness and reassurance.

But this is all within the range of the artist's identity as man. And I have already indicated my conviction that the design of Joyce's novel goes far beyond this. It is as naturalistic a novel as it needs to be, provides as much psychological realism as the modern conception of probability in the life novel requires. But no analysis of the kind I have suggested here—with the "eye" symbolism, for example, reduced to its sexual significance—no matter how much more complete and detailed than this one pretends to be, can adequately explain the metaphorical structure of the novel, or give us the true character of the artist *qua* artist whom Joyce portrays. Neither would any analysis of the mythic substructure, some elements of which I shall mention briefly, any investigation of the traditional sources of the metaphor, a reduction of character and situation to their archetypal components, however broad such a study might seem, do any better justice to Joyce's essential purpose. If I may risk so cavalier a fusion of the Dionysian and Apollonian opposites that these two names represent to some minds—climbing the Jungfreud can do no more than provide us with a platform, a kind of Kill-Devil Hill, for the final flight in pursuit of Dedalus. It must not be confused with the flight itself. Perhaps levitation is invariably a symbol of sexual wish fulfillment in dreams—but it is something more in the nature, finally, of an old-fashioned *vision* with which we are dealing in Stephen's interpretation of his mythic lineage. No combination of the methods of psychological and mythographic analysis can provide any more fruitful results, in coming to terms with the total form and intent of the novel, in explaining what is the matter with Stephen, what he is about, than could an approach that might attempt, say, to relate everything to the sociology of modern Ireland.

For Joyce's artist, his poet, to repeat, is primarily wordsmith, maker of metaphors. The world is dissolved and remade into language. To the institutions, traditions, ceremonies, to the beasts, trees, stones, even to the buildings of the world, Joyce is their Orpheus, giving them tongues to speak. Even the world's myths. Woe to the critic who mistakes his direction here and would translate the metaphor of the book back into myth—as if he were translating the English New Testament into Greek. Myth to the poet is dead metaphor, petrified metaphor, that must be brought to life again, made into new metaphor.

John Nims, appealing in part to Ovid and in part simply to etymology, has called attention to the fact that the plumes in the wings of Daedalus are *pens*. The flight itself is speech, is song. And, to return now to the beginning, although it is to be long before Stephen discovers his mythic father in his study of Ovid under the English priest, yet in the first of his actions in rejection of Simon there is, as Hugh Kenner has noted, an assertion of the independence of his poetic imagination, a

remaking of the song that accompanies his father's story of the
moocow and baby tuckoo. "He was baby tuckoo. The moocow
came down the road where Betty Byrne lived: she sold lemon
platt. O, the wild rose blossoms / On the little green place. He
sang that song. That was his song. O, the green wothe botheth."
It is in the mysteries of the *word* that his natural father is
incompetent to instruct him.

In the first recorded episode of his life at school, the game of
football, Stephen in momentary revery at some pause in the play
recalls how Nasty Roche one day had asked him:

> —*What is your name?*
> *Stephen had answered: Stephen Dedalus.*
> —*Then Nasty Roche had said:*
> —*What kind of a name is that?*
> *And when Stephen had not been able to answer Nasty*
> *Roche had asked:*
> —*What is your father?*
> *Stephen had answered:*
> —*A gentleman.*
> *Then Nasty Roche had asked:*
> —*Is he a magistrate?*

And immediately following upon this reminiscence, of his
inability to identify his father, there is, as he returns to tentative
contact with the game, "creeping about from point to point on
the fringe of the line," the first of Stephen's reflections upon the
multiple meanings of words.

It is the one dominant theme throughout, the central, strong
thread of the entire design of the narrative—this continuous
fascination of Stephen's with language, his yearning for the
power of words, with which he may know himself and make
himself free, discover the order and significance of his existence.

The mystery of multiple denotation. "That was a belt round
his pocket. And belt was also to give a fellow a belt." The
problem of moral and social connotations, the power of words to
define the lines of social intercourse. "He'd give you a toe in the
rump for yourself. That was not a *nice* word. His mother had
told him not to speak with the rough boys in the college." The
primitive strength of onomatopoeia, and the evocative power of

speech sounds, to call up visual images—how one *sees* with words.

*Suck was a queer word. . . . The sound was ugly. And when [the water] had all gone down slowly the hole in the basin had made a sound like that: suck. Only louder. To remember that and the white look of the lavatory made him feel cold and then hot. There were two cocks that you turned and water came out: cold and hot. He felt cold and then a little hot; and he could see the names printed on the cocks. That was a very queer thing.*

His retreat from the conflict of the team exercise in sums, from the cold abstraction of mathematical thought, into musing upon the color images evoked by the York and Lancaster badges, the image of the roses, and so again into the excitement of a vision of a world in which the given qualities of a thing might be altered by the mere combining of words, by manipulation of syntax such as he had accomplished in his infant rendering of the song. "But you could not have a green rose. But perhaps somewhere in the world you could." Names, of things visible and invisible. His own name, on the flyleaf of the geography, and the attempt to define the self by locating it—"Stephen Dedalus, Class of Elements, Clongowes Wood College, Sallins, County Kildare, Ireland, Europe, the World, the Universe." And, significantly following immediately upon this, the names of God and the mystery of the multiplicity of languages and the unity of His being who knows and answers His name at once in all tongues—God, we may say, in the character of master linguist. The nature of abstractions. Politics. And the problem of abstract loyalties—the division of loyalties within the family circle. "That was called politics. There were two sides to it: Dante was on one side and his father and Mr. Casey were on the other side but his mother and Uncle Charles were on no side. It pained him that he did not know well what politics meant." The mysteries of the rhythmical order of words, of the nature of verse. The sentences in the spelling book, that were "like poetry but they were only sentences to learn the spelling from"; the verse about him that Fleming had written in the geography book—"he read the verses backward but then

they were not poetry"; the strange emotional power of the
rhythm in the line of the song Brigid had taught him—"Bury
me in the old churchyard." "How sad and beautiful! He wanted
to cry quietly but not for himself: for the words, so beautiful
and sad, *like music*. The bell!! The bell! Farewell! O farewell!"

And so it is, not simply in this first chapter, but, in less
obvious forms, throughout the novel. The lips of the harlot, in
the scene at the end of Chapter II, "pressed upon his brain as
upon his lips as though they were the vehicle of a vague speech."
And later, in Chapter III, driven to terror by the sermons at the
retreat, by the words of the priest, the "blasts of the angel's
trumpet," remembering how he had written, "in the joy of
guilty confession," long foul letters and left them about in fields
and hedges and doorways where a girl might find and read them,
he knows that now he has again, to another end, to "confess, to
speak out in words what he had done and thought, sin after
sin . . . utter [it] in words to the priest. Confess! Oh he would
indeed to be free and sinless again." He is surrounded, pursued,
and beckoned on, by voices—the voices of the world that would
hold him, the weary, innocent voices of the children at home
singing the glees, the voice of the priest who speaks to him of a
vocation, the voice of the mad nun crying Jesus! O Jesus!—and
the voices from beyond the world, the cry of the boys to him
from the water, and the voice in the eyes of the wading girl
whom he sees as a vision of mortal beauty. "Her eyes had called
him and his soul had leaped at the call." He hears an
unintelligible speech in the cries of birds, in the sound of horses'
hooves on the road at night. When, after ten years since the first
vague effort, he writes verses to Emma, he thinks of "the virgin
womb" of his imagination, in which "the word is made flesh."
And the world appears to him in the image of a censer, from
which the smoke rises as the words of prayers ascending to
heaven. Everything, from the sight of rain-laden trees in a certain street to the bite of a louse, evokes its corresponding verbal
rhythm, its attendant phrase, in his mind. Bitter in his consciousness as he talks to the Dean of Studies that the very English he
speaks is a foreign tongue—"his [the Dean's] before it is
mine"—and unable at the same time to respond to the sentimental romanticism of Davin's appeal for revival of the Irish

language—aware that the "monkish learning, in terms of which he was striving to forge out an aesthetic philosophy, is held no higher by the age he lived in than the subtle and curious jargons of heraldry and falconry"—Stephen tells Lynch that for the second, as-yet-unformulated part of his philosophy, the part concerning "the phenomena of artistic conception, artistic gestation and artistic reproduction, I require a new terminology and a new personal experience." And the two, the terminology and the experience, are actually one. For Stephen, experience *is* language.

But if, I trust, all this is now clear enough, that Stephen's basic and constant concern is with language, to know and control the word that he may know himself and fulfill his destiny—we have still to trace out the course of his quest, his progress through the labyrinth of his experience, and attempt some judgment of its probable success. There is, again, the matter of his choice of guides, the equation I earlier suggested, of the search for the word with the father search.

The structure of the novel can be seen as a series of appeals for guidance, and subsequent disillusionments, on Stephen's part. Sensing his father's inadequacy, after the episode of Roche's questioning which I have quoted, already in his first year at school "feeling sorry for him, that he was not a magistrate," even at the time that, confined to the infirmary as a result of being pushed into the ditch by Wells, he tries to follow the only, meager advice that poor old, windbag Simon was able to give him, "whatever he did never to peach on a fellow"— Stephen humbly accepts, first, the superior authority of the priests. They, he is determined to believe, are the keepers of the word, and can teach him. He is prepared to accept their learning as superior even to that of the venerable Dante.

But, he had made this acceptance, in the first place, chiefly upon the basis of a supposed unanimity of respect for the clergy among his family. And, his confidence once already profoundly shaken by the terrifying scene at the Christmas dinner table, when the fact of an irreconcilable conflict between the two persons (other than his mother and father) whom he has always most venerated is made apparent to him—he then returns to school only to be beaten and humiliated, called an idler and a cheat, in an act of flagrant injustice that the good Father Arnall (the teacher in whose favor he has abandoned his first devotion to the wisdom of Dante) is either unable or unwilling to prevent—only to discover, in short, that the priest, whatever his claims to learning, to possession of the word, is not a man of his *own* word. To be sure, Stephen makes his visit to Father Conmee and is reassured, has his confidence in the ultimate unity of authority and justice in the Church, through appeal to the hierarchic principle, restored—and, as a further consequence, is accepted for the first time by the other boys, not only as a peer, but as a hero. But the reader must suspect, even at the time, that the reassurance is only momentary. The anguish that he has suffered in the pandying, and in the sight of Mr. Casey's face after the argument with Dante, are terrors too great to be so easily soothed for long. And in the next chapter, long afterward, when his father tells him of his meeting Father Conmee and his decision to send him back to school to the Jesuits, of the now Provincial's recollection of Stephen's complaint against Father Dolan and the "good laugh" the community had about it afterwards, the suspicion is justified. There is unanimity, all right, between his father and the priests, but at a level that is not calculated to do much credit to either party in Stephen's eyes. The praise that Simon has brought him now from Father Conmee is the final betrayal, worse even than Father Arnall's silence during the outrage of the pandying.

Thus, there is for Stephen—confined to the companionship of unimaginative boys and pathetic old men, Uncle Charles and the trainer, with their Irish pieties of sentimental song, religion, and sport, caught in the impotence of his daydreams out of the Count of Monte Cristo and unable to find the words by which he might, in the verses to E-C-, "meet in the real world the unsubstantial image which his soul so constantly beheld"—not much hope for any further assistance from the priests. And, after a confirming experience, at the college entertainment, of the essential identity of his father's and the Jesuitical character—"he thought he saw a likeness between his father's mind and that of this smiling welldressed priest; and was aware of some desecration of the priest's office, of the vestry itself"—an incident which, in effect, establishes the rejection of his father during the visit to Cork as a rejection also of the priests as fathers-surrogate—his next appeal is to the harlot. The scene, as Kenner has noted, is a parody of a religious ceremonial. "The yellow gasflames arose before his troubled vision against the vapoury sky, burning as if before an altar. Before the doors and in the lighted halls groups were gathered arrayed as for some rite." He goes in to the woman, receives that communion of her kiss which seemed "the vehicle of a vague speech," and for a time is able to suppose himself communicant, conversant, with some reality outside himself.

But the women are not, in fact, it soon appears, very real to him. Not these any more than the vague figure of E-C-, whom, it should be noted incidentally, we never see very clearly in the entire novel, but always only retrospectively, in brief, fleeting glimpses, hardly as substantial as Mercedes—and whom, after all, he abandons with so little regret to Cranly and the priest, forgiving the betrayal so easily, one suspects, because he has never really known or wanted her as a woman in the first place. We discover, in his examination of conscience before the confession, that his lusts have continued to be principally autoerotic. And it is in this that we might see, further, why his next appeal, the attempt at a renewal of his faith, is foredoomed to failure.

For what he attempts to do, really, is to appeal exclusively to the Church as mother, as woman, as it were over the heads of, or evading, the masculine authority. His devotions are chiefly to the Blessed Virgin. And in the image he has of her, she appears clearly, I think, as merely another idealized embodiment of the same insubstantial feminine figure who has appeared before under the names of Eileen, Mercedes, and Emma. (Note, for example, in this connection, Stephen's childish realization of the meaning of the phrase "Tower of Ivory" in the touch of Eileen's hands, and the allusions to the Annunciation, etc., in the poem addressed and dedicated to Emma.) To her, as such, Stephen's devotions can be only a manifestation of his continued and still frustrated need for real communion, escape from the prison of his shameridden conscience, and not a means of satisfying the need. The devotions are only, in effect, a continuation of the retreat, and inevitably less and less gratifying as he must resume his everyday affairs—having, finally, just the opposite of the effect for which he had hoped, that he would learn to "love his neighbor" and discover the beauty in the common things of his environment.

The final point is that no appeal to the feminine can be effective, for the release desired, the freeing of the creative energy, realization of potency, without prior reconciliation with the masculine authority—the recognition by the father that is the assurance of maturity. And, since Stephen cannot effect such a reconciliation with the representatives of that authority, the priests, while he must at the same time realize that the way of access for his prayers, by virtue of their administration of the sacraments, is in their keeping, he has at last to abandon this way entirely—to seek a wholly new dedication, again, a new father.

Not in the course of Stephen's life, for some considerable time has passed, but in the novel, then, there follows very shortly upon the episode of the interview with the director about his vocation, and his implicit refusal of the call to the priesthood, the visit to the seaside when Stephen is hailed by the boys, and, "flattered in his mild proud sovereignty," entertains for the first time the full vision, as a prophecy for himself, of the "fabulous artificer" whose name he bears and whom he addresses, in the final page of his diary that closes the book, explicitly as "father." It is clear, actually, that he has already, here at the end of the fourth chapter, accepted him as such; and that he feels himself recognized in the acceptance. And then, fired with the sense of his destiny and his strength, he is able at last to assert it in the silent meeting with the girl, subduing her with his eyes to effect the communion "with a creature of his own kind" (now that he knows what that kind is, the fabulous bird kind) that he had sought in the skulking wanderings, the "sins" of his youth.

This experience is, in effect, for this novel, the end of the father search. There are no further steps in the series of appeals and rejections—but only, through Chapter V, additional evidences of Stephen's assumption of the mythic identity.

But in this long final chapter there must be, for any reader, an effect of falling-off that needs to be accounted for. Why did

Joyce not end the novel with the triumphant vision of mortal beauty? Why doesn't Stephen simply take flight immediately, in full glory?

Is the still-prolonged plodding through the physical and intellectual mire of Dublin simply present as a necessary testing of the strength of the vision, a proof that Stephen can carry his new identity unscathed through the ruck of the world? Or is there some evidence of radical misgivings, a fatal hesitancy, a gradual blurring of the vision that anticipates the sorry situation at the beginning of *Ulysses*—when Stephen appears again in Ireland with his wings plucked, a weary wanderer by a sea now thoroughly gray and cold, in the character of Kinch, the fearful Jesuit, the bullock-befriending bard?

Not to prolong the rhetorical questioning: I think that there is a distinct weakening of the heroic character in the final episodes. One evidence of this is the fact that Stephen is still, long after the vision, unable to find a language for the second part of his aesthetic theory. He is still only sullenly resentful of his enslavement to the borrowed languages of his country and church, to the antiquated philosophical jargon of the "jolly round friar" Aquinas, without any clear notion of how he is to escape it. Not only is he at a loss as to how to finish his essay, but it would appear that he has not written much more verse either. There is little to support his claim to the title of poet except the courtesy of his friends.

Further, there is a suggestion toward the end that he has put on yet another mythic character which is rather difficult to reconcile with that he assumed in the vision by the sea. If Cranly is, as Stephen would have it in one of his diary entries, Saint John, then Stephen, even here in anticipation of the role assigned to him later by Buck Mulligan's ballad, must be Christ. Once again, he is unable to escape the limits of his education, unable finally to dedicate himself to the service of a new master, but only to blaspheme against the old.

But these are not, as might seem, simply ironic afterthoughts on Joyce's part. There is, if we have read carefully, and kept clear from the first the distinction between Stephen and his creator, no need to feel baffled by the ending.

All along, actually, much has been going on in the novel, in his own thoughts and emotions, which Stephen is not aware of, or at any rate can never be supposed in a position to interpret. For one thing, there is a side to the character of Dedalus, the "fabulous artificer," that Stephen has consistently ignored, or at least kept out of his conscious musings on the image of his spiritual father. It is always only the flying Dedalus that Stephen pictures to himself. If, as John Nims again has pointed out, Stephen may be supposed, from his studies in Ovid, ever to have known that Dedalus was also the architect of the Cretan labyrinth in which the monstrous Minotaur was imprisoned, and before that of the wooden cow in which Pasiphae hid herself to be covered by the bull—he has either forgotten it, or deliberately repressed it.

But *Joyce* has not forgotten it. From the beginning of the novel to the end—in the story of the moocow and baby tuckoo; in the episode of Stephen's disillusioning visit to the dairy yard; in the nightmare where the goatish demons of his lust surround him, and indeed these horned and tailed figures are obviously reminiscent of that same experience of his childhood; in the scene at the seashore (immediately preceding his vision of the fabulous artificer mounting the air) where the boys hail him as the crowned bull; in the diary entries where the "terrible queer creatures at the end of the earth," the old man himself of Mulrennan's account, and again the creatures of Stephen's nightmare, are strangely merged in the figure of the demon-angel with whom he prophesies he must struggle—there is a dark undercurrent of reference to this other aspect of the myth, of the character of him whom Stephen has chosen as father, that does much to account at the end for the apparent inadequacy of his preparations for the priesthood in which he has ordained himself.

For one thing that is surely represented here in this dark side of the legend, in the allusions to the Minotaur and the labyrinth, the hidden shame of both Minos and Dedalus himself—though there may be a great deal more, too, in it—is the flesh and its lusts, and the subrational processes of the mind. And what Stephen has consistently done, from the altars of Clongowes to those of nighttown, though theoretically he would see himself as the artist "forging anew in his workshop out of the sluggish matter of the earth a new, soaring impalpable imperishable being," is simply to ignore, as any part of the matter of himself, that matter—to deny rather than to redeem it. The image in which, during his terror at the retreat, he saw his own lust—as a monstrous, snaky life attached parasitically to him, feeding upon him at the direction of its own, separate mind and will—though he senses even then the heresy of such a notion, is never really changed for him. Perhaps at the very end, in the prophecy of the struggle he must enter into with the demon-angel, there is suggested some possibility of his coming to terms with it in the future. For he speaks of "gripping him by the sinewy throat till . . . till what? Till he yield to me? No, I mean him no harm."

But whether he is to or not is a question of no critical consequence, so long as we see that he has not yet; and that it is precisely by the extent of this failure of Stephen's to attain full stature as artist that we can measure the greatness of Joyce.

If Stephen has failed to understand or to accept the third significance of the plume, as phallic symbol, Joyce assuredly has not failed. He knew that it had to be redeemed, of course, along with all the rest of the flesh. But, in this respect, the phallus is no different from feathers. Feathers without the bird cannot fly either. Stephen turns away in fastidious disgust from his own thoughts when from the censer of his world there emerges a recollection of Moynihan's crude capping of the professor's joke on the elliptical billiard balls. But Joyce knew the price, and had paid it long before he wrote *A Portrait of the Artist as a Young Man*. The final triumph of his "penisolate war" is in that joyous language of *Finnegan's Wake*. But the "snaky life" is already in process of redemption in the *Portrait*, if we can manage to hear this as *his* song, not Stephen's. The serpent is already on the wing, for the land where "the green wothe botheth."

# 5 *The Great Gatsby:*

## One in Two

*The Great Gatsby*, it has been generally agreed, is the high point of F. Scott Fitzgerald's career. He himself regarded it as such, asserting by his use of the word in the title his hope for it as the one, whole embodiment of his own slender greatness. Everything that he wrote before in some sense leads up to this book, and everything afterward represents a decline from it, a blurring and disintegration of the single moment of perfected vision.

But most interesting, I think, is his specific identification of "Winter Dreams" (1922) as a preliminary version of the novel. With respect to the plot situation of the two stories, the likeness is not very close. In "Winter Dreams" there is a comparatively, but only comparatively, poor boy from the Middle West who loves and loses a glamorous, rich girl of his home community; himself gets rich and moves to New York; and, at the age of thirty-two, comes to disillusioning awareness (not by seeing her again, but only by hearing of her from a chance acquaintance) that the image of the girl he has carried in his mind during all the intervening years corresponds to no reality. This is all. But the basic similarity of theme is at once apparent. And James E. Miller, in *The Fictional Technique of F. Scott Fitzgerald*, comments at some length on the relationship of the two works. Here, I want to stress only one point: how Dexter Green, of "Winter Dreams," is a kind of single-character version of the double hero of *The Great Gatsby*.

Fitzgerald confessed that he often had the experience of seeing his fictional heroes, in the process of writing, turn into himself. And he once remarked also that he and Zelda sometimes seemed to him actually to be characters from one of his novels. He had, then, more than the usual difficulty in maintaining the distinction between art and life; a difficulty related to, or including, that of keeping his vision as artist clear of his ambition merely to be a successful writer, to get rich.

Dexter Green is one of the early, less effective masks of himself, in which he tried to overcome the inner conflict simply by making the hero a businessman, with no more than minimal pretensions to literary intelligence, eminently successful, and experiencing no doubts of the adequacy of his ambitions except in love. But given, on the one hand, Dexter's single-minded purposefulness in making money, it is improbable that he should have the capacities of sensibility, of self-scrutiny, expressed in his feelings about Judy Jones. Conversely, given the sensibility, it is difficult to believe in his business acumen. There are two men in Dexter, neither realized; and the fact that the same two were in Fitzgerald, also unrealized, that the fiction is accurate, "true," in this sense, does not make it any more convincing.

The reason they are not realized (and to some extent we sense this from the one story) is that Fitzgerald always had, actually, a profound moral suspicion of success, especially of great financial success, as inevitably corruptive of the finer sensibilities, at the same time that he admired it and dreamed of having it—and a further suspicion that the kind of attraction which a Dexter Green felt for a Judy Jones bore the same taint—so that the situation in "Winter Dreams" was a twofold falsification of the essential problem. But when he hit upon the plan of *The Great Gatsby* he found the means effectively of dramatizing, and resolving, the conflict that was insupportable in the one person (either Green or himself) simply by dividing the one into two. Nick Carraway, the "I" of the story, is not a writer but a man we can imagine capable of writing, a man of sensibility and scruple, son of respectable and reasonably well-to-do but not patrician parents, relatively unsuccessful, both in business and in love, so that he can afford to take a detached and skeptical attitude toward success. In Jay Gatsby we see the man of power and unscrupulous ambition, an outright gangster, so that the moral status of his wealth is unambiguous, enormously rich, entirely self-made from origins of total obscurity, and completely blind to the folly of his desires.

The two come together, of course, finally. They discover and complete themselves—on Carraway's part, at least, consciously—in each other. There is the side of callousness and success in Carraway's failure, in his respectability; the side of honor and the capacity for magnificent defeat in Gatsby's ambition. That is the story. And both of them are Fitzgerald. But the point is there would have been no story, or not so finely successful a story as the one we have, if they had not first been separated—and the author allowed, for a time, room to stand invisibly between them.

But the book is more, too, than dramatization of a personal problem. For the conflict within Fitzgerald was (perhaps we should say *is*) the conflict of an American era. The question whether Scott Fitzgerald did, as he sometimes supposed, help largely to *make* that era, is one of the permanently unanswerable questions of cultural history. At any rate, the age and the man mirror each other. And insofar as his association with Gatsby results for Nick Carraway in a discovery of his own identity, it amounts also to a rediscovery of America.

Specifically, Nick finally identifies the Middle West as the essential America—i.e., the visionary America—and himself as Middle Westerner. But, more generally—and less, necessarily, in terms of space than of time, for the land itself is long since possessed, and no longer "something commensurate to [man's] capacity for wonder"—he discovers himself as resident, so to speak, citizen, of a particular "moment" of Western history, which the whole social milieu of postwar America, and the opportunity it affords for the career of a man like Gatsby, epitomizes.

It is, obviously, a rootless society. For, again, the sense of rootedness—the identity of career with place, the identity of the individual with the regional character, the possibility of setting spatial limits to a man's aspiration, his "capacity for wonder"— depends upon the supposed existence of *new* places, new physical regions, that might be discovered and explored.

When the First World War had demonstrated beyond all possible doubt or forgetfulness that no such regions did, in fact, exist—that it was, and had been for a long time, "one world," the New World already, as Nick Carraway calls it at the end of this novel, "the old country"—man's ambition suffered inevitably a radical displacement. It is not simply that the characters of *The Great Gatsby* are all constantly "on the go"—with the automobile as the central symbol of their erratic existence—but precisely that the movement *is* erratic, has no definite, forward direction, is merely to-and-fro. The course of ambition, of empire, is turned backward, upon itself. Gatsby, the new pioneer, the new empire builder, turns not farther westward but back eastward. Nick Carraway discovers the further irony that the trek to the East, for himself and Gatsby, *was* westward, that the story he has told is "a story of the Middle West." But the final point is, of course, that the *West* (or Middle West)—in contradistinction to its public, historical significance—is for Carraway, Gatsby, and the Buchanans, the place of their origin, their personal *East*. Gatsby's quest for the love of Daisy is, as he admits to Carraway, an attempt to relive the past, a journey, again, that carries him backward in time, in the history of his personal experience. In short, East is West and West is East, in the sense simply that the course of the expansion of civilization having come full circle there is no empirically meaningful orientation of calendar to map, no necessary, practical relationship, such as there once was, between the direction of economic or social purpose or aspiration, the thrust to the future, and the direction of either mass or individual migration, the changing of place of residence.

And thus, the geographical terms of the novel have, it seems to me, a *purely* mythic significance, and are everywhere subject to the paradoxical reversals of myth. (Even Nick's decision at the end to return to the Middle West surely does not represent any naïve, practical identification of the region itself and its social usages with the system of moral values he seeks to establish or recover for himself, but is only a conscious, symbolic gesture, the dramatic "sign" of his purpose. If *Middle* West, in distinction from West—with the humor of Gatsby's vagueness about the region of his origins—has any special significance, it is just as "middle distance," aesthetic distance, the point of visionary nowhere.) Indeed like Kurtz—the alter hero of Conrad's novel from which Stallman and others have shown that

Fitzgerald derived so much of his design—not only Gatsby himself, but all the characters here, are so thoroughly rootless that they have quite "kicked the world out from under them."

And, if it is easy enough to see in this connection the significance of such overt symbolic usages as Fitzgerald's naming of the two sides of the bay, East Egg and West Egg, and the fact that Gatsby never gets any farther than West Egg and lives in a "mansion" as opposed to the "palaces" of the East-Eggers, and the allusion to the story of Columbus and the egg—we need still, if we would take his measure purely as novelist and not just as critic of his age, to examine some more subtle characteristics of his style. There is in the descriptive imagery, for example, supporting the vision of the uprooted society of the period, an elaborately contrived, recurrent *motif* of things and people seen as suspended above the ground, floating or hovering in air.

The dumping ground between West Egg and New York, where the figures of men appear to people watching from the trains to rise out of the gray "farms of ashes" like wraiths of dust or smoke, insubstantial and shadowy, gives its character finally to the entire world of the novel. The scene is dominated by a signboard bearing the picture of two gigantic, blue eyes framed by a pair of yellow spectacles—advertising the services of Dr. T. J. Eckleburg, "some wild wag of an oculist," as Nick calls him, who has "moved away" or "sunk down himself into eternal blindness," leaving the image on the signboard to "brood on over the solemn dumping ground." He is later identified by Wilson, with unconscious irony, as "God," who "sees everything." The monstrous, disembodied eyes become symbolic of the God-abandoned state of the whole society. Wilson, Gatsby's nemesis, who runs the service station in the midst of the underworld of the dumping area (the *nameless* place—"What's the name of this place?" the cop asks after the fatal accident, and someone replies "It ain't got no name"), is with clear appropriateness the most notably ghostly figure of the novel. He is described always as ashen, completely colorless both in character and appearance. And when Nick Carraway is first introduced to them, Myrtle Wilson "walks through" her husband to shake hands with Nick and Tom Buchanan.

But Daisy and Jordan too, and even the furnishings of the

room in which he finds them, have for Nick on his first visit to the Buchanan's house this quality of impalpability—with the difference only, to be sure, that in their case the effect of ethereality is more immediately pleasurable than in the description of Wilson's world. The joining of the two worlds, of this at first merely "dreamy" one and the other of nightmare, is to come later. But (aside from the mere factual reference in this first chapter to Tom's keeping "a woman" in New York) it is ominous here of the final catastrophe that Nick should see the room as he does; "the breeze blew through the room, blew curtains in at one end and out the other like pale flags . . . , and then rippled over the wine-colored rug, making a shadow on it as wind does on the sea." Even the couch, "the only completely stationary object in the room," is like "an anchored balloon," on which the two young women are "buoyed up." And they, Daisy and Jordan, are "both in white," and "their dresses were rippling and fluttering as if they had just been blown back in after a short flight around the house."

Variations on the same motif are apparent everywhere in the descriptions of Gatsby and the settings and company of his parties. "In his blue gardens men and girls came and went like moths among the whisperings and the champagne and the stars." ". . . as the earth lurches away from the sun . . . the groups change more swiftly, swell with new arrivals, dissolve and form in the same breath . . . girls . . . glide on through the sea-change of faces and voices and color under the constantly changing light." "A tray of cocktails floated at us through the twilight." The climactic statement of the theme in this chapter (chap. iii) comes significantly in the description—surely the most exquisitely comic episode of the novel—of the automobile accident after the party, when a car bearing two of the drunken guests crashes into a wall on the driveway and loses a wheel. There is a mix-up about who was driving, the onlookers thinking for a moment that only one man (Owl Eyes, as Nick calls him) was in the car—and then, when the door has opened again, ". . . there was a ghostly pause," and "very gradually, part by part, a pale, dangling individual stepped out of the wreck, pawing tentatively at the ground with a large uncertain dancing shoe." The bystanders explain to him, or try to explain, that "wheel and car are no longer joined by any physical bond," but persisting in his own utter detachment from physical reality he suggests that they try to "Back out. . . . Put her in reverse," and when again someone protests "But the *wheel's* off!" he replies, with a heroic indifference to the laws of inertia and gravity that is matched only by Gatsby's defiance of Time, "No harm in trying."

And, to come now to Gatsby himself. It is he who, at least in the first part of the novel, is the most insubstantial, the most ghostly, of all. In Nick's account of his first sight of his neighbor, a shadowy figure on the deserted lawn at night, he tells how, seeing him stretch out his arms toward the water, he too "involuntarily glanced seaward," and when he turned again to look for Gatsby, found that "he had vanished." He comes and goes at the parties in the same disconcerting fashion, showing up out of nowhere for a few minutes' talk at a table, or standing alone on the steps of the house, and then disappearing. And at Nick's house, momentarily panicked at the actual prospect of seeing Daisy again after so many years, he briefly pulls the vanishing act once more just as Nick is showing Daisy in.

Now, there are some important qualifications to be made in this characterization of Gatsby. He is to become a more and more substantial figure, as the others thin out in the course of the novel. And even as early as the account of the party in the third chapter, there is a prefiguring of this in the picture of him standing alone on the steps of his mansion, "his hand up in a formal gesture of farewell" to his departing guests, and looking out serenely over the din of horns and the confused movements of the crowd around the wrecked car. In his very isolation, and against the background of the "sudden emptiness" of his great house, he is the more sharply and surely defined. And, in the seemingly unreal setting of his party, with the moon itself something "produced like the supper, no doubt, out of a caterer's basket," and so on, there is a certain important quality of the *artificial* that from the first subtly distinguishes the insubstantiality of his world from that of both the Buchanans and the Wilsons. The improbability, the impalpability, is here in a measure palpably contrived. To some extent, clearly, it is a deliberate and purposeful trick being worked by Gatsby, an elaborate and controlled effect of *legerdemain*, not a true manifestation of the preternatural.

But final consideration of these matters may best be deferred until we have examined the connections of the impalpability motif with another recurrent theme. Insofar as human identity is a matter of certainty of origins, there is an obviously necessary loss of identity on the part of persons living in such an uprooted society as this one of the period Fitzgerald describes. The problem of identity centers throughout, of course, in the treatment of Gatsby himself. His guests like to give each other the shivers with stories about him—that he was a German spy during the War, and so on. There is his own fantastic story to Nick on the way into New York the day they meet Meyer Wolfsheim, of his inherited wealth, and experience as a globetrotter, big game hunter, war hero and Oxford man; the mystery of how he makes his living; the entire fantastic accumulation of lies and half-truths that has been, to some extent by his own efforts, built up around him. The central thread to be followed in the whole, rather simple design of the novel's plot is that of the question: Who is Gatsby?

A part of this theme is the rejection of the father—Gatsby's renaming himself, making the more distinctive-sounding *Gatsby* from *Gatz*, and, having grown to his present estate through, first, his association with the fathers-surrogate Cody and Wolfsheim (who tells Nick "I made him"), being now finally characterized by Nick as a Son of God, about his Father's business. And, if it is true, as Marius Bewley has pointed out, that he has in this something of the character of an American culture hero, the culture in question is most particularly that of the immediate postwar period. His mythic personality reflects the temper of his age, and is to a great extent, in the design of the novel, a heroic composite of all the virtues and vices of the secondary characters.

Everyone, to a greater or lesser extent, shares in the loss of identity. All the guests at his party are more or less nameless. They are simply "girls," or "men," in the ever-dissolving and reforming groups around the tables and bandstand, the "sea-change of faces." Or, when one or another is, for a fleeting moment, identified individually, it is either by succinct reference to profession, with perhaps one or two adjectives ("the movie director," "the undergraduate," "a notorious contralto"—Tom Buchanan, with an irony that cuts both ways on the question of the relative certainty of his identity, is annoyed at being introduced as "the polo-player"); or else by a caricature, more or less elaborate, of physical appearance (Owl Eyes and his companion in the wrecked car, the "pale, dangling individual," the drunken girl singing the blues whose tears wash the mascara down her cheeks to form "notes" that someone suggests she sing); or again by characterizing, satiric nicknames supplied impromptu by Nick ("Owl Eyes," "the three Mr. Mumbles") or, much to the same purpose, the ostensibly "real" names he has recorded on the old timetable (James B., "Rot-Gut," Ferret; S. W. Belcher; the Smirks; and Klipspringer; along with less fanciful ones like O'Donovan and Myer).

Nor are the three-dimensional characters besides Gatsby exempt. It is sufficiently clear from the start that Nick Carraway is a bit overanxious about identifying himself with his family, and their standing of three generations in the St. Paul community, and with one particular great-uncle, whose appearance and character he is supposed to have inherited. Jordan Baker, when Nick first meets her, is at length "identified" simply as the face whose "pleasing contemptuous expression had looked out at him from many rotogravure pictures of sporting life at Asheville and Hot Springs and Palm Beach." Her family, according to Daisy, is "one aunt about a thousand years old." Whatever "her story" was that Nick had once known something about, he has, he tells us, "forgotten long ago." And, after a few brief threats fully to emerge, she is at the end of the novel about ready to be folded away once again into the rotogravure section.

Tom Buchanan, for all the hard-muscled, fleshly reality of him, is unable ever to emerge into entire, adult existence from his dream of "the dramatic turbulence of some irrecoverable football game." With some panic, apparently, in contemplation of his own or the world's advancing age, he has "begun to nibble at the edges of stale ideas," and takes solace in half-baked theories of Nordic supremacy. Even at the crisis of his conflict with Gatsby over Daisy, in the suite at the Plaza, he is altogether incapable of seeing the connection between his own infidelity and the present threat to his marriage. None of the personalities involved, least of all his own, is real to him; and he babbles in incoherent generalities of the degeneracy of the times and how, "nowadays," "family life and family institutions" are sneered at by "people."

And perhaps it need hardly be stressed, as the final pathos of Gatsby's situation, that Daisy, simply, is not what she seemed. She is fundamentally spurious. She lacks entirely the moral responsibility that is one essential measure of identity, and is capable of keeping faith neither with her husband nor her lover. She is, after all, what Nick has a brief intimation of in the first chapter, a great deal like Tom—and the two of them are in the end bound together inseparably by a lie.

The lie, specifically, is Daisy's concealment of the fact that it was she, not Gatsby, who was driving the car when Myrtle Wilson was struck. But, through the accumulated significance of the automobile as symbol, and with regard to the moral relationship that exists among the five of them (Daisy, Tom, Gatsby, Myrtle Wilson, and Wilson), constituting as it does at once a betrayal of her lover to his death and an acquiescence in her husband's adultery—the lie is evidence of her general and fundamental dishonesty, of her failure in every sense to acknowledge herself and her responsibilities.

This entire chapter, of the excursion to New York, the showdown between Gatsby and Tom, and the killing of Myrtle Wilson, it should be noted, is a tragedy of errors, a series of mistaken identities. In the first place, Gatsby and Tom exchange "attributes," so to speak, their automobiles, for the trip into the city—which leads, in turn, to Myrtle Wilson's mistaking Jordan Baker for Daisy. There are further, psychological mistakes in the scene at the hotel: Tom's failure to see, to recognize, both Gatsby and Daisy for what they are; Gatsby's own to understand the difference that the years and her marriage have made in Daisy, and so on. And, finally, once more in the realm of objective fact, Wilson tracks down the "wrong" man.

Now, all of this, the uncertainty of identities, is the moral and psychological counterpart of the theme, or motif, of dissolution, of impalpability and the airy suspension of things, that we have noted in the imagery of physical description. The two are found frequently in very close connection—as, for example, in the episode of the wreck after Gatsby's party in Chapter III, where the imagery of ghostliness in the description of the second man's emergence from the car accompanies a statement (here comic, in anticipation of the later, tragic event) of the theme of identity and responsibility in the crowd's mistaking Owl Eyes for the driver.

What is argued, ultimately, is a radical coincidence of order, of stability, in the physical realm, with moral and psychological order. Nick observes that Wilson has been made physically sick, reduced to a still more deathlike pallor and numbness of movement than he usually has, by his suspicion of his wife's infidelity—the "something funny" he has found out of which he speaks to Nick and Tom when they stop at the station on the way to New York with Jordan earlier in the day of Myrtle's death. But Wilson's state reflects the general, social or cultural condition of the world represented in the novel.

In Fitzgerald's treatment of the "waste land" and "hollow men" themes that are the commonplaces of the principal fiction of the Twenties and later—(we need not concern ourselves further here with his probable, specific "sources" for such symbols as the dumping ground or Nick's fanciful picture of Gatsby as the turbaned "character," "leaking sawdust at every pore" as he pursues a tiger through the Bois de Boulogne)— modern man, in his cultural displacement, his loss of contact with traditional values and modes of conduct, has lost hold also on the reality of his physical environment. Automobiles and even houses are the least-significant signs of the disorder of his imagination. Beyond the absurdity of Gatsby's vast chariot of a car, and of his movie-set house with its conglomeration of "period" styles in architecture and furnishings—and the Buchanan's East Egg "palace" is, after all, as spurious in its fashion as his "mansion," as much a pastry creation, with its "wedding cake" ceilings, as ridiculously anachronistic, with its garages converted into stables for Tom's polo ponies—beyond the distortion of form in these manufactured things, there is an assault upon the order of things in nature, the created and procreated. Grass, trees, the lesser lights of heaven—Gatsby's *"blue* lawns," the moon out of a caterer's basket—become also artificial, and man's very flesh to him, at last, in Webster's phrase, "fantastic puff-paste."

But what, now, is the greatness of Gatsby? In what does he "redeem the time," "redeem the dream," to make him essentially different from the others in Nick's view—from Tom and Daisy and Jordan, or even from his guests whose improbable names are written into the blank spaces of Nick's old railroad timetable?

A brief examination of Fitzgerald's treatment of the time theme as such might be helpful. Nick's choice of notepaper for recording the names of Gatsby's guests is obviously symbolic here. It points up, simply, the cultural disinheritance of these people, with their names either of late-immigrant or, in the case of ones such as Belcher and Ferret, of no discernible genealogical origin, but seemingly the result of some primitive linguistic process of the new barbarism, a system of character naming, perhaps with the involvement here and there of a rudimentary totemism. They are people who came from, and are going, nowhere. The fading pencil scrawl in the blank spaces of the timetable deftly characterizes the nature of their existence as one in a historical vacuum.

Robert Stallman has interestingly analyzed Gatsby's own fall as the result of his failure to come to terms with time, of his making or attempting to make "a hole in time." And there are several instances in the novel of a special association of Gatsby with symbols of time—one of them as plainly, almost blatantly significant as the writing of the guest list on the railroad schedule. When Gatsby comes back into Nick's house at the "teaparty" arranged for him and Daisy, and meets again for the first time in many years his old sweetheart, her with whom he assures Nick that he not only can, but firmly intends to, "relive the past," in his nervousness he leans against the mantelpiece and very nearly knocks over with his head "an old, defunct mantelpiece clock." Gatsby catches the clock in time to keep it from falling, sets it straight again on the shelf, and stammers inordinate, embarrassed apologies. Then, when Nick has reassured him that no harm is done, that the clock is an old one, useless anyway, they are all three caught in a brief, desperate silence—while Nick tells the reader that "I think we all believed for a moment that [the clock] had smashed in pieces on the floor." A short exchange of remarks ensues on the subject of how long it has been since Daisy and Jay have seen each other—Gatsby remembering that it is precisely "five years this November"—and so on. And, of course, we know that Gatsby is *not* to have Daisy, will not be able to restore the lost romance.

But what Nick's thought during the moment of silence clearly means is that he—as well, he believes, as the others right then—is almost convinced that Gatsby can pull it off, can "relive," or recapture, the past—somehow bring time to a final stop. It is only for a moment that he even believes this—and he knows, of course, that it hasn't been and can't be done. But the question, once again, is what there is about Gatsby that can compel Nick, even if it is only momentarily, to believe something that his reason and his experience of life deny.

The answer has to do, I think, first with the matter of Gatsby's relative *control* over the spuriousness and artificiality of his environment that I mentioned earlier—with the sense one has that he is not just a part of the vast, vulgar artifice of the age and its society, but, at least to some extent, himself the artificer. The difference between him and the Belchers and the Smirks and the Chromes is that they are the rabbits, and he is the magician.

He is a version of the hero of Marvell's poem—though he cannot make his sun stand still, yet he will make him run. And this, the entirely willed character of his self-deception—the fact that he is not simply "careless," like Daisy and Tom, but positively called and dedicated to self-destruction—is as I see it the basis for the implicit final interpretation of the lie by which he saves Daisy, the last act of self-deceit, as something in the nature of self-denial. It is the necessary and only possible basis for Nick's supposing that he could have had, just before his death, as he crossed the lawn to the swimming pool, one final moment of tragic enlightenment, of recognition of the real externality of things—"and found what a grotesque thing a rose is and how raw the sunlight was upon the scarcely created grass." It is the basis on which Nick—Gatsby's biographer, the man of articulate insight whom the man of purpose and action needs to complete his character—makes and justifies his own, untragic "choice of nightmares."

The choice, of course, was not possible for Fitzgerald. He could not so conveniently and honorably kill off the Gatsby of himself. For one thing, he was unable, as we have noted, ever to know whether he had like Gatsby made, or was only the victim of, his age. He had to go on to other novels, falling back once more on the mere substitute, third-person identity of Dick Diver in the post-Jamesian confusions of *Tender Is the Night*; and to begin too late, as might have been foreseen, *The Last Tycoon*—both of them documents of the worship of failure. But in *The Great Gatsby* he was able just once to have it, as America has always wanted it, both ways: himself as first *and* third person, the failing success identical with the successful failure, the responsibilities of the future both demanded and refused.

# 6 *To the Lighthouse:*

## Vision Without Promise

It would seem impossible to construct the problem of human identity apart from consideration of the mysteries of sex and procreation. The sexual character of the human individual, however inevitably mixed, no one person purely male or purely female—and, indeed, this indecisiveness only serves to emphasize the importance of the dichotomy—is radical. Chiefly in being aware of this character in other persons, which is the procreative potentiality, whether affirmed or denied, deprived or richly endowed, the capacity to bring forth many out of the one, do we recognize the otherness of ourselves.

Virginia Woolf's novel has as its ultimate theme precisely what Andrew Ramsay defines, in answer to Lily Briscoe's question, as the burden of his father's philosophical preoccupation—"subject and object and the nature of reality." But Lily is speaking both as woman and as artist when she replies that "Heavens, she had no notion what that meant," and is instructed then by Andrew to "think of a kitchen table . . . when you're not there." The table of which she entertains a vision, "a scrubbed kitchen table . . . lodged now in the fork of a pear tree . . . its four legs in air," a "white deal" table—"deal" is perhaps a pun on "ideal"—becomes the concrete symbol of the abstracting, rational intelligence, or of reality as seen by that intelligence. It is the first in a long series of things "thought of when no one is there," in its initial, mere absurdity ironically anticipating the later terror—of the vision of the vacant house in the middle section "Time Passes," where the eye of the lighthouse beam and the shadows of birds pass over the empty mirrors, and of Mr. Ramsay's and Lily Briscoe's bereavement in the final section, seeking communication with the invisible presence of the dead Mrs. Ramsay. But the matter of first importance to be noted about that table, as symbol of the abstracting intelligence, of one way, rendered manifestly absurd, in which things invisible (what is there when no one is there) may be dealt with—and, by the token of its absurdity, demanding the attempt to reveal, in the rest of the novel, presumably a better way—is its specific identification with the masculine mind.

The table as such, perhaps, is inevitably feminine. As such, it is, or truly represents, reality. But the positioning, so to speak, of the symbol, its awkward lodging in the pear tree, obviously renders it absurd, and makes it representative of the abstracting, i.e., masculine, intelligence—the kind of intelligence that, in Lily Briscoe's view, violates reality.

Now, one is tempted to start making qualifications, stating reservations, right away. Lily Briscoe, besides being an artist, is an old maid, which assuredly qualifies her character as woman. And, I might seem to have implied that her point of view, however we are to define it, is dominant throughout the novel; whereas, in any obvious way, it actually does not become so until the final section. Moreover, especially in the conclusion, her function is somewhat to mediate between the opposed claims of Mr. and Mrs. Ramsay, after a fashion to reconcile them, rather than unequivocally to champion the latter's cause in her absence. But, to whatever extent that sensibility is or is not finally identifiable with Lily's, not to speak yet of Mrs. Woolf's—and notwithstanding the force of such an argument as Glenn Pedersen's, which would make Mrs. Ramsay the villainess of the piece—the initial effect of the entire opening section "The Window," by far the longest, is surely to glorify the feminine sensibility, in the person of Mrs. Ramsay, at the expense of the masculine, her husband's.

The pattern of a dialectic opposition is clear. These two are not simply a man and a woman—rather distressingly not that, indeed—a husband and a wife, but Man and Woman, the Masculine Principle and the Feminine Principle. They represent two, clearly opposed truths in competition for the world, for the future, as represented specifically in the proposed trip to the lighthouse but more generally in the future lives of their children, for truth.

Mr. Ramsay's is the truth of things as they are. He "never tampered with a fact." Mrs. Ramsay's is the truth of perhaps, of things as they might be. They will go to the lighthouse tomorrow "if it's fine." "But it won't be fine," says Mr. Ramsay. "But it may be fine—I expect it will be fine," says Mrs. Ramsay.

And, although we suspect from the first that Mr. Ramsay's judgment will be vindicated by the weather on the tomorrow— the set of the wind, the falling barometer, cannot be and must not be argued with—we are given clearly to understand that this does not mean he is *right*. For it is the "won't be" that betrays the inadequacy of his kind of truth. He may pretend that it is only facts with which he is concerned, with things as they are, but actually he is radically discontent with present reality; he has no real interest in *is* except as the basis of *will be*. The supposed, uncomprising factuality, objectivity, of his mind is revealed as a pathetic egotism. Is, when pushed to will be—cannot, to must not be—becomes, obviously, the instrument of moral tyranny.

Hardly less even than his sycophant Charles Tansley, "the little atheist" whom the children so despise, Mr. Ramsay is a figure of ridicule in this first section of the book. It is only the element of pathos in his egotism, only the evident fact that he himself is the chief victim of his own tyranny of mind, that makes his antics in any way "funny," and serves somewhat to redeem him as a sympathetic character. But the emphasis is derogatory. He is a disruptive presence, demanding, mean, indifferent to anyone's peace of mind except his own—repeatedly breaking in to destroy the serenity of the mother's communion with her child, abrupting with his wild, self-dramatizing declamations upon the field of Lily Briscoe's vision as she sits on the lawn trying to paint. And the meanness, the cruelty, the demanding relentlessness, is specifically identified again and again with his character as *male*. The sensibility of the woman, of Mrs. Ramsay, is the "fountain and spray of life," a "delicious fecundity," into which "the fatal sterility of the male plunged itself, like a beak of brass, barren and bare." And again, "James felt all her strength flaring up to be drunk and quenched by the beak of brass, the arid scimitar of the male, which smote mercilessly, demanding sympathy."

The very, shameless intensity of his need for sympathy is what most prevents its being, at least from the reader, elicited. And to the extent that Mrs. Ramsay is willing to provide it, despite his unworthiness, her charity serves only further to ennoble her. "There was nobody she reverenced as she reverenced him." But this reverence, although it is wholly admirable in her, is at the same time one which Mrs. Woolf has made it plain would be very difficult for anyone else to understand or share.

To be sure, we get some few hints at a quality of nobility in him discoverable to others than his wife. Lily Briscoe, comparing him at first unfavorably to Mr. Bankes, remembers suddenly how he had "come down in two coats the other night and let Mrs. Ramsay trim his hair into a pudding basin," and is filled for a moment with the recognition of "a fiery unworldliness" in the man which makes him seem then infinitely superior to the neat, scrubbed, bachelor botanist. And we catch something of the same in the story of the walk he had taken many years before with Bankes, when he stopped in the path to point his stick at the mother hen with her chickens and muttered "Pretty— pretty"—the gesture in which his friend had sensed "an odd illumination in to his heart," and, admiring it, yet at the same time had foreseen the drying up of their friendship, what was to come about as the result of Ramsay's marriage and the encumbrances of "clucking domesticities." The passage elicits a subtle variety of sympathies, for Bankes as well as for Ramsay. It has the true, high pathos, of an insight into one of the ineluctable sadnesses of life—how the love of man and woman always, inevitably, if it is to be fulfilled, destroys the love of man and man—which is momentarily beyond considerations merely of individual personality, and of the relative merits of character. But, in the end, the tendency of it is to confirm Lily Briscoe's intuition of Ramsay's superiority. The "glories of isolation and austerity which crowned him in youth," which had made him, in the time of the flower of their friendship, most admirable to Bankes, we are led to feel have been worthily put off. Bankes "commiserated him, envied him," in his having so divested himself. And it is the envy that is proper; the commiseration is the thinnest mask of Bankes's own, mere self-commiseration, in being deprived of the friendship. Ramsay's petty, eccentric vanities are nothing beside the botanist's settled habits of self-solicitude, with his valet and his objections to dogs on chairs.

But this can do little to offset the effect of the other episodes, of Ramsay's cruelty to his wife, and of his absurd, childish daydreams of self-dramatization, as the hero of Balaclava and what not. It is clear enough how pettiness and vanity, in the truly great, may be evidence of actual humility. But the question is, whether Ramsay really is a great man. Humility, especially when it so successfully disguises itself as vanity, requires so much charitable insight on the part of others to be discovered as humility, is not likely to seem much of a virtue unless there is reasonable cause for pride. What, in short, does Mr. Ramsay have to be humble *about?*

The crucial passage is the one describing his effort to run the "alphabet" of thought—to push on from Q, where he is stuck, to R. He does not make it, of course. And we see clearly the grounds of his fear about his status as professional philosopher. We are told repeatedly how he frets over the suspicion that "young men do not care for him," that Charles Tansley's opinion of him as "the greatest metaphysician of the time" is pure sycophancy. But the final, ironic point is not just that he is a lesser thinker than someone who could, perhaps, go on to R, or even all the way to Z. Bernard Blackstone, without being able to make much of his insight, has observed that the "shutter," "the leathern eyelid of a lizard," which obscures Ramsay's vision of R, is the veil of his egotism. So, rather obviously, it is. Throughout the episode, in the midst of the intellectual struggle, he is so preoccupied with the pathos of his lonely heroism—daydreaming about himself as the leader of a party of shipwrecked seamen, of imperiled mountain-climbers—that he cannot keep to the discipline of his mental task. But the point is not that Mr. Ramsay, in particular, is so grossly self-infatuated that he cannot reach that goal of R. (I take it that R "stands for" Reality.) The point is, rather, that the entire system, the entire conception of thought as the "piano keyboard" or the "alphabet" is a construct of egotism—i.e., of the intelligence acting in the service of the ego—and therefore doomed to failure. No one who thinks in this way is going to reach R, for the simple reason that the Reality so conceived, so reduced, does not exist. R is an illusion.

"For if thought is like the keyboard of a piano, divided into so many notes, or like the alphabet is ranged in twenty-six letters all in order . . . ," Mrs. Woolf says. But we could hardly be given more clearly to understand, than by that "if," that thought is *not* like that.

But this, although it somehow universalizes Ramsay, does nothing to dignify him. No matter how universal the tendency of mind that he represents—and Mrs. Woolf pretty clearly regards it as the basic tendency of all, at the very least, English metaphysics—the tendency stands, in him, condemned. The "on to R" skit is a merciless caricature of rationalistic metaphysics, of the kind of thinking that would, precisely, be good enough for directing polar expeditions, rescuing shipwrecked seamen, governing India, any endeavor in which the object is simply to "get things done," but which is utterly ineffectual when it comes to the fundamental problems of existence. (The farce is more than a little embarrassing, perhaps, in a way not intended by the author. Mrs. Woolf simply doesn't know very much about the way philosophical investigations are conducted. Her philosopher is a straw man. But the intention is unmistakable.) There is, therefore, an irreducible element of condescension in the "respect" Lily Briscoe professes to feel for Mr. Ramsay's mind, in Mrs. Ramsay's "reverence" for him. He is pitiable, nothing more, in his humiliations; for his greatness, to which the willingness to suffer humiliation, the thoughtless simplicity, should attest, is revealed as monstrous self-delusion.

And, to repeat, that false tendency of mind which would push the processes of rationalism—i.e., the processes of ego-assertion, of practical intelligence—into realms where they do not and cannot apply—i.e., precisely into the realm of the metaphysical, properly so-called—Mrs. Woolf clearly identifies with the masculine intelligence.

The philosopher's wife, on the other hand, is perfection of

beauty and wisdom. All (with Mr. Carmichael, to whom we shall come later, the notable exception) dance attendance upon her. She is mysterious, to be adored, at once completely self-contained and completely self-giving. Because she seeks nothing, all things come to her. Her beauty is indefinable; the "nonsense" of Charles Tansley's thoughts as he carries her bag, "stars in her eyes and veils in her hair, with cyclamen and wild violets," is in fact about as sensible as anyone's efforts to capture it could be. William Bankes is hardly more successful—"one must remember the quivering thing, the living thing . . . , and work it into the picture," but ". . . he did not know, he did not know, . . . he must go to his work." She is careless of it, "is no more aware of her beauty than a child," thinks Mr. Bankes; "she clapped a deer-stalker's hat on her head, she ran across the lawn in goloshes to snatch a child from mischief," so that ". . . one must endow her with some freak of idiosyncrasy—she did not like admiration—or suppose some latent desire to doff her royalty of form as if her beauty bored her and all that men say of beauty." But its indefinability, and her unawareness, her carelessness, are of course to be understood just as the firmest proof of it.

Children, goloshes, and deer-stalker's hat notwithstanding, she is accorded, and accepts, the homage due a queen. Mrs. Woolf repeatedly invokes the metaphor of regality in the account of her presiding at dinner.

In her beauty, her grace of bearing, she is queenly. But in some as it were neo-Platonic conception, the beauty is but the outward light of an inner virtue. She is queenly in her roles of protectress and of giver. "She had the whole of the other sex under her protection"; that, of course, above all, and the passage implicitly states the metaphor of royal patronage—"for reasons she could not explain, for their chivalry and valour, for the fact that they negotiated treaties, ruled India, controlled finance." But, besides the children, her guests too are her subjects, and the poor people of the town whose sickbeds she visits, going about dispensing favors from the mysterious bag that Charles Tansley was permitted unworthily to carry for her. (The household, with the children and guests, the latter significantly divided into the two circles of those who are actually staying at the house and those who have taken rooms in town, contains her court; the town itself, and the lighthouse, are her realm.) She is queenly as molder of destinies—as if, not so much merely prompting, but decreeing the engagement of Paul and Minta, appointing in fancy her son to a seat on the Bench.

But the matter of final importance is the implicit identification of beauty, of the virtue that shines forth in the beauty, with wisdom. Lily Briscoe, to be sure, is uncertain of the term. "Was it wisdom? Was it knowledge? Was it, once more, the deceptiveness of beauty, so that all one's perceptions, half way to truth, were tangled in a golden mesh? or did she lock up within her some secret which certainly Lily Briscoe believed people must have for the world to go on at all?" "And yet, she knew knowledge and wisdom were stored up in Mrs. Ramsay's heart." And the term, then, wisdom, will serve as well as another. The important thing, regardless of the precise term, is that she has a truth—or a source of truth, a way to truth—which is necessary "for the world to go on at all," which is opposed to the way of her husband's thinking, and which is plainly "preferred" to his, or regarded as superior.

It is also plain that the area of her concern is precisely that defined as her husband's—"subject and object and the nature of reality"—or, in terms that perhaps more accurately suggest the character of her "approach," existence and being. She is, in brief, albeit unwittingly, a metaphysician. Or, Mrs. Woolf has embodied in her, "symbolically," the statement of a metaphysical doctrine.

One need not too long hesitate to attach labels—except with due caution to note that the doctrine is one which in itself expressly condemns the habit of attaching labels. The pseudo-Bergsonism is apparent, and has been often observed. (James Hafley, in his generally excellent book on Virginia Woolf, *The Glass Roof*, presents the most sensible account of this matter to date.) Mrs. Ramsay's experience of knowledge as unity—her identification with the third stroke of the beam from the lighthouse, "the last of the three, which was her stroke," with "inanimate things, trees, streams, flowers," how she "felt they expressed one, felt they became one, felt they knew one, in a sense were one"—is a variety of intuition. Her mind at rest, in the "core of darkness," "when life sank down for a moment," inhabits Bergsonian time, entertains the experience of self as pure flow of consciousness, the *durée réelle*, and is indifferent to the limitations of spatialized experience. "Her horizon seemed to her limitless. There were all the places she had not seen; the Indian plains; she felt herself pushing aside the thick leather curtain of a church in Rome. This core of darkness could go anywhere, for no one saw it."

If the act of self-knowing or self-contemplation, Mrs. Ramsay's ecstatic composure in her momentary solitude when the household quiets down at the end of the day and she listens to the sea and watches for the stroke of the lighthouse beam, is vaguely "Bergsonian," we must be careful to recognize that the explicit identification in the novel of the capacity of mind for such an act with the feminine, with something deriving from popular notions of woman's intuition, is Mrs. Woolf's own idea. She is also largely on her own in seeming to interpret, finally, the act of creative intuition as identical with the artist's creativity. When Lily Briscoe, in the last section of the novel, is made consciously and directly to draw the analogy between Mrs. Ramsay's composed and composing presence and herself at her easel—"that woman sitting there writing under the rock resolved everything into simplicity . . . brought together this and that and then this . . . made . . . something which survived after all these years complete, . . . stayed in the mind affecting one almost like a work of art," and again, "Mrs. Ramsay making of the moment something permanent (as in another sphere Lily herself tried to make of the moment something permanent)"— the novelist has exploited for her own purposes a notion that is nowhere more than implied in the writings of the philosopher. But, with these reservations duly made, with due recognition above all that we are dealing with a novel, not a work of formal philosophy, it is not unenlightening to recall Bergson when we attempt to define the issue of the conflict, contest indeed, between Mrs. Ramsay and her husband. I have so far deliberately avoided a terminology that smacks exclusively of the Bergsonian; but there is no harm in thinking of nearsighted Mrs. Ramsay as representative of "intuition," of farsighted Mr. Ramsay as the "intellect," so long as we do not suppose that everything in the book can or should be made to fit the formula. The reference will be most useful when we try to determine where Mrs. Woolf herself "stands" with regard to the conflict between the Ramsays.

About the fact of Mrs. Ramsay's triumph, at least in the first section of the novel, there can be little question. She is, we are given clearly to understand, made of far sterner stuff than her husband, is in truth far more of a realist than he. If one might have suspected at first that she is merely the sentimentalist in her opposition to his pretentiously uncompromising factuality— wanting to reassure James, that "it may be fine"—the suspicion is soon dispelled. When, in the course of her meditations as she sits knitting, the voice of an insincere, conventional faith momentarily asserts itself—"We are in the hands of the Lord"—she quickly and firmly rejects it. It is not her voice. "Who had said it? Not she." "How could any Lord have made this world? she asked . . . there is no reason, order, justice: but suffering, death, the poor. There was no treachery too base for the world to commit; she knew that. No happiness lasted; she knew that." And her husband, passing by the window and seeing her, cannot "help noting the sternness at the heart of her beauty," and is pained and baffled by it. Finally, indeed, he cannot bear it. He must, in defense of his own weakness, the failure of his own philosophical faith to sustain him, come in again and plead silently with her for sympathy, try to compel her to some show of compromising softness.

And when she does, finally, seem to yield—by admitting that she was wrong, that the stocking she is knitting will not be finished, and that, in any event, she knows the weather will not permit the trip to the lighthouse next day—we realize that it is, at the center of her being, no real yielding at all. She can afford to say she is wrong, because she is on another and higher plane so indubitably right. The discovery of self, in the "wedge-shaped core of darkness," is a loss of self. (Specifically—Mrs. Woolf is very precise—it is a loss of *personality*. "Not as oneself did one find rest ever, `. . . but as a wedge of darkness. Losing personality, one lost the fret, the hurry, the stir. . . .") Just so, when she surrenders to her husband, yields, admits he is right, the surrender is in truth a triumph.

" 'Yes, you were right. It's going to be wet tomorrow. You won't be able to go.' And she looked again at him smiling. For she had triumphed again. She had not said it: yet he knew."

These are the final lines of Part I, "The Window."

The unfinished stocking, it is plain, is the web of Penelope. Insofar as, in remaining unfinished, it foretells Mrs. Ramsay's death, it is the thread of her fate, untimely cut off. But, most immediately, in the context of her admission that it cannot be finished, that the trip cannot be made, of her triumphant surrender, it is the web of her wifely fidelity—in which she draws Odysseus finally home.

And yet, I have so far deliberately overstated the case for Mrs. Ramsay as embodiment of the author's view. Not only have we the evidence of Mr. Carmichael's refusal, even to some extent Lily Briscoe's own hesitancy, to join in the dance of praise; but it might reasonably be questioned whether the effect of this final, living picture of Mrs. Ramsay, in triumph over her husband, is altogether flattering to her.

"Little question," I said, about her triumph. But enough, perhaps. Is it, as I have suggested, altogether the same thing when in her solitude the loss of self becomes self-discovery, truest communion, and when in her confrontation with her husband her seeming surrender becomes a triumph? Cannot the latter be interpreted merely as a psychological maneuver on her part, which—however true-to-life it may be, familiar from our experience of the ways of women with their men, and as such to be appreciated among Mrs. Woolf's many discernings of the kind—is not meant further to exalt the character of Mrs. Ramsay at this crucial point, but rather to diminish it, subtly to reveal its one, fatal weakness, its "tragic flaw"?

As her husband has stood watching her, she has been aware that he would have her tell him she loves him. "Will you not tell me just for once that you love me? He was thinking that, for he was roused, what with Minta and his book . . . their having quarreled about going to the Lighthouse." But she cannot. She smiles at him, anticipating her admission, the gesture of submission to his superior practical judgment, and reassures herself— that, "though she had not said a word, he knew, of course he knew, that she loved him." But there is a mocking tone of anxiety in the very repetition of the assurances. "He could not deny it." And when we come to the final words—"For she had triumphed again. She had not said it: yet he knew."—although, at first glance we might suppose the "it" to be the same as before, supply unthinkingly the phrase "that she loved him" after "knew," a second look might arouse some misgivings. Perhaps that is not it at all. Perhaps the only thing he really knows is that "she had triumphed again"—which, except from the viewpoint of a colossal egotism, is hardly the same thing as loving.

There is reason to suspect that Mrs. Ramsay *is* a colossal egotist. We have identified her husband's way of thinking with ego assertion. But does not the metaphysical certainty she secures in her experience of "losing personality"—what she gains through the *via negativa* (in the term of Blackstone's rather oppressively enthusiastic analysis) of her submergence in the "core of darkness"—become the weapon, consciously and deliberately used, of a purely personal victory in her conflict with her husband? In that victory, she is inevitably compromised; her queenliness is suspect of tyranny. And we have not far to search for other evidences of compromise.

Her vaunted realism—"there is no reason, order, justice: but suffering, death, the poor . . . there was no treachery too base for the world to commit; she knew that. No happiness lasted; she knew that"—is compromised over and over in her actions. In deference to James's wishes, she will not remove the *memento mori* of the pig's skull from the children's bedroom; but neither is she content to leave it there to frighten Cam, "branching at her all over the room," but covers it with her shawl, as if, though she herself knows best of all it cannot, the mantle of her benevolent wishes might hide the shadow of death itself. In "Time Passes," the wind, the slow decay of the fabric, have begun to unwrap the shawl. She has decreed the marriage of Minta and Paul, sent them out to walk beside the sea and become engaged. But the heirloom brooch (Minta's grandmother's), symbol of tradition, of the tie between past and present and future, is lost. And in "The Lighthouse" we learn that the marriage was not successful. It might have been foreseen that it would not be. But, whether it could have been or not, the point is plain that such considerations—i.e., in the ultimate interest of the parties concerned—rarely enter into Mrs. Ramsay's thinking, this, as Lily Briscoe sees it, "mania of hers for marriage." She is concerned only to make the match, is all but totally irresponsible with regard to its probable outcome. Again, the benevolence is subtlest despotism—is betrayal, and not only of Paul and Minta, but self-betrayal, betrayal of the deepest certainties of her own self-knowledge. "No treachery too base for the world to commit"? But, of course, "she knew that"! She knows it, one begins to suspect, best of all from her own example.

The argument might be pursued primarily on the evidence of the second and third sections of the novel. Several critics have noted the implications of "Time Passes"—that time and decay, wind and water and sand, the birds and beasts and plants, seem to have conspired to defeat Mrs. Ramsay's design. Her children die, in childbirth, in war; the house deteriorates, in a few more seasons would fall into utter ruin; and the island, as island of human order or human time (planned time, projected, plotted time) in the undifferentiated sea-flow of Time, would be obliterated. And if one asserts that this obliteration is precisely what Mrs. Ramsay alone was capable of foreseeing, unflinchingly facing in the depths of her secret wisdom, in the "core of darkness"—and that, therefore, she would have been most vindicated by such an outcome—still, that only states the fact of her self-betrayal in another way. For, outside the core of darkness, she herself has planned, has projected, plotted, has sought to protect, to determine destinies. The design, however paradoxically, was hers. It is only a little more accurate to insist that the conspiracy of time and decay is a conspiracy *with* her, to the end of her self-defeat.

Further, in the final section, "The Lighthouse," Lily Briscoe feels for some time a continuing resentment against Mrs. Ramsay. She, whose viewpoint becomes more and more the point of final reference for the reader, congratulates herself, and one feels with every right to do so, on having defied the tyranny of Mrs. Ramsay's matchmaking. (Mrs. Ramsay had tried to pair her off with Mr. Bankes.) She indulges, again righteously, a certain bitter joy of triumph over the tyrant in the knowledge that the marriage of the Rayleys has turned out badly. If the edge is taken off her triumph by the realization that Mrs. Ramsay herself is dead, safely beyond reproach, yet the effect is only to arouse further feelings of indignation against her—for having, as it were, escaped her responsibilities in death.

But all this is anticipated, actually, in the first section. Pedersen has indicated in part the importance of the recurrent references to the fairytale of "The Fisherman and His Wife" which Mrs. Ramsay is reading to James. It is apparent that the reader is expected to remember Grimm's story; and the "moral" of it serves covertly to define the relationship between Mr. and Mrs. Ramsay, the issue of their conflict over the proposed trip to the lighthouse. The philosopher—who keeps interrupting the reading of the story, who precisely does not believe in fairytales, who suspects as dangerous nonsense the kind of defiance of the facts of nature his wife practices in continuing to encourage James and to prepare for the trip in the face of the falling barometer and the set of the wind, but who lacks the courage of his convictions, so fears the woman's displeasure that he humbly offers to "step over and ask the Coastguards" on the chance that he might be wrong—has rather exactly the character of the Fisherman. And Mrs. Ramsay, at second glance, looks very much like Ilsabil. It is not simply that, living in a hovel, she would play the Queen. (Or "King," as in the story. The theme of discontent with the limitations of sex is also involved.) In Grimm's story, the final outrage, which calls down the wrath of the wizard Fish upon the woman, to punish her pride and send her back to the poverty from which he had rescued her, is her demand for control over the movements of the sun and moon. I.e., she has demanded the power to interfere with the laws of external nature, specifically, to prohibit the passage of time. Just so, Mrs. Ramsay would make of the self-certitude that she has drawn from the sea-depths of her intuitional experience an instrument, in her personal relations, of her possessive will—and again, as we have seen, in a way that specifically involves a defiance of time, the "spatialized time" which is championed by her husband, with his watch on which he wears a compass as a fob.

The stylistic effects, or manifestations, of Mrs. Woolf's time consciousness in this book and others—the pattern of the development of her style, her narrative technique, from the earlier works to the later, in terms of a growing preoccupation with the time problem—have attracted sufficient critical attention. I am concerned here primarily with questions of another, although closely related order—namely, with the moral-psychological implications of the time-experience that she attributes to Mrs. Ramsay (the experience of the self, in Bergsonian terms, as, or as consciousness of, duration), and that, it would appear, is so nearly identical with her own, central, artistic vision.

That vision, that experience, provides a sufficient aesthetic order. The lives of the Ramsays and their friends are composed, rendered, in the novel. We "get the picture." And it is not difficult to see what the peculiarly plotless character of the narration—the apparently aimless moving about, backward and forward in chronological time, from moment to self-contained moment of consciousness, the emphasis everywhere upon reaction rather than action, upon what the characters are seeing, thinking, feeling, rather than upon what they are doing, with an attendant reliance upon the structure of symbolic motif to provide thematic unity—has to do with our getting it so clearly as life-picture. The life-sense is inseparable from the time-sense, the new order of narrative. But the question is: whether the order provided is *merely* aesthetic. The novel itself, I think, clearly raises the question whether Mrs. Ramsay's vision has validity in the moral sphere—i.e., in the sphere of personal relationships wherein the persons are conceived, or conceive of themselves, as responsible, moral agents.

The drift of the observations we have been making, about Mrs. Ramsay as the Fisherman's wife, is to suggest that it has not. If, in the "core of darkness," she can achieve self-realization through the loss of self, a self-communion, yet she cannot realize her husband, cannot lose herself in him. Although that night, of the end of Part I, "The Window," is not the last night, we have no indication that the situation has changed before the day when, in "Time Passes," "[Mr. Ramsay, stumbling along a passage one dark morning, stretched his arms out, but Mrs. Ramsay having died rather suddenly the night before, his arms, though stretched out, remained empty]." The word of love, which he required, apparently has remained unspoken to the end. The gesture of surrender remains suspect as mere gesture, tainted with egotism. "She had triumphed again." Mrs. Woolf would seem to suggest that in the love relationship there is no true self-giving, but always a loss, a subduing, of one or the other. "Alone," with "inanimate things," it is possible; "they expressed one; . . . became one; . . . knew one, in a sense were one." But not, it appears, with another person. Mrs. Ramsay can, to be sure, with her husband, "read his mind"; she knows what he is thinking, and why. But this penetration is nothing finally resembling that sympathetic intuition by which she becomes one with the trees and streams and flowers. It is an insight that enables her only to prepare an attitude, a strategy for her "triumph." We are left, at the end of "The Window," with something very like the Sartrean view of a permanent and inevitable state of conflict between human selves—that situation in which one or the other must be violated, must become object to the other's subject, a being-in-itself to the other's being-for-itself, and thus less than fully human.

We are presented, that is, with a view of man's essential loneliness. Death, the death of Mrs. Ramsay and of the others who follow her, merely confirms in an obvious way the estrangements of life. In the long view (God's view, except that there is no God), the state of things in "Time Passes" is the normal state. Even before the family have left the house, before the last candle (Mr. Carmichael's) is out, the forces of destruction are already at work, the winds tugging at the loosened wallpaper as the household falls asleep. We have been reminded over and over that the battle for order and stability is at best a desperate one, lost from the start. When they have finally gone, and the house is left unprotected, the ineluctable process is not essentially changed, but simply proceeds at a faster pace. The mirrors, symbol and instrument of the vanity of man's self-regarding desire, are simply presented in their true aspect when they are empty, reflecting only the beam from the lighthouse, the shadows of birds passing the windows. For—the root meaning of the word is instructive—vanity, of course, is emptiness.

And the image presented in this middle section—of the

frailty of man's habitation, frailty of his hopes, his loneliness
and loss and emptiness—is not to be redeemed. Even when the
house has been precariously snatched back from oblivion,
cleaned, restored, reopened—by the efforts of Mrs. McNabb
and associates, the old creature herself ironically a looker in
mirrors, whose mad cheerfulness, the croaking gaiety of her
ancient music-hall songs, is a mockery of human hope, her mere,
instinctive strength to endure an all but subhuman virtue,
travesty of fortitude—we understand clearly that this does not
imply a restoration of the family life that had inspirited the
place in the years before. We understand, indeed, that only by
the merest accident, not by any guarantee of fate, is anything at
all saved. Just as easily, it is implied, it could have gone the other
way, the house, the island itself, could have been obliterated.
There is no reason to assume that man and his world should
even endure, not to speak of surviving, in the fullest sense, of
prevailing. And with the opening of Section III, "The Lighthouse," there is an unremittingly enforced sense of a restriction
and a narrowing, a depriving. The very tone of the prose is
saddened, severe, more restrained. Few of the group introduced
in "The Window" have returned. And even they have little to
say to one another. Each has withdrawn all but entirely into
himself.

The dominant impression, almost to the very end, is this one
of a nearly unbearable loneliness—of pervading, unbearable
silence, with undertones of panic. It is the absence of Mrs.
Ramsay, of course, that has cast the spell.

Lily Briscoe cries out silently to her, once almost aloud,
afraid that Mr. Carmichael has heard her; and, the cry going
unanswered, it is for a moment as if the world were on the brink
of annihilation. Here, and in the scene with Lily and Mr.
Ramsay—when she feels his silent appeal to her, demand,
rather, for the solace he would once have taken from his wife,
and in outrage at the shamelessness of his desire, the proposal to
use her, poor dry old maid that she is, as a substitute for the dead
woman, mentally to rape her, she is unable to speak—the mood
is something very near to madness. It is no accident that Mr.
Ramsay's beautiful boots, which in the extremity of her desperation she seizes upon as a subject of conversation, pulling herself

out of the insufferable silence, should be explicitly referred to as symbol of "sanity." "They had reached, she felt, a sunny island where peace dwelt, sanity reigned and the sun for ever shone, the blessed island of good boots." The sense of terror achieved here, I think, is more authentic in its kind than anything Virginia Woolf had done in *Mrs. Dalloway*, where in the characterization of Septimus Warren Smith she attempted directly to represent a state of insanity.

But, to repeat, we shall have missed the principal point if we interpret either the second or the third sections of the novel simply as contrasts to the first in situation and mood. The title of the long, first section, "The Window," provides the dominant symbol of that, in opposition to the mirror of "Time Passes." The window is symbol of perception and of intercourse. It is the aperture between the realms of subject and object, between the human consciousness and the world of external reality—and between the separate consciousnesses of different persons. Mrs. Ramsay sits at the window and looks out at her husband on the terrace, apprehending his state of mind; he, passing by, looks in at her and sees that "sternness at the heart of her beauty." And so on. But we have observed the reasons for suspecting that the window may have been, all along, no better than a mirror, its transparency an illusion, that neither Mr. nor Mrs. Ramsay can really know, really "see," the other.

The most appalling implication of the experience of bereavement Lily Briscoe suffers upon her return to the island, suffers only besides and not with Mr. Ramsay, is that Mrs. Ramsay, as her true self, never was really there, never was truly *visible*—that the loneliness, the self-imprisonment of consciousness, the impossibility of communication, are the permanent conditions of human existence. And there is, finally, the implicit, terrible reproach to Mrs. Ramsay, that if she cannot be charged with responsibility for these conditions, at least she had, and has failed, the responsibility of her knowledge. You knew, Lily Briscoe says in effect to the shade of Mrs. Ramsay, and you did not tell us. You could have forewarned us, but you did not.

But what I have said now would seem to be that both Mr. and Mrs. Ramsay are wrong—that neither provides a view of existence which can justify anything other than despair. Where, then, do we stand? Is there not some further design, something perhaps in the nature of a proposed *synthesis* of the contrary points of view, in the final section, that will yield a less melancholy interpretation of the novel's meaning.

There is, of course. We shall have still to defer the question of whether it is successful. But the intention is obvious.

Mr. Ramsay, with Cam and James, does in the end reach the lighthouse. In the course of the trip, his children's pact of enmity against him is dissolved. They come to know him, to recognize and acknowledge his fatherly authority; and by the same token they achieve self-recognition, are freed from the bondage of their childish hatred into mature awareness and acceptance of their own, each other's, and his separate identities. When, as they prepare to land, Mr. Ramsay says to James, "Well done," in the classic phrase of paternal recognition, we realize that all three of them have grown up during the journey. And the growing up is nothing more or less than the simple realization by each of one's primary responsibility to the truth of one's own feelings. When this has been accomplished, then they are able to establish a true community of good will, inseparable from the sense of individual, personal independence.

Moreover, there is a tacit but unmistakable implication that the voyage, with all the attendant blessings of its accomplishment, has been undertaken by Mr. Ramsay in homage to the memory of his wife. It is a pilgrimage, a memorial ceremony. In winning the confidence and admiration, the recognition, of his children, he has not won them away from her, but rather for her. This, we are surely to understand, is but the completion of her own, original design, in the trip she had planned years before. To be sure, she is absent now. But we are not to forget that she had never intended to go along on the actual voyage. Then, too, the children were to have been sent out in his care alone. Now, at last, it is his day. James comes to his father's knowledge, sees the lighthouse, reality, the real situation of man in the universe, at this farthest outpost of human society, as his father would see it—looming up, "stark and straight, glaring black and white . . . a stark tower on a bare rock"—sternly rejecting the council of "old ladies . . . [who] went dragging their chairs about on the lawn . . . saying how nice it was and how sweet it was and how they ought to be so proud." His father is right, rather: "as a matter of fact, James thought, looking at the Lighthouse standing there on its rock, it's like that." And yet (Cam, always looking back as they sail, watching the island disappear, but keeping it in her mind in the image of the censer, the hanging garden, which recalls the imagery of Mrs. Ramsay's comforting stories about the pig's skull, embodies the invisible presence of the mother—she is even shortsighted, like her mother), Mr. Ramsay is given his day and his due somehow only at his wife's behest. If it had not been for her, they would never have gone.

And, finally, at the same time that the boat makes its way across the water, Lily Briscoe is winning her struggle to fill the blank space of her canvas, pushing toward the resolution of her own conflict with Mrs. Ramsay, reconciliation to the fact of her absence, the betrayal of her death. The parallel is all but too strictly enforced; we are obviously to assume that Lily's intimation is correct, that the boat is landing, Mr. Ramsay is saying "Well done," preparing to leap ashore, in the moment just before she makes the final stroke with her brush and utters again, with respect to her own struggle, the "consummatum est." " 'He has landed,' she said aloud [to Mr. Carmichael]. 'It is finished.' " And on the next, and final, page: ". . . it was finished. Yes, she thought, laying down her brush in extreme fatigue, I have had my vision." And much of the same paradox is involved in the two accomplishments, of the homage to Mrs. Ramsay which is identical with her rejection, of the acknowledgment of her presence which is identical with acceptance of her absence.

It is precisely when, realizing that the drawing-room step, where the shape of Mrs. Ramsay reading to James had once provided an essential mass of dark color in her intended painting, is empty now, she no longer cares—when she can say to herself, "she did not want Mrs. Ramsay now"—that she has her. In the conversation with Mr. Bankes in "The Window," when she tries to explain her intention with the half-finished painting, a particular point is made of the "triangular purple shape . . . a purple shadow" to which she has "reduced . . . the mother and child." Now, in "The Lighthouse," when she has started the painting afresh (the old, unfinished canvas has been lost somewhere during the intervening years), someone comes to the drawing-room window while she is working and casts again "an odd-shaped triangular shadow over the steps." There is a moment of obscure intensity in the account of Lily's mental reactions to this phenomenon when we might suppose she is seeing the ghost of the dead woman. But, actually, the final point is exactly and only that the shadow, not the shade, has reappeared—and that this, the shadow, now just as before, is all she really needs. For the purposes of her art, the completion of this "picture" which is identical for her with the reconstruction of the past and, in retrospect, penetration of its meaning, she requires only the mass of color—regardless of who, or what, has provided its counterpart in the actual scene before her. As I have suggested, this experience clearly parallels that of Mr. Ramsay, in Lily's intimation of his state of mind, when precisely by no longer demanding, needing, no longer taking thought of, the denied consolation of his wife's presence, he is enabled to start on the voyage which will do her greatest homage in his own self-fulfillment. But, further, Lily has also unwittingly reproduced, in the "triangular shadow," exactly the image embodying Mrs. Ramsay's experience of self-intuition—the "wedge-shaped core of darkness."

That shadow is, in the most profound sense, the very shape, the very presence, the very self as presence, of Mrs. Ramsay. It is not less but more real than the substantial, flesh-and-blood shape of her, in her maternal beauty, and than any apparition, ghost, of that. And we are to understand that the truth of this vision of reality—the reality, again, of the self—is attested principally by what would seem, according to our usual, ego-centered conception of time (Mr. Ramsay's time, as opposed to Mrs. Ramsay's), its brevity. "The great revelation," Lily has reflected earlier, "had never come. The great revelation perhaps never did come. Instead, there were little daily miracles, illuminations, matches struck unexpectedly in the dark. . . ." Lily's vision, her painting—"it would be hung in the attics . . . it would be destroyed. But what did that matter?"—is just such an illumination, a match struck in the dark. If it pretended to be otherwise, sought to be longer lasting, we should suspect its truth.

And yet, with this much by way of an account, I think reasonably sympathetic, of the book's attempt to resolve itself, we must ask again the question that I said seemed to be raised by the characterization of the central figure, Mrs. Ramsay—i.e., whether her vision of the self has validity in the moral sphere, the sphere of relationships among persons conceived, essentially, as moral agents. I think it has not, and that the reading of the conclusion we have undertaken, the paralleling of the experience of Mr. Ramsay and his children on the boat trip with that of Lily Briscoe at her painting, really only confirms rather than alters what might have been suspect as the result of oversimplification in the previous analysis—i.e., that the order provided by the vision is purely aesthetic, in a deliberately extramoral sense.

The issue indicated is, essentially, the same as that of the conflict between Mr. and Mrs. Ramsay. And the way the conclusion of the book "resolves" it is by finally denying its reality.

Pedersen's study furnishes a useful corrective to the conventional readings of the novel which accepted Mrs. Ramsay as unqualified heroine, her point of view as identical with that of the author, and Mr. Ramsay as villain-fool. But it will hardly do simply to reverse the formula, to make Mrs. Ramsay, as I said, the villainess—she is, according to Pedersen, "a matriarch encouraging an Oedipus complex in her son, . . . deny[ing] the husband and negating the father"—and to present Mr. Ramsay, once the baneful influence of his wife is removed by her death, as hero. There is, I have indicated, an apparent intention on Mrs. Woolf's part to redeem Mr. Ramsay, and correspondingly to reveal the flaws in his wife's character. But it is an intention that falls far short of what Pedersen wants, and that, even in its own measure, is scarcely realized. Mr. Ramsay, with the philosophical attitude he represents, has been too effectively caricatured throughout not to appear somewhat fatally ridiculous even at the end. And too much essential sympathy, or admiration, for Mrs. Ramsay has been built up; her point of view is too closely identified, expecially in the last section, with the finally dominant one of Lily Briscoe herself, to permit the interpretation that she is somehow simply routed in disgrace at the conclusion, to be replaced in the heroic role by her husband. The opening statement that Pedersen's article is designed to prove—" 'Someone had blundered.' The vision of Lily Briscoe reveals that it was Mrs. Ramsay."—is a vast oversimplification.

So too, although not so relentlessly pursued, is Hafley's contrary assertion: "Seven times in [the first] part of the novel, the phrase 'Someone had blundered' is repeated. Either Mr. Ramsay or Mrs. Ramsay is wrong, and the remainder of the novel shows that it is Mr. Ramsay who 'had blundered.' " Pedersen and Hafley are both right, and they are both wrong.

But this still does not mean that any formula of synthesis or reconciliation of the two opposed points of view, Mrs. Ramsay's and her husband's, can accommodate the book's final effect. In his discussion of *Orlando,* Hafley quotes a statement of Bergson's:

*Intuition and intellect represent two opposite directions of the work of consciousness: intuition goes in the very direction of life, intellect goes in the inverse direction, and thus finds itself naturally in accordance with the movement of matter. A complete and perfect humanity would be that in which these two forms of conscious activity should attain their full development.*

I do not, as Hafley seems to, find even in *Orlando* anything resembling an image of such perfection. And, assuredly, it is not achieved in *To the Lighthouse.* In a sense, this is what Mrs. Woolf "pretends" to do—to show us Mrs. Ramsay's intuitive experience of "The Window," wherein she becomes one with the beam of light, now as it were harmoniously "completing itself" in the actual (i.e., "material," "intellectual") voyage of her husband with the children to the lighthouse. Or, to put the matter another way: I said at the outset that the function of Lily Briscoe was "somewhat" to mediate between the two, "after a fashion" to reconcile them. But the qualifying phrases were deliberate. The pretended harmonization is a trick, a skillful manipulation of symbolic motifs; there is scarcely anything in the way of psychological realism to account for the strange sea-change of personality undergone by Mr. Ramsay and James and Cam in the brief time of the voyage; that sudden achievement of maturity, upon second examination, must seem little short of a miracle. And what Mrs. Woolf really and finally does, through Lily Briscoe, is to get rid of Mr. and Mrs. Ramsay—of those troublesome *married* people, precisely, both of them, and of their offspring into the bargain.

The man and the children are abandoned somewhere out there in the haze, into which the lighthouse itself has finally disappeared from Lily's view. And the woman is reduced entirely to the symbol of the intuitive principle.

Whatever else might be said about her, it is surely no accident that Lily Briscoe is an artist, and that her viewpoint is the last one presented, the definitive and conclusive one. In effect, any questions of a seeming moral import left over from the scene of the family party's arrival at the lighthouse—questions, that is, of their probable capabilities for the future, the dimension of moral responsibility—are simply "referred" in the end to the aesthetic test, translated into aesthetic terms, out of time. Lily Briscoe, the last person we see, is the artist, and the artist, in the most literal sense, alone. There is nothing left but her and her painting. The human person, in what we are accustomed to calling his representational image in art, necessarily evokes a response which is in some part moral. This image, as we have seen, is deliberately excluded from Lily's painting. Mrs. Ramsay appears only as the triangle of shadow. Humanity, even in the guise of possible, future viewers of the work, has been pushed out of the picture; she doesn't care if the picture is destroyed, hung in attics. And there can be little question but that that "picture" is, in some at least wishful sense, the novel.

But perhaps the most significant aspect of dehumanization in the final scene is the desexualization. In this we witness the final abandonment of the issue, the conflict of masculine and feminine—the problem, simply, of marriage and the family—which purported to be the book's central, dramatic concern. Lily Briscoe's only "companion" on the lawn at the end is Mr. Carmichael; and he is invisible then. The characterization of

Carmichael, also an artist, the poet about the nature of whose poetry we are deliberately told nothing—Lily Briscoe has not read his work, but "thought that she knew how it went," in a way designed simply to indicate that it does not matter what it is about, the subjects and themes, the character of its technique—is a device for reinforcing certain implications of Lily's experience which might otherwise remain obscure, or seem to have only particular validity.

His presence establishes the point that the order provided by the visual art, the painting, an order which is entirely self-justifying and is not required to render "life" intelligible, is essentially the same order in verbal art. Mr. Carmichael makes, in the penultimate paragraph of the novel, a gesture as Lily sees it of universal benediction—"spreading his hands over all the weakness and suffering of mankind . . . ," and then lowering one hand slowly, "as if she had seen him let fall from his great height a wreath of violets and asphodels which . . . lay at length upon the earth." It is clear that his capacity for making such a gesture, his godlike character (Lily sees him as "looking like an old pagan god"), consists simply in his entire inscrutability. He is silent; to the repeated exasperation of Mrs. Ramsay in the first section of the book, he needs nothing; of all the persons surrounding her, he is the only one who seems, not in any simple sense to dislike her, but to be utterly indifferent to her. He and Lily, we are repeatedly told, communicate silently in this final scene on the lawn. "They had not needed to speak. They had been thinking the same things and he had answered her without her asking him anything." But *what* they communicate would seem to be, at last, simply the truth of the impossibility of communication. And essential to this ineffable process of nonknowing, nonintercourse, between the two artists, is the character of the so-called "androgynous" in them that has become one of the central clichés of Woolf criticism.

Actually, despite the intent of Mrs. Woolf's own theorizing on the matter, "androgynous" is the wrong term, with reference to what we find either in this book or her others. She is not a feminist, certainly, in any usual, plain sense. Again, all that is left at the end of her sympathy for Mrs. Ramsay, the woman, as opposed to her husband, is the notion of the superiority of the intuition to the intellect. But neither, then, does she succeed in constructing characters in whom the male and the female are dynamically combined. She needed, as a counterpart to her female painter here, a male poet. But she needs him, finally, to prove that the sexual distinction is, in fact, of no importance— no more essentially meaningful, precisely, than the distinction between verbal and nonverbal art. Lily, the juiceless old maid, is a not-woman; and Mr. Carmichael, a kind of Tiresias figure who has ceased even to prophesy, surviving timelessly into a life simply *beyond* sex, is a not-man.

This implicit doctrine of the asexuality (not androgyny) of art may well be the one, necessary key to the final impression—it must be recorded, at last—of dryness, thinness, for all their surface richness of design and subtle nuance of feeling, the impression of morbid triviality, that the novels of Mrs. Woolf leave. We have noted now Mr. and Mrs. Ramsay, from the very first, appear not so much as male and female, man and wife, but as embodiments of ideal principles, thesis and antithesis, of masculine and feminine. And this peculiar aridity of effect is felt more and more strongly in the final section. In a novel so bristling as this one with sexual symbolism—the lighthouse itself, the window, the red-hot pokers at the edge of the lawn, the stroking of the light beam which bursts "some sealed vessel" in Mrs. Ramsay's mind, the insistently triangular shadow, "wedge-shaped core of darkness" that she is, even Mr. Ramsay's beautiful boots, which poor Lily adores—it is astonishing to realize how little, primary sexuality there is.

It is impossible, I think, to escape the implication. For the purposes of art—and art is everything, the only ultimately dependable source of order, source of being, self-fulfillment, "the one thing that one [does] not play at," art is directly and unequivocally represented, in Lily's painting, as the true perfection of Mrs. Ramsay's intuitive wisdom—Mrs. Woolf thought that sexuality must be reduced entirely to symbolic status. And this is at one with the denial of communication, the denial of the possibility of an intelligible moral order, the denial of concern with the moral dimension in human relationships, i.e., the dimension of potentiality, of the future. Mrs. Ramsay is, purely exists, only when she is dead, only in the past. We have communication, only with the dead. It is at one with the implicit equation, let us say, of the Crucifixion and Creation—of *consummatum est,* Lily Briscoe's "It is finished," with *fiat,* the creative word—the equation of darkness, the triangular shadow, with the perfection of light, of vision. ". . . it was finished. . . . I have had my vision." But, finally, it is at one with the total denial of value in the art work, as such. Because the art is seen as identical with the vision (process of execution and completion of vision are coterminous, in Lily's experience), the status of the finished work is indifferent. It literally and entirely does not matter that Lily is a poor painter, that the painting is a poor thing. No reliable criteria for critical judgment exist.

*To the Lighthouse* seems to me the high point of Mrs. Woolf's achievement as novelist; yet one can discover in it the pattern of the decline to follow. What she did here, in effect, was to theorize her craft out of existence. For it is questionable whether novels, in anything of the traditional sense, can be written on the basis of a conception of the human being as a purely aesthetic mechanism—mechanism of aesthetic response—whose life has no purposeful, moral continuity.

Beyond the joking escape fantasy of *Orlando,* which simply says that man, under the given conditions of his existence, sex and mortality, is impossible, *The Waves* is an exercise in sensibility completely detached from the concerns of human community. The other characters exist only in the mind of Bernard; and his mind is in no meaningful sense to be distinguished from that of the author. At least the facts of society and social institutions, and the frightful fact of sex, are acknowledged again in *The Years* and *Between the Acts,* but with an inevitable sense of despair, of hopeless confusion. For no outrage, even, no attack on society for its cruelties to the individual (*The Years*), conceived in the conviction that the individual truly lives only between the acts of his community performance, that his being is radically unrelated to fellow beings, can be clearly purposeful. Such a view, moreover, would seem to deny the possibility of a dramatic action, without which the novel as such is hardly conceivable.

# 7 *A Farewell to Arms:*

## The Death of Tragedy

The Hemingway hero is always isolated. He is often literally an alien; but even when he is not, he is never, in one way or another, at home. He is uncommunicative. Even in situations in which it is possible for him to speak his native tongue, he has little to say, and usually cannot make himself understood when he does attempt conversation. If he is not physically impotent, then there is some other barrier to the establishment of a satisfactory relationship with a woman, in which he might hope either to reproduce or otherwise to fulfill himself. His friends are either unwilling or unable (usually unable) to help him in any showdown—or, if they do, it is by some irony of circumstances beyond the power of their intention. And, finally, he is isolated in the moment of experience. His experience has no continuity and no purposive design. The past, what little of it he permits himself to remember, has no bearing on the present; and there is no future. There is only the flux—and against it, a rather desperate devotion to private ritual.

Lieutenant Henry, protagonist of A *Farewell to Arms*, elaborately qualifies on all counts. Not only is he fighting in a foreign country, and under a foreign flag (although, technically, Italy is an American "ally"), but he has apparently no intention of going home after the war. He never discusses his family, except for a few vague references to some unhappy misunderstanding; and his communications to relatives and friends are limited to postcards now and again and the sight drafts on his grandfather. In this connection, the pathetic irony of his reference to Catherine's ability to "make a home of any place she is in," and of their calling the hospital room a "home," is immediately apparent.

In many ways, he feels a greater affinity for the Italian

people, and their country, than he ever has felt for his own. And he is assured by Rinaldi that he is "really an Italian, all fire and smoke and nothing inside." But this remark, in its context and emphasis, carries its own obvious irony. And it is, of course, the fact that he speaks Italian with an accent that is the immediate cause of his arrest by the battle police during the retreat. Moreover, the Count Greffi recognizes that it is, after all, a strain for Henry to carry on a conversation for very long in Italian (especially when he is "tired"—physically tired at the moment, and also tired of the war, fed up, as the Count subtly realizes, with the whole Italian adventure), and so in his exquisite courtesy puts himself to the trouble of speaking English—or "American" as Henry insists upon calling it—for a time.

But the language difficulty points finally to a much deeper and more subtle problem of characterization and style. Lieutenant Henry is inarticulate even in English (or "American"), and especially so with Catherine. The all-but-unrelieved banality of the lovers' dialogue has a certain relevance to the qualities of other parts of Henry's narrative. The "separate peace" that he would make is, of course, finally impossible. The ambiguity of the title is finally resolved. The two worlds of "arms" are ultimately the same, and the game of both is played according to the same deadly rules—"they put you in, and tell you the rules, and the first time they catch you off base, they kill you." And so, to a certain extent, the childishness of the love patter merely corresponds to the flatness and understatement of Henry's report of the war. He is antiheroic in bed just as he is in battle—fearful of the emotional consequences of eloquence.

The world has frightfully betrayed the talk of "honor" and "loyalty" and "patriotism" in war. Men die trapped in a hole while eating cold macaroni and cheese. The guns "cough," and make "a noise like a railway engine starting." (The industrial metaphor is a recurrent, antiheroic usage.) Passini is reduced to a twitching leg-stump and a childish voice crying "Mama." And, picking up the implicit metaphor of the broken toy, when Frederick Henry tries to sit up "something inside [his] head moved like the weights on a doll's eyes."

And so are they, Frederick and Catherine, fearful of the

heroism of love. This too may be betrayed. Better to be childish from the first, to take pleasure in, and to talk, simply, of food and drink and the feel of the sheets—to resist nuances, and to let the inexpressible remain inexpressible, to surround the mystery with a ritual of deliberate, adjectival triteness. "Isn't it a lovely day?" "We had a lovely night." "It's a splendid room." "You're a grand girl." "Wine is a grand thing." "We have such a fine time."

But it is something more than a matter just of correspondences. The whole treatment of the war is in a sense a gigantic, perverse, and hideous metaphor of love. And, in the plot design—with some retrogressions, of course, and at the very end the ironic reversal, with the scene of childbed becoming a battle scene—the movement is from war toward love. The issues of the war (the private issues, that is—but in this war, there are hardly any other kind) are developed in their true significance, and resolved, finally and only, in the love affair.

In the imagery of the account of Passini's death, for example, the mutilation and the crying for Mama, there is an element of sexual symbolism. And Frederick's own wound, although less severe, is notably of the same kind as Passini's. It is the classic euphemism of the wound in the "thigh." (In Henry's case it is the knee that is principally involved; but this must be intended as a subtle refinement, reinforcing the notion of fate's giving him a temporary respite before the ultimate blow, but with enough now to warn him that is it *only* temporary.) Or again, Frederick is wearing a pistol on the occasion of one of his first visits to Catherine, and the weapon—with its too-short barrel, its uncontrollable kick which makes accurate firing all but impossible—clearly symbolizes a type of impotence, or sexual incompetence, that psychologically if not physically characterizes the wearer.

And so on. In other stories, Ernest Hemingway is more refreshingly literal in his identification of the good, the true, and the beautiful with the vital—and the precise character and consequences of the blow below the belt are more clearly definable. But the relatively greater subtlety of his "symbolic" usage here hardly demands further multiplication of examples for analysis.

Thus, Henry is prepared by his experience of the war, of the life of one kind of arms, for the maimed and furtive conduct and the dismal outcome of the love affair. (Or we, at any rate, are prepared, to see how essentially spurious is the lovers' healthiness, and so the inevitability of their ruin, with the affair ending, as it began, in a hospital—although we might reasonably wish that the stillbirth were more satisfactorily explicable than only, it would seem, as a matter of "poetic" justice.)

To come back now to the theme of communication: it is important to note that the breakdown is progressive, and the condition of Frederick's verbal impotence much worse in the bedroom than in the billet or dugout. To be sure, he is never much of a talker. But he has decidedly more to say to Rinaldi, the priest, and his men, than ever to Catherine. His conversation has larger and more varied dimensions; he is more witty, more articulate in every sense.

Now, in part, this is merely a matter of Hemingway's rather old-fashioned attitude toward women. He has good women and bad women, and some small variety of types in either classification. But a self-respecting man simply does not talk very much to any of them, and feels no compunction about lying to them. If, in fact, there is any means of differentiating between good and bad in this respect, the good woman—i.e., the woman who, in Catherine's phrase, "gives a man what he wants"—is precisely the one who demands the least conversation, and who, like Catherine, positively enjoys being lied to. The more a man is obliged to talk to a woman, and especially to talk intelligently and truthfully, the more suspect is her virtue—i.e., the less is she likely to give him what he wants. The stability of relations between the sexes is built on the preservation of feminine illusions.

But, if for lack of evidence to the contrary one must suppose that Hemingway believes such a state of affairs to be universal and unalterable, he seems nonetheless to find some of its consequences regrettable—and indeed to see it as threatening the extinction of man. Or, if not causative, the conversational banality, which I have called the verbal impotence, is at any rate clearly symptomatic of the failure of the sexual union.

And, while Lieutenant Henry does converse more intelligently with his male friends, there would seem to be no possibility of a satisfactory solution to the problem in a simple division of energies—whereby a man might seek the exclusive society of men when he needs to talk, and of women when he needs sexual release. For, once again, the world of war and the world of love cannot be so easily separated. And in this novel, if not in all of Hemingway's, the finest friendships of man and man are tainted with the threat of homosexuality. The comrade threatens to become a lover.

Rinaldi's first, halfhearted pretense that he is jealous of Frederick as a rival for Catherine's favor is obviously spurious. The evidence of his homosexual attraction to "Baby" rapidly accumulates. And it is essentially his repressed desire and jealousy that poisons not only his own, but the priest's relationship with Frederick. Although Rinaldi himself knows as well as Frederick that there is no literal truth in his later accusations that Henry and the priest are "that way," the very suggestion is enough to make Henry uncomfortable in the priest's company. Under this strain, as much as under that of the general war weariness, their relations progressively deteriorate, conversation becomes more and more difficult and less and less candid, the pained silences are longer and longer each time they meet, as his affair with Catherine advances.

In other words, Henry is forced by his involvement with Catherine to reject both Rinaldi and the priest. And the ironic effect of this in turn, of Frederick's guilty consciousness of it, is finally to promote his isolation from Catherine herself. During one of the long evenings together in Switzerland, toward the end of her pregnancy, when Catherine notices that Frederick is preoccupied and inattentive to what she is saying, she presses him to tell her what he is thinking about—and, of course, it is Rinaldi and the priest. Repeatedly, during these weeks, she has to be reassured of his contentment in being with her. Their conversations become more and more tediously circular, revolving drearily and hopelessly about the one, obsessive theme; and the more often the reassurances are made, the more Catherine exerts herself to be "like" Frederick, wanting to cut her hair short and so on, the more they protest to each other their oneness, their completeness in and with one another, the more apparent is it that they are lying, the more surely are they estranged. And the problem is more deeply rooted than in the particular circumstances of their fugitive life and Catherine's pregnancy. The woman is not, and cannot be, pregnant or otherwise, "like" the man. Short hair and a slim waist are not enough. The exclusive company of a woman is not, and cannot be, under any circumstances, a sufficient life for the man, as both Catherine and Frederick know. Try as he will to enforce his "separate peace," to cut himself off from his loyalties to his old comrades and deny his concern for them, some part of Frederick is still Lieutenant Henry and remains "at the front"— i.e., in the world of men. And yet Catherine, the woman, must demand the oneness, the wholeness of attention and content- ment, whether she believes it possible or not, and Frederick must pretend that he can satisfy the demand, that the part of himself is the whole.

Frederick, in short, is damned if he does and damned if he doesn't. Neither life, the life of the front nor the life of the bedroom, is complete in itself. Each is needed to complement the other. To attempt a final choice between them, as he has done, is fatal, for a man must live wholly, or not at all. And yet, such is the universal disorder and corruption—of which Dr. Rinaldi's homosexual tendencies and his fear of syphilis, that is, of contamination by women, are the specific signs in this connection—that the two worlds are set in rivalry, and Henry is forced to make the fatal choice.

But I have suggested here and there my feeling that what Hemingway represents is something he sees as the universal and permanent human situation—a situation that is, perhaps, brought into clearest focus in the circumstances of war, but that is by no means totally the product of war and its disruption of the normal order of society. In one of their frequent, whimsical moods of self-pity during their stay in Switzerland, Catherine and Frederick admire the fox they have seen, with his big tail that he can wrap around himself as a covering when he sleeps in the open. Frederick thinks it would be splendid to be equipped with such a tail. Catherine is doubtful, on the grounds of the inconvenience it would put one to in dressing. And when Frederick suggests that they might go to a country where it would make no difference if they wore clothes designed to accommodate tails, Catherine replies that they "live [i.e., *already* live] in a country where nothing makes any difference." Now, at least one meaning of this precious little exchange (if the sentimentality is of a kind familiar in Hemingway, there is a virtuostic subtlety and multiplicity of implication here that his dialogue rarely attempts) is that Frederick feels so lost and homeless in the world that he would fain escape his very humanity. The condition of the beast, the creature with the tail, his "house" that he carries with him, seems enviable. And Catherine's reply, that they live already in a country where nothing makes any difference, implicitly recognizes and protests against this significance of his remark. She means that this "country," of their love, is the best of all possible worlds, that if not here, then nowhere is there wholeness and perfect freedom of life. And, if we are permitted to question the comfort of Catherine's words, to wonder whether a world in which "nothing makes any difference" is really a very desirable one, the implication remains clear, I feel, that Hemingway means us to see this world, for better or worse, complete or incomplete, as the only one available. For man, so long as he is not permitted to grow himself a tail, this is it.

And with this point established, I think we may fairly come back to raise more searching questions than we have so far allowed ourselves about the stature of Hemingway's art. In recent years, it has become critically fashionable to attack Hemingway. No one, of course, likes to appear merely fashionable; and I should have wished for a different climate of opinion in which to exercise my own animadversions. But I trust it is apparent that my general approach to the problems is different from that which characterizes most current criticism. More particularly, I have chosen not to represent him as the once great novelist who pathetically outlived his vision, as is so often the case, but to focus upon this book, A *Farewell to Arms*, in which he is usually acknowledged to have been at his best. Basically, whatever is wrong with *For Whom the Bell Tolls*, *To Have and Have Not*, *Across the River and into the Trees*, etc.—everything that *The Old Man and the Sea* I think signally failed to redeem—was wrong from the beginning.

John Peale Bishop once defended Hemingway's apparently negative view of humanity and the human condition on the grounds that, although the world he represents is almost exclusively that of war and war's aftermath, a world in disorder and confusion, suffering the loss of traditional values, there is always a full *consciousness* of the loss to provide the measure of man's ultimate dignity. (Sean O'Faolain's more recent defense, in *The Vanishing Hero,* is much to the same purpose.)

But is there such a consciousness? I question whether Hemingway's atraditionalism, the cultural-historical isolation of his typical hero, is not so complete that he seems unaware even of the possibility of a life other than this desperate and sterile one of Frederick Henry.

That Frederick and Catherine's conversation is a deadly bore for the most part, banal, trite, and childish, verbal proof of their general, spiritual and mental impotence or *malaise*—of which the physical disaster of the stillbirth and the mother's death are the symbolic consequence—I have taken as a fact of the novel that must be readily apparent to any reasonably sensitive reader. But where is there any evidence that these two would have anything more interesting to say, would be capable of a life of richer sensibility, in a world at peace?

It ought to be noted that Frederick Henry is not, in comparison to many other of Hemingway's characters, an especially primitive type. I take it he is meant to be about as mature, intelligent, and well educated a young man of good American family as Hemingway is capable of portraying. He even regards himself, it would seem, as in a small way an "intellectual."

But his few efforts at introducing any kind of intellectual subtlety into his conversation, and again especially when he is with Catherine, are inevitably painful in their sophomoric self-consciousness. Perhaps the best example is his quoting to Catherine, in the hotel room the night he is to go back to the front, Marvell's lines—"But at my back I always hear / Time's wingèd chariot hurrying near." The effect—with the lovers' situation at the moment, parting after a furtive hour together in the cheap hotel, with the motorcar honking in the street below just as Frederick speaks, and so on—is clumsily reminiscent of Eliot.

But how clumsily, indeed! Hemingway trifled now and again with most of the intellectual fads of his period, and unquestionably he supposed that he was doing something here, in the entire novel, comparable to *The Waste Land*. But the vital difference between the final effect of such juxtapositions of reference—the ancient grandeur and the contemporary triviality, the chariot and the motor car—in Eliot and in Hemingway, lies in the fact that Eliot (or Pound or Yeats or Joyce, or F. Scott Fitzgerald, for that matter) has an understanding of and a commitment to the traditional values embodied in the allusion, that inform and dignify his view of the present at the same time that they afford startling recognition of the contrast of past and present. An order for the grasp and assimilation of contemporary experience is provided in the poet's very metaphoric act of noting how the present has disordered the world of the past.

In Hemingway, no such understanding and commitment are apparent. And the effect of the allusion is simply one of a puerile, romantic cynicism. Catherine's sad little coed response to the quotation, pointing out that the poem "is about a girl who [unlike her] wouldn't live with a man," in the quality of the language and the way it interprets the poem, merely vulgarizes Marvell without doing anything to enlarge or dignify her own and Henry's situation. And Frederick's response, far from correcting her bad taste, is simply to retreat into his tough attitude of intellectual indifference, as if he were rather ashamed of having "gone literary" in the first place. "My head felt very clear and cold," he reports, "and I wanted to talk facts." ("Facts," presumably—the question of when the baby is due, where Catherine will go, etc.—is in opposition to "poetry.")

If this is a fair sample of Hemingway's grasp of traditional values—and I think it is; it certainly represents Frederick Henry at about his most perceptive, and I see no great aesthetic distance maintained between author and hero in this novel—then John Peale Bishop's defense breaks down pretty rapidly. And it breaks down, I would emphasize, not merely on a point of criticism of Hemingway's limited moral horizons, of his "world view," but—insofar as, with his habit of presenting such obvious stand-ins for himself as heroes, we can make the distinction at all—on a question of his literary craftsmanship. The argument from a supposed, submerged consciousness of lost values—they could have been grand lovers in the old days, or might be in the future if the world ever again achieves an ordered peace—simply will not hold up as a justification of the present, plain dullness and mawkish triteness of Catherine's and Frederick's dialogue.

Religion comes off with Frederick Henry about as well as poetry. He has a kind of distant, wistful, half-ashamed and apologetic respect for it; a vaguely superstitious nostalgia which permits him, or at least does not forbid him, to carry the St. Anthony medal in his pocket although he balks at wearing it, and to feel "somehow" that the baby ought to have been baptized. He and Catherine are pleased now and again (with the priest's encouragement to Henry) to make a religion of their love, to speak of their devotion to each other in the conventional terms of religious usage, while at the same time, of course, they refuse, or are denied, the possibility of religious sanction of their union. He can never enter wholeheartedly into the game of priest-baiting with Rinaldi and the captain, and is frankly tempted by the invitation to the priest's home in the Abruzzi.

In all of this, there is a discernible pattern, involving once more the theme of a loss, or collapse, of traditional values. Bereft of his former belief in a supernatural power sustaining the visible church and its ceremonies, the modern man nonetheless continues to cling rather pathetically to a few vestiges of ceremonial practice and of respect for the representatives of the institution. Frederick's attraction to the Abruzzi, as the priest describes the place and the life of the people there, is perhaps most interesting as an expression of his religious consciousness. As Carlos Baker has observed, the mountains, as opposed to the plains, are generally symbolic in the novel of permanence and stability of order. And the life of the priest's family and their community, an old-fashioned one in which men have a natural honor and respect for one another, and in which "one is permitted to love God . . . and it is not a dirty joke," further characterizes in Henry's mind the Abruzzi, where he had one and only one opportunity to go and did not, as the place of the old, lost order of traditional society.

But, on re-examination, the symbolism is really rather vague. The values which Frederick associates with the place are perhaps more primitivistic than appropriate to an ideal of civilized tradition. And insofar as it represents an idea of the proper relationship of man to God, it seems almost Eden-like, a place of legendary innocence and natural purity of manners, forever and always lost—hardly in any way to be associated with the religion of fallen man, with traditional Christianity. Moreover, Frederick has the primitivist's primary fascination with the country as such, with the trees and the streams and the roads iron-hard with frost. If the kingdom of God could ever be found, it would be some definite place, not a spiritual state.

The mind of the hero, then, to reiterate, seems to me essentially and fundamentally atraditional. And, since not only his part of the dialogue but the entire narrative is presented by him "in character," the whole texture of the prose is limited to the operations of his isolated sensibility. There is, of course, a general repudiation of the techniques of traditional rhetoric—variations of sentence structure, overt development of metaphor and other tropes, variation of diction to avoid monotonous repetition, elaborate modification of nouns and verbs, use of the subjunctive and of the perfect tenses, etc., etc. But the familiar Hemingway device, for example, of stringing a series of simple, independent clauses together with *ands* has also an appropriateness to the hero's isolation in the moment of experience. He does not want to remember or to try to penetrate the future; and so he sees, or does, or has done to him, one thing at a time in a straight line of succession, and tells about it in the same way, with a minimum of qualification, subordination, anticipation, and concern for cadence.

Perhaps, of all modern heroes, Hemingway's is most uncertain of his identity. For Lieutenant Henry, the loss of the sense of identity is progressive. From the first, an alien, estranged from his family, his very status as an American citizen frequently doubted by the Italians, he is a shadowy figure. But so long as he remains in the army, even if he does not know what he is fighting for, he can define himself fairly satisfactorily at least in terms of the military code of duty. And the first major admission to himself of his uncertainty is made when, escaping the battle police, he plunges into the river (symbolic, of course, of the flux of time). Drifting with the current, catching at whatever comes to hand to keep afloat until he is carried into the bank by an eddy, he emerges finally to confirm his sense of purgation and release from responsibilities by cutting the stars off the shoulders of his uniform. There follow various episodes pointing up the theme. He reflects that the mended knee is Dr. Valentini's, not his. "Doctors did things to your body and then it was not yours anymore." And, "the stomach was mine, and the head, but not to think with, but only to remember, and not too much remember." Later, he is offered forged papers by the restaurant keeper, and borrows civilian clothes from his friend Sim. Wearing the clothes on the train, he "felt a masquerader." "I had been in uniform a long time and I missed the feeling of being held by your clothes." And so on, until the final phase begins with his flight with Catherine across the lake into Switzerland.

Here, they are both impostors, posing first as cousins and then as husband and wife, as students of art, as tourists in search of winter sport. They are obliged to act out a farce of weighing advice on where they should stop for the best sports—the crowning irony being that they know the act deceives no one. They have come from nowhere and are going nowhere. The passports, the last identifying documents, are confiscated. And beyond all this, the merely accidentally symbolic circumstances of their visit—what Frederick calls the "comic opera" aspect of their arrival—there is their growing sense, in the winter isolation, of Switzerland's being actually another world than the one they have left, and finally their effort to "lose themselves" in each other, or as it were to make one person out of the wreckage of their two identities.

The effort, for reasons I have already discussed, is a failure. Catherine is nothing to him when she has died—"It was like saying goodby to a statue." She is devoid of personality, and obviously, walking back to the hotel through the rain in which

Catherine has seen them dead, Frederick is dead also to himself.

But if—whether from the necessity of his own nature or otherwise—having limited himself to the anonymous and crippled sensibility of such a man as Frederick Henry in telling his story, Hemingway produces what seems to me a radically maimed prose, a style that does not simply reflect but is the victim of the spiritual malady that afflicts his characters, there is one way in which he can and does keep the true artist's superiority to his creature. He is, at least in this one novel, and very often in his short stories, a master of plot and of patterns of symbolic action. I mean, for example, such an implicit, overall structural metaphor as that I have tried to describe based on the ambiguity of "arms"—or the balanced, cadenced, larger sweep of the action back and forth between the worlds of war and love in Italy, and finally across the lake into Switzerland where the essential inseparability of the two is revealed—or the development of the identity motif, not so much in the words, as simply in the episodes themselves. Wyndham Lewis's famous observation that Hemingway's characters are not those who do, but to whom things are done, is hardly to be disputed. And, although it pleased Hemingway to speak of the novel as a tragedy, it seems to me that Frederick Henry fails to achieve the vision of self-knowledge, the final sense of identity, that is inseparable from the disaster in genuine tragedy; that he is rather, as I have said, dead to himself at the end, utterly without identity. But it is Hemingway who decides what will happen. And in acting out the fate he has designed for them, there is a sense in which the pathetic little hero and heroine of A *Farewell to Arms* do become larger than themselves, are engaged almost in a truly tragic action without being capable of tragic emotions and insight. The beauty of the whole design does much to redeem the inanities of dialogue and narrative texture, and the weakness of characterization.

And yet, it is not quite enough. A novel is not a bundle of artistic effects, for some of which we can give good marks, and bad for others. Hero and action cannot be separated in this way. The book as a whole does fail of the tragic vision. The famed "athletic" prose is, actually, a maimed language, admirable chiefly for the pathetic virtue of its triumph over its disabilities. Its ultimate appeal is as the embodiment of a cult-attitude, largely indifferent to the formal requirements of a work of art—and that a cult to which it is difficult to belong after extreme youth, one expressive, as Henry James said of an enthusiasm for Poe, "of a very primitive stage of reflection." Once the required cultist disposition is outgrown, or simply outlived, the language is seen to be disintegrative—not contained in the form of the work. In the portentous littleness of the short-story form, the illusion of vast meanings unspoken is more easily sustained. But the novels, even the best, early ones, become in a fundamental sense unreadable. Like an Eisenhower who made a political success of contempt for politics, Hemingway established his literary reputation, his enormous popularity, essentially on a contempt for letters.

# 8 *William Faulkner:*

# The Legend Behind the Legend

There is scarcely a better way of getting at anything of central significance in William Faulkner's work, than by comparing him first to his contemporary and fellow Nobel prize-winner, Ernest Hemingway. This is not my specific subject here —but the divergence of these two careers, starting from the somewhat common ground of *Soldier's Pay* and *A Farewell to Arms*, presents to the historian of modern American literature probably the most interesting and important problem with which he might concern himself.

We have noted that Hemingway is the perfect type of the expatriate writer, the self-conscious internationalist, who is never at home except somewhere away from home—the chief spokesman for the sense of rootlessness that is the principal characteristic of the general, American mentality in the twentieth century. But, as has often been pointed out, the Southerner is a different kind of American. If he too, especially and increasingly since the First World War, has suffered with his Northern and Western fellow Americans, and with Occidental man in general, an uprooting, a disruption of the sense of local community and of the continuity of economic, social, and moral values from one generation to the next, at least he has been more than other Americans profoundly and agonizingly *conscious* of his loss. And precisely that agony, that tortured consciousness, of the order of the human community, and of the threats posed against the order (by fate, by history, by the mere desire and design of any individual man at a given time and place), is at the center of all Faulkner's work.

It is, in brief, the regional consciousness. That the South has long been (it is now, for better or worse, ever more rapidly losing its special status) the only part of the United States that in any true, distinct sense of cultural community could be called a "region," is a commonplace observation. But essential to the regional consciousness as a whole—a fact rather less often noted—is the Southerner's even narrower sense of identity with the local neighborhood. To the resident of Yoknapatawpha County, not only Yankees are outlanders, but also Alabamans, Georgians, Texans, Louisianians, even people from other parts of Mississippi. The nearby city of Memphis, Tennessee, or still more, New Orleans, in the mind of the typical Faulkner character is remote and vaguely forbidding, as "foreign" almost as New York or Paris.

I do not mean to say that the regional consciousness is necessarily deficient in its sense of the universal human community, its concern with universal human values. In the moral sphere, for example, the people of Faulkner's fictional town are by no means blind or indifferent to the plight of the stranger— the reception of Lena Grove, in *Light in August,* is a good illustration. Indeed, one sees that the regional sense, the certainty of one's own identity in the local community of values, is essential for recognition of the common humanity of the stranger. Only when one is certain of his own domain, of belonging to a certain place and a certain kindred, of where, so to speak, the gates stand, is he capable of recognizing the larger obligation to the stranger within his gates. And, by the same token, regionalism as an aesthetic principle, the regional consciousness of Faulkner as novelist, is not to be understood as a principle of isolation.

He is, of course, far from being a *provincial* writer—a mere, quaint local colorist. There is local color in plenty—in language, characterizations, settings. The novels and stories are a mine of folklore. But, the more intense and rich for its very narrowness, Yoknapatawpha County, as Robert Penn Warren has pointed out, is finally the world's stage. Faulkner the regionalist stands, as I see it, much more firmly than Hemingway the internationalist in the mainstream of the Western literary tradition.

If he is not put off at first by the surface peculiarities of setting and characterization, the folkloristic detail, the frequent use of dialectal speech, anyone acquainted with, for example, the Bible, the ancient Greek drama, Shakespeare, and Milton, will shortly find himself on at least as familiar ground with Faulkner as with Proust, say, or James Joyce. His themes are all the ancient themes; and even his style, for all its rich individuality, is one that we must recognize finally as built upon old, familiar rhetorical principles.

I shall come back a bit later to examine a particular example of his dependence upon traditional "mythic" materials, the Biblical references in *Absalom, Absalom!, Light in August,* and *The Sound and the Fury.* But one thing I mean by his traditionalism—again, reflective of his Southern regionalism, his conformity as artist to the pattern of the Southern "mind," and again radically distinguishing his art from that of a Hemingway—is his complex time-sense. Faulkner is, of course, one of the great modern experimentalists in style, eminently in the vein of that obsessive preoccupation of which Wyndham Lewis was the testy prophet in *Time and Western Man.* But, at his best, the experimentalism only confirms and supports the traditionalism.

In Hemingway's novels, as we have observed, everything happens in a straight line of succession and is told about in the same way. One event leads only to the next; there is never the slightest intention of inquiry into possible, past causes of what transpires in the present, nor even very far into future consequences. In Faulkner, we have precisely the opposite situation. The key to the significance of present events lies *always* in the past—or perhaps it is to the past in the present or, as Warren has suggested, to both in the future. At any rate, if human affairs are intelligible at all, Faulkner tells us, they are so only in consideration of the constant tendency of man's mind to break out of the confinement of chronological time. Man lives, and is engaged in significant action, in some sense simultaneously in past, present, and future.

Hence, the characteristic, spiral movement of the Faulkner narrative, beginning—as with the arrival of Lena Grove in sight of Jefferson and the smoke of the burning house, at the start of *Light in August*—at some tentative point of "present" action, and moving out in widening circles neither really forward nor backward in time, but only *about* the subject. The movement of the entire narrative (though with some decided exceptions to the "peacefulness") is somewhat like the journey of Lena herself as Faulkner describes it: "backrolling now behind her a long monotonous succession of peaceful and undeviating changes from day to dark and dark to day again, through which she advanced . . . *like something moving forever and without progress across an urn.*" (Italics mine.)

Hence, too, the complex, rolling convolutions of the syntax, the long suspensions and subordinations. The very sentences, in their syntactic construction, wind and "double back," foxlike (Faulkner's preoccupation with the situation of the hunt is radically related to his stylistic practice), upon the trail of meaning. Hence, his fondness for characters such as the Reverend Gail Hightower, for whom his long dead grandfather, the Confederate cavalryman, is more alive and present always than his Jefferson parishioners or his wife—for the men, in one critic's phrase, of "frozen passion," such as old Doc Hines, living and acting always in a kind of timeless state of obsessive fury. Hence, his "ancestor worship," the preoccupation with the bloodline, and with the theme of incest, whereby the normal order of generation is turned back upon itself. Hence also, the recurrent theme of confused identities—on a fairly simple level, as in the consequences of Lena Grove's momentary confusion of the names Burch and Bunch, or, in a more complex and subtle usage, in *Absalom, Absalom!*, the merging of the identities of Quentin Compson and his Harvard roommate, Shreve, with those of Henry Sutpen and Charles Bon, whereby the sense of historical time is lost, and Quentin's narrative becomes an enchantment, narrator and listener disappearing, as it were, into the story.

If Faulkner is in one sense, as some critics have seen him, a fatalist—one of his favorite themes, of course, being the inevitability of the defeat of purely rational purpose; one thinks of the ruin of Thomas Sutpen's plans by the "accident" of his first wife's lineage—there is nowhere in his novels the kind of utter passivity that we find in Hemingway. Faulkner has, to be sure, created a wide variety of merely representative types among his secondary characters. And there are a few, even principal figures, who either by their own or others' abuse of their humanity have been turned into will-less automatons, rendered in a sense soul-less. But none of his fictions is without some who, if they are doomed, live always in what Warren has called the "agony of will." They struggle mightily, at least convincingly enough for dramatic purposes (the drama that Jean Paul Sartre's oversimplified analysis of Faulkner's time philosophy fails to account for), *as if* there were such a thing as the individual will. Heroism for Faulkner is not, as for Hemingway, simply a matter of meeting one's fate bravely, i.e., of dying bravely. His major characters live, as if life had some value other than as a preparation for death.

Moreover, the code, or codes, according to which they live, although they may be extremely complex, are open to examination. In Hemingway the interest is almost exclusively in the action, and inarticulateness is a virtue, the mark of *aficion*; in Faulkner, a good half of the excitement is in the effort, on the part both of characters and of author, to explain, to justify, always at least to inquire, into the motives, moral and psychological, of men's actions. The mere loquacity of Faulkner and of many of his characters is, of course, one of the things that most strikingly differentiates his work from that of Hemingway, the original man of few words. But below the surface effect, of an overplus of words on the one hand and verbal poverty on the other, there is, I think, a difference of basic assumptions on the nature and function of language. Faulkner, unlike Hemingway, has faith in the ultimate power of language as instrument for the discovery of truth, especially truth of human motives. Faulkner assumes that actions always *have* motives—which is to say, that man acts, and is not, as Hemingway would have it, simply acted upon; that he is not isolated in the moment of experience, but that his total experience both as an individual and as a member of a community has some continuity, entailing a certain measure of moral responsibility; and that, through the power of language, such motives can be discerned and rendered intelligible.

The "Southern Renaissance," of which Faulkner was belatedly acclaimed the hero by the critics, was essentially a renascence of the Word. And Faulkner is a man of words—many words, sometimes far too many. But, although he could borrow stylistic techniques from James Joyce, for example, they were always thoroughly assimilated and transformed to the purposes of his unique, humanistic-religious vision. He has none of Joyce's historio-theological, verbal aestheticism, the worship of the word as such. His hero is never himself, the poet—but man, man talking.

But a problem in Faulkner's work perhaps more urgent than any other demanding critical reconsideration—and, again, a problem intimately related to that of his time-sense—is the significance of his Biblical references. Historically, of course, his Bible-mindedness is just a part of his regionalism. Yoknapat-awpha County, insofar as it represents a sociological reality, is a part of the Bible Belt. But in the total design of his fiction, his purpose with the references obviously goes far beyond an intent of mere historical realism.

Malcolm Cowley, in one of the basic critical studies of Faulkner, defined his "legend of the South," distinguishing the legendary from the factually historical, and demonstrating convincingly that Faulkner's chronicle of Yoknapatawpha is "no more intended as a historical account of the country south of the Ohio than *The Scarlet Letter* is intended as a history of Massachusetts or *Paradise Lost* as a factual description of the Fall." But perhaps Mr. Cowley's choice of works for comparison, these two highly individualistic products of minds steeped in the traditions of Protestant Christianity, is significant in a way that was not part of his conscious intention. His description of the "legend" is accurate enough, as far as it goes. (And he is certainly right in his objections to such a rigidly *allegorical* reading as George Marion O'Donnell's interpretation of *Sanctuary* as an account of the Rape of the South by the forces of modern industrialism.) But it seems to me that beyond or back of this, in several of the major novels—beyond the legend constructed of the materials of the immediate, regional history, which is still, necessarily, at least half in historical time—the Biblical references provide a further dimension of symbolic significance that is ultimately ahistorical.

The relatively strict allegory of *A Fable* (true allegory, not the kind of thing forced upon the social symbolism of *Sanctuary* by O'Donnell) represents a late development in the technique of Faulkner's long-standing, near obsession with Biblical themes. (In attempting any generalizations about his work, one must realize that his career divides into several, well-defined periods— and discard those things that are either outright, potboiling junk, written off the top of his mind, or abortive experiments.) But in at least three novels from what must by any standards be regarded as his great period—in *Absalom, Absalom!*, with the Old Testament frame of reference set up there by the title, and in *Light in August* and *The Sound and the Fury*, with their more exclusively Christian emphasis—a kind of loose system of religious allusion constitutes what I consider his principal device for giving a basic order and intelligibility to the fiction, for rescuing the story, so to speak, from the chaos of immediacy and temporal particularity, and for providing a sense of permanent, or timeless, human significance and dignity in the frequently bizarre actions of his provincial characters.

Unquestionably, as Cowley suggests, *Absalom, Absalom!* is a kind of summing-up of Faulkner's recurrent fascination with the "legend of the South," the supreme embodiment of his tragic insight into the regional history. In this connection, Quentin Compson, hearer and reteller of the story, represents the intelligence and the conscience of the modern South in contemplation of its history.

This novel takes us back to a period in Quentin's career presumably just previous to that in which he is represented in the earlier book, *The Sound and the Fury*. And it should be noted that Quentin here, as in the other story, is a man attempting to escape from time. The story, told to Quentin in large part by Miss Rosa Coldfield, is a "spinster's tale," the narrative of a woman shut away for forty-three years, cut off from the normal life in chronological time; and it is informed from the first, in some sense deliberately (on Faulkner's part) distorted, by the terrors of her old maid's imagining. The theme of virginity, in several modes, is a central one here as in *The Sound and the Fury*. And, clearly, a considerable part of the motivation of Quentin's interest in the story of Henry and Charles and their sister is to be found in the analogy it provides for his own situation with Caddy. (For understanding of Faulkner, it is not only justifiable, but frequently necessary, to read in the situation of one novel upon that of another in this fashion.) But, once again, Quentin's obsession with virginity is only one expression of his preoccupation with time.

It is an essential irony of the book that Thomas Sutpen, the "demon" of Miss Rosa's virginal nightmares, should emerge finally, as Cleanth Brooks has shown, as himself a type of the innocent. Sutpen's is the innocence of pure rationality. The flaw of his design is, of course, simply that it ignores other, nonrational human values in his relationship with both his wives, with his children, with Miss Rosa, and finally with Wash Jones and his granddaughter. But all this is a way of saying that Sutpen is another character unable to adjust to the fact of time, to the facts of life in time.

Unable properly to accept it, he attempts to exploit time—as in his participation in the Civil War just to maneuver for advantage in his struggle with his sons. He participates, but he does not morally share the public agony. The War functions in the novel as a product and expression of "public" time, which finally thwarts Sutpen's private design.

In some aspects, obviously, the time theme is practically identical with the theme of identity. It should be made clear that to say Faulkner is a traditionalist does not mean that he identifies tradition, as such—i.e., whatever is merely "time-honored"—with Good. It often appears in his work, indeed, as an evil force. The ultimate good, rather, is human dignity. He is concerned with the struggle of the human being to define himself, to attain individual dignity, identity, both in and against tradition. This is, in one form or another, the basic drama of all his major characters' lives. It is Quentin Compson's struggle with his family, both in *The Sound and the Fury* and in *Absalom, Absalom!* It is Thomas Sutpen's struggle with Jefferson, and his sons' struggle with him, the Father. It is Joe Christmas' struggle with race and church, with "society" at large. The basic pattern is repeated through an endless variety of dramatic situations, mutations of symbolic motif, guises of preoccupation with social and psychological subthemes.

The episode of the arrival of Sutpen, the "man of mystery," in Jefferson is reminiscent of many other scenes in Faulkner's fiction—for example, the account of the first appearance of Joe

Christmas at the planing mill, in *Light in August*. In the present instance, however, the incident embodies many of the conventions of the popular frontier tale, or the Western movie. And it is very important to observe Faulkner's consciousness of the ironic combination and conflict of frontier and traditional values within the society of pre- and Civil War Mississippi. Sutpen is the would-be exploiter of this historical situation, his design to some extent representing the familiar, frontier American dream, of a man's *being* what he is able to *make* himself—but with the fatal irony that here it is a design, and an attempted self-characterization, in imitation of the values of traditionalism. (Cf. the situation in *The Great Gatsby*, the frontier quest, the thrust to the future, turned back to the past.)

We have remarked already how Quentin and Shreve, in the telling, "disappear" into the story, merging their identities with those of Henry and Charles. Throughout the novel, there is great difficulty in keeping up with names and relationships. This deliberate obscurity is clearly relevant to Faulkner's constant and complexly ironic concern with the theme of the brotherhood of man. Chiefly by virtue of its bringing together the themes of incest and miscegenation in the one situation of family conflict (the brother-lover also a Negro), themes that were still separate in *The Sound and the Fury*, there is embodied in *Absalom, Absalom!* Faulkner's most profound study of the "human family"—and of the agony of the individual to find and justify himself within that family. That is the book's greatness.

But my specific point, again, is that we cannot fully grasp the significance of any of this—everything comprising the time-identity theme—without recognition of the Biblical references. They are least obtrusive in this novel, but decisively there. Time in the novel is not just time—not even the two times, the twentieth and the nineteenth centuries, regarding each other—but Time. The account of Sutpen's origin, and of the family's descent, during his boyhood, from the West Virginia mountains into the Virginia tidelands, is a metaphor of the Fall—the expulsion from Paradise. The mountaineer society is an all but totally undifferentiated one, hardly even as to generations. Shreve points out that West Virginia did not then exist as a state. It is, rather, a "state," the Edenic state. And for *tide*lands we are to read *time*lands. Sutpen's disturbance of conscience, and his tragic design, are born of his inability to grasp the values of life in time—the mysteries of race and class status, etc., etc. He is not just Southerner, nor American, nor even Modern Man, Western Man; but Fallen Man, refusing to accept the conditions of his fallen state. And Henry and Charles and their sister are not just the children of Thomas Sutpen, in the nineteenth century, in the South, acting out their private tragedy against the public catastrophe of the Civil War. Nor do they "live again" only in Quentin and Shreve, and in Quentin's unspoken obsession with the image of the ruined Caddy. They live, and have lived, as the children of David. They are Absalom, and his brother and his sister.

Behind the psychology and the history and the society—all richly realized, as they have to be, we are dealing with symbolic realism, not allegory—is the myth of the culture. Let us turn now to the strictly Christian aspect of this in *Light in August* and *The Sound and the Fury.*

The bare facts of the system of references in these two novels have been noted by a number of critics. But most commentators seem either to have been puzzled or somehow embarrassed by their own insights here, and have shied away from any real effort to accommodate them in their final view of the novels' integrity of artistic design. (The one notable exception is Hyatt Waggoner, in his recent, excellent book, *William Faulkner.*)

But the facts, as always, have got to be accommodated. It will hardly do, as Irene Edmonds, for example, has suggested ("Faulkner and the Black Shadow," in *Southern Renascence*), to dismiss the matter as some tentative, half-formed idea that Faulkner had in mind when he began work on *Light in August* but that somehow got lost in the course of the writing. What this means (Miss Edmonds' further suggestion that Faulkner could not find the "moral courage" to complete the parallel between Christ and the part-Negro Christmas is too fanciful to demand refutation) is purely and simply that Faulkner is a fumbling and tentative artist. And that is a proposition I am reluctant to accept without further demonstration, not to speak of its failure to square with the facts both of the one novel's construction, where the intent of the symbolism is as apparent in the middle and the end as in the beginning, and of the previous appearance of the same themes in *The Sound and the Fury*, arguing a strangely intense and recurrent preoccupation with a matter of such supposedly slight concern.

Nor should one be put off by such a warning as Mr. Robert Jacobs' that only the "sentimentalist" would insist upon the parallel between Joe Christmas and Christ—for what *this* means, if anything, the facts being what they are, is that Faulkner himself is a sentimentalist; and the obloquy of such an association as that one would be happy to risk at any time. Jacobs and William Van O'Connor (both of these also in contributions to *Southern Renascence*), arguing against the interpretation of Christmas as "victim," i.e., as Christ figure, primly remind us that he is "a pervert and a murderer." But such considerations as this, all too typical, miss the whole point of Faulkner's artistic purpose in the use of the symbolism, if not the point of Christianity itself.

As if it should ever be possible to imagine a human personality "good" enough to represent Christ! It is precisely the central irony of the characterization, and of Faulkner's view of the degeneracy of the "Christian" society, that has produced such a person, a paradox centrally intended if anything is, to show us the image of Christ most clearly in this man of evil. For we must also remind ourselves that behind Christmas' perversion of character are the mad fanaticisms of Doc Hines and McEachern, the all but unspeakable depravity of whose perversion of religious thinking has victimized the child Joe—and, further, that it is, at least permissively, through the weakness and vacillation of the "good" but faithless minister, Hightower, that he suffers his final immolation.

The reader who does not see Joe Christmas as always, primarily, the victim, as a man not choosing but driven to the evil he himself commits—and who misses the irony of his being taken for the Devil when he invades the pulpit of the Negro church, a mistake, we ought hardly need to be reminded, that was made concerning Christ Himself—has failed to understand anything of the book's essential design. The point is, finally and simply, that this kind of Christ, this monstrous mockery of Him, not willing Savior but tormented and compulsive victim of history's perversions of Christianity, is the only kind that properly can appear to a society that has already completely rejected Christ.

But let us, now, briefly review some of the facts of the allusional structure in *Light in August*—and then go on to deal with certain difficulties of the design that seem to me of greater, real importance than those usually pointed out.

On the strength of his name, as well as the mysterious circumstances of his birth, his doubtful parentage, his age at the time of the climactic action of the novel, and his "passion" and death, Joe Christmas has been generally recognized as a Christ figure of some kind. Also related to this conception is the supposition (whether it be fact or legend, the product of Doc Hines's fanatical imagining, we can never be entirely sure) of his mixed blood. It is, at any rate, a psychological fact, of the greatest importance for the development of Christmas' personality. And it is this, obviously, more than anything else, that makes him, again like Christ, a "stranger in the world."

Faulkner has several times in his fiction suggested an identification of the sufferings of the Southern Negro with the suffering of Christ. But for the particular, individual identification, it is clearly significant that Joe Christmas should be both white and black—belonging to both races, and therefore, of course, to neither.

In this, we have not only a type and figure of the double ministry of Christ, but also of His two natures, human and divine. I can only mention in passing the elaborate light-dark symbolism of the novel, centered in the figure of Joe Christmas, with his black trousers and white shirt—light above the waist, dark below, his consciousness of the smell and feel of the Negro's shoes that he wears during his flight as the ineradicable mark, dark taint, of his blood doom, and his deliberate wearing of them as a symbol of acceptance of the doom, etc., etc. But the general significance of all this, within the framework of the Christian references, is readily apparent.

However, one cannot pursue such a line of analysis very far without running into some disturbing, apparent inconsistencies. Assuming that the novel does operate on at least two levels of significance, the naturalistic (or "literal") and the symbolic, how, then, do the other characters fit into the scheme? Lucas Burch has been generally recognized as a Judas; and someone has made out a case for the Reverend Hightower as a Pilate. But there are a number of other loose ends. And especially difficult is the case of Lena Grove, Byron Bunch, and Lena's baby. This trio are clearly intended as a representation of the Holy Family. There is the journey of the unwed, expectant mother; her difficulty in finding a place to stop and bear her child in the strange town; the foster father, who accepts his role with something, clearly, of a fateful insight; the birth of the child in a former stable; everything complete down to the final detail of the salesman's narrative at the end of the book, in which we discover that Lena is still "virginal" after the birth.

It appears, in short, that we have not one but two Christ figures in the novel: Joe Christmas and Lena's baby; and that Faulkner is rather hopelessly confused in his allegorical intent with the story. Where do we stand? Is the symbolic time of the narrative Passion Week or the Christmas season?

Perhaps these questions can best be left until we have first had a look at *The Sound and the Fury*, where there is a strikingly similar situation. The most obvious of the Christ figures in this novel is the idiot, Benjy Compson. The conception of the idiot as the favorite of God, as in the simplicity of his mindlessness presenting an image of divine innocence, is, of course, a traditional one. And in near literary history, we have such figures as Prince Myshkin of Dostoyevsky's *The Idiot*. (Dostoyevsky's work, in many different ways, has often been compared to Faulkner's. In the present instance, there is, to be sure, the significant difference that Myshkin, except for the periods of his recurrent illness, is a man of normal and even superior, adult intelligence—whereas Benjy is literally, in the strict clinical sense, an idiot. Faulkner's character, and the prose style embodying his mindless interior monologue, are probably most directly derived from the so-called "cult of the child-mind" familiar elsewhere in modern American literature. But distinctions of this kind need not primarily concern us here.)

Further, innumerable internal evidences support the intent

of the characterization. There is the mystery of his name, changed from Maury (the name of his uncle) to Benjamin (at his brother, Quentin's, suggestion) when the mother at last acknowledges the fact of his idiocy and cannot endure the impropriety of having the uncle's memory so perpetuated.

There is the sense that the entire family have—this, of course, enforced by the changing of the name—of Benjy's being a kind of divinely appointed burden, his very innocence and helplessness a constant and unbearable reproach.

There is the mysterious fact of his spiritual or psychological insight, knowing, by some super- or subhuman, sixth sense of smell, when Caddy has lost her virginity and when Damuddy has died.

There is his character of the sacrificial victim: his inheritance, the cow pasture, sold to supply the money for Quentin's year at Harvard, he himself deprived of freedom when he is committed to the state insane asylum, and his blood shed in castration (compare the castration-crucifixion symbolism in the death of Joe Christmas), to secure Jason's final escape.

There is the feeling on Caddy's part and still more on Quentin's—recognizing, as they do, his mysterious power of discernment—that it is Benjy to whom, ultimately, they are morally responsible or answerable, he whom they have "offended" with their sins.

There is his association with the Negroes, whom, as I have previously indicated, Faulkner habitually identifies with true religion. Benjy is, throughout the novel, cared for by the Negroes, with some sense of his being one of their own, rejected by his race. And in the Easter Morning service at the Negro church, where he is taken by Dilsey, his presence, plainly awesome to the rest of the congregation, is clearly to be interpreted as embodying Dilsey's apprehension of the divine presence among them.

And, finally and most directly, there are Dilsey's words to him: "You's de Lawd's chile."

But once again, as in *Light in August,* a second glance at the symbolism reveals certain apparent inconsistencies. The climactic action of the novel—involving the conflict between Jason and the second Quentin (the daughter of Caddy), with Jason's pursuit of the girl and the carnival pitchman around the town, the theft of the money from Jason's room, and Quentin's final flight—takes place on Good Friday and Easter. And there are a number of half-submerged hints at a symbolic level of significance in the timing of the episodes and in certain descriptive details.

In the insistent references to the time of day on Friday afternoon—clocks are heard striking, or someone looks at a watch or a clock or asks the time at least a dozen times between noon and three o'clock—and, coupled with these, to the "show" that is going on in the town, for which everyone in Jefferson and in the country for miles around has left work for the day—a good part of the intention, unquestionably, is a fairly simple kind of satire on the neo-Pagan character of this "Christian" community. It is the farthest thing from anyone's mind—Jason's especially, of course, who is spending the three hours trying to defraud his niece, play the stock market, and protect his mother's good name, but also from that of the community at large—that the day is the anniversary of our Lord's death, of that other carnival, whose drama has traditionally embodied the central myth of our culture.

But if we can take it for granted that Faulkner is never *merely* a satirist, and push below the level of satire to tie up the personal or family tragedy of the Compsons with the system of mythic references, then the difficulties begin rapidly to multiply.

If there is something more than the negative intention of satire—however covert, and unwitting on the part of the participants, some re-enactment on the naturalistic level of the divine drama—then who is the Christ figure here? Plainly, it cannot be Benjy, who hardly figures at all in this part of the story except in Jason's interior monologues.

And since, I should think almost as plainly, it cannot be Jason, who only in the most outrageously ironic sense could be conceived as undergoing a "passion" in these three days—we are left with the girl, Quentin.

And yet, unlikely as it may seem, this must be Faulkner's intention. The symbolic evidence is in the account of the discovery of Quentin's flight on Sunday morning. The opening of her room by Jason, racing up the stairs to take the keys from his mother, pushing her and old Dilsey aside in the fatalistic eagerness of his premonition (the very use of the keys ironically superfluous against the certainty of his foreknowledge), is the discovery of the empty tomb.

Every essential detail is supplied: the "dead" anonymity of the room, the mocking odor of sweetness, the discarded garments hanging from the dresser drawers, the face towel bearing the rouged imprint of her lips and cheeks, the resurrection symbol of the newly blooming pear tree at the open window. And if from this point we go back to look for other signs of Quentin's preparation for her role here, they are not, after all, difficult to find.

She too, in a special sense through the fact that she bears the name of her suicide uncle, Quentin, is a doomed person, a victim chosen and appointed by fate. "I knew the minute they named her Quentin this would happen," Mrs. Compson says, after they have broken into the room. She is, again in the strict tradition of such figures, of uncertain parentage, the identity of her father, as Jason repeatedly reminds us, never is known for sure. And certainly it is she, if anyone, who is the principal victim (besides Benjy) of Jason's viciousness, who is robbed of her inheritance and betrayed by him to her doom of ostracism and exile, giving herself, as her mother had before her—denied the love of her own people—to the embraces of the stranger.

That Quentin is one of the "good" characters, one "on the side of the angels," at least, we need no more evidence, I think, than to note that she is loved by Dilsey—the universal Great Mother figure of the novel, whose affections are always the sure index to Faulkner's intention. The fact that she is, apparently, something of an habitual free whore is nothing, of course, against our argument. The tradition of saintly harlotry is well-established in modern literature—we may think again of Dostoyevsky, for example. Only if we adopt the attitudes of Jason, the man whose positive vocation it is always to throw the first stone, should we think her disqualified as surrogate of Christ by her whoredom. The simple point here is that the harlotry is not anything chosen by Quentin, but obviously is her doom. The acceptance of the pitchman is her appointed agony.

Quentin represents in the novel, to put the matter as briefly and directly as possible, the idea of *love*. It is, to be sure, largely a negative representation. Love is precisely what she is likely never to get. But it is always and only this for which she yearns, and for which she undergoes the agony. And insofar as Jason surely represents, in his losing conflict with her, the antagonist of love, is pre-eminently the man incapable of loving—the man of hatred and lust, enslaved to time and the desire of material possessions—the outcome of the struggle is not, perhaps, entirely negative.

Mrs. Compson is wrong, we should observe, in the implications of her words to Jason and Dilsey on Sunday morning, when they find the empty room. "Find the note," she keeps saying. "There's bound to be a note. Quentin [i.e., the uncle] left a note *when he did it*." (Italics mine.) But it is not suicide this time, as she suspects, but quite the opposite. It is not Good Friday now, but Easter. The tomb is empty.

(I do not mean to suggest that the male Quentin is another Christ figure—he the dead Christ, she, with his name, the risen. The effect of the fish symbolism in the June 2, 1910, episodes—immediately preceding Quentin's suicide—is to characterize him as the lost soul; the man whose own intellectual understanding of his predicament prevents him from accepting the redemption. Faulkner's Christ figures are all of sub- or extraintellectual intelligence. The girl Quentin is resurrected from her own death on the Friday, though in some sense, as his namesake and the product of his imagined sin with Caddy, she redeems his death through her triumph.

At least at the naturalistic level, we can hardly miss interpreting the situation as a victory for the girl. Whatever her future with the pitchman, it cannot possibly be as loveless as the home with Jason that she is leaving. Whether she is to get anything in return, however possibly unworthy the recipient, she has at least found the wherewithal to give; and, plainly, the stolen money, her "dowry," is only the talisman of her self-giving.

But perhaps the character of Quentin as Christ figure can be seen most clearly by indirection, in a study of the antagonist himself. We must surely, at any level of interpretation, be convinced of the defeat of Jason in the final action, and take the keenest delight in it. Nowhere in modern literature is there a more terrifying portrayal than this account of the disintegration of a man facing the collapse of his schemings, finding himself, so to speak, pulled into the gears of his own machinations. Jason blustering, threatening the sheriff when he refuses to help him, trying to claim the protection of the law in his effort to recover the money that he has broken every moral law in the first place to possess—his own part of it, as well as what belongs legally to Quentin. Jason with his pounding, blinding headache, his brain aboil with rage and frustration in the sight of his collapsing dreams. Jason in demonic fury chasing about the countryside after the fleeing girl, bursting into the carnival wagon, raving like a madman at the old workman, and in his turn cursed and threatened and driven out. Jason at last, when he knows finally that everything is lost, that no one will lift a hand to help him, sitting beside the road in the automobile, the proudest of his stolen possessions, the chief symbol of his glory in his petty tyranny, now merely "a small car," in which he waits in the quietness of despair, an object of the idle curiosity of passersby returning from Easter church services, and having finally to suffer the indignity of accepting assistance (and that at the man's own terms) from one of the despised race of Negroes. Jason, above all, seeing his precious *time* run out on him.

*He sat there for some time. He heard a clock strike the half hour, then people began to pass, in Sunday and Easter clothes. Some looked at him as they passed, at the man sitting quietly behind the wheel of a small car, with his invisible life ravelled out behind him like a wornout sock. After a while a negro in overalls came up.*

Jason is, perhaps, finally somewhat pathetic. And he has been all along humanized enough to enable us to participate empathically in his feelings, to recognize, dramatically, his situation. Especially, all but in spite of ourselves, we have to appreciate his humor. Faulkner is altogether Shakespearean in his ability to make his villains men of wit, without any sense of incongruity. And the drollery is often inextricably bound up with the terror. But there is never any sentimentalizing of the characterization, no suggestion of anything finally to redeem the evil of the man. He remains a rustic Iago, or Judas, if you will, who plainly does not deserve to live, but, if anything, simply lacks the dignity to die.

And in this characterization of the man-of-evil, the man of the devil opposed to the Christ figure, the chief mark of his role, as I have suggested, is his enslavement to time. (He is associated everywhere with symbols of time: the car, the stock ticker, the newspaper.) His brother Quentin was the victim of time—the watch and clock symbolism figures as prominently in that part of the novel as in Jason's section. And so is it time that finally destroys Jason. But the difference is that Jason has willingly chosen time as his master, and thus receives only the just wages of his service when the mechanism of its tryanny is at last turned against himself. Quentin had sought a Hell in which he could be with Caddy, in the pure flame, out of time. Jason is already in Hell; like Milton's Satan, he carries his Hell with him.

But to go back to the question of the apparent confusion of the symbolism, the rather, at times, elusive character of the symbolic references, the fact that there are not one but at least two Christ figures in each of the novels, and in *Light in August* the merging of the liturgical seasons, the fact that there is never any strictly dependable coordination of annual and liturgical calendar: The answer, I think, lies in something like the observations I made some years ago in an essay on T. S. Eliot's *The Cocktail Party*. My argument was that the apparent division of the Christ role there, between Harcourt-Reilly and Celia Coplestone, was not confusion at all, nor any vagueness of artistic purpose on Eliot's part, but simply sound theology. And I think that the same is true of Faulkner's design in *Light in August* and *The Sound and the Fury*.

If a convincing consistency is to be maintained at the naturalistic level, as it is in Faulkner's novels much better than in Eliot's play, then there can be no question of investing only one of the characters with all the godly attributes. So long as the persons of the drama are to be seen as human beings, acting within the limits of creaturely capacity and subject to the laws of time and space, we can see the image of Christ, and the career of His ministry, partially and momentarily in one or another of them, but never wholly and perfectly in any one. And, by the same token, no pattern of events in mere human lives can exactly parallel any part of Christ's career. Insofar as His drama is repeated in day-to-day human affairs, it is not in the original chronological order. Mystically, the God dies and is born simultaneously.

Moreover, it is sound cultural history as well as sound theology. For the pattern of the Christian myth does, in our society, survive only in fragments. And it would be, again, unrealistic to impose its order too rigidly upon a representation of modern society, as if it had the same force and immediacy for us that it had, say, for the society of Dante's time. This is, of course, especially true for the particular, regional society about which Faulkner writes, where observance of the liturgical calendar scarcely exists as part of the local religious tradition.

We do not expect of Faulkner the intellectually punctilious, history-of-ideas conscious religiosity of an Eliot; certainly not the fanatic aestheticism of a Joyce, in contemplation of the collapse of the traditional, theological order of symbolism in the world, imposing as substitute a purely verbal, metaphoric order. Faulkner had not (in some ways an advantage to him) the kind of education that would demand either of these strategies, produce the conditions of either of these particular kinds of spiritual anguish; he has had no experience of a Catholic society. But what we do expect, and get, concomitant with his more passionate *immersion* in the chaos of decadence, is a strong and immediate sense of the spiritual potentiality of man—and informed with at least enough Bible-consciousness, if nothing else, for us to recognize the potential man as a member of the same species as the makers of Western civilization.

I might, in conclusion, put the matter this way. There is not much comfort for the orthodox believer (Catholic or Protestant) in Faulkner's use of the Christian references. His Christ figures are largely negative representations. The girl Quentin, for the best example, remains a shadowy figure, certainly insubstantial in contrast with the characterization of the antagonist, Jason. It is in his representation of despair, not of hope, that Faulkner is characteristically most convincing. (I mean, specifically, theological despair and hope. At the purely human level—if there is such a level—Faulkner's pervasive humor decisively undercuts the pessimism.) They are Christs without followers; again, it is Jason, the Judas of the piece, in despair, not a disciple in joy and hope, who hastens to enter the empty tomb. Or, one might say, he succeeds better in creating the atmosphere of the Old than of the New Testament, not only in *Absalom, Absalom!*, but in those novels in which the Christ is already present. We have from him a picture of modern man in whose waking consciousness, moral and intellectual, the images of the Christian myth persist only like the fragments of a dream—and, usually, a bad dream.

Institutionalized Christianity is, for Faulkner, a part of that tradition which, as I took care to emphasize earlier, he treats always as being at least as much burden as blessing. In its original intent, it is a religion of liberation, a faith specifically promising the regeneration of the individual, the opportunity of each man to realize his unique identity and responsibility for his destiny. But, that this intent has been often obscured, if not entirely reversed, in the history of the cult's practice—its involvement with other human institutions—Faulkner is scarcely the first to have observed. It is no doubt distressing to be told, so forcefully as Faulkner tells us, that the Christ of the myth, the personally redemptive Christ, is least of all likely to be found in His church; that, in the hands of His followers, His teachings have been made the instrument of enslavement, of a vicious and soul-destroying community prejudice. But the distress is not novel.

In any event, we are concerned here with his books as works of the art of fiction. I have wanted, first of all, to argue their intelligibility as fiction. And my argument has been simply that in order to understand their form we must first consult the time-scheme, as radically related to the concept of character, of the self—and, further, that the time-scheme, Faulkner's time-sense, his conception of the interrelationship of past, present, and future, both in the history of the individual and in public history, is explicable only with reference to the Christian (or Judeo-Christian) myth of the Fall and Redemption. For no work of art is produced outside a cultural context; our culture (including Mississippi!), if it is anything definable, is still the Christian culture, albeit in fragments; and the Christian myth is centrally and essentially a time-myth, the myth of the God of Eternity "in love with the things of Time," of the light of the infinite shining within the darkness of the finite, of the One within the many.

I do not say this argument embraces the only possible approach to Faulkner, the whole area of possible critical interest. But I do insist that any approach which seeks simply to ignore or evade, to explain away, these evidences, is fundamentally in error. One might as well refuse to face up to other troublesome matters: that the novels are about the South; or that they are written frequently in a very difficult prose; or, simply, that they are written, and in an unconscionable number. Christ, in whatever embarrassing disguises, is there, and must be confronted.

# 9 *Brideshead Revisited:*

# God, Man, and Others

*Brideshead Revisited* is a book of nostalgia. The title of the novel—not only with "revisited," but before we know whether it is a place, person, or what, "Brideshead," its overtones quaint and virginal—tells us that much. And so, further, does the "Et in Arcadia Ego" of Book One. It is a sigh of gentle melancholy for the lost past of England; for the order and sanity, above all the *charm*, of the old, true Oxford, of country estates with fountained parks and well-stocked wine cellars, of an art that need not question or assert its validity beyond attesting to the supreme virtues of the national character; for everything "before Hooper," the new Englishman who feels that his countrymen "could learn a thing or two" from Hitler.

But it is also the record of Charles Ryder's effort to transcend the nostalgia. Book Two, "A Twitch Upon the Thread," and the Epilogue are designed to show us the protagonist brought into a new, more realistic relationship to tradition, finding a way spiritually to accommodate the hated present. The way, of course, is Catholicism; specifically, and insistently, *Roman* Catholicism, but discovered as an intrinsic part of the English tradition.

Considered in the light of Evelyn Waugh's total career, the book simply reveals the positive values of his English traditionalism (the nostalgia) on the one hand, and of his recusant religious faith on the other, that were always present behind the negative statement of the satires on contemporary society and its debasement of the image of man which brought him his principal fame. The novel attempts, further, to indicate that there is no conflict between these two sets of values; that, as I have said, the Catholicism is in fact derivable from, is essentially part and parcel of, the English tradition, transcending but not contradicting it, and providing the necessary means of bringing the traditional values living into the present.

The point is worth repeating, because a number of critics who have seen the relationship of this "romance" to the earlier satires, and duly pointed out that Mr. Waugh was a Catholic long before *Brideshead Revisited,* have continued to express regret, chagrin, and apparent surprise at the "irrelevancy" (the term is Sean O'Faolain's) of his admiration for titles and the pleasures of inherited wealth—the "lushness," the snobbish, romantic sentimentalism of his nostalgia—both to his religion and to his satiric gift. I share the regret and the chagrin at discovering how much of the traditionalism is sheer snobbery, and that of the crassest, most undiscriminating sort. One can be a snob in better or worse taste, at least. Mr. Waugh's taste, as we might not have expected from any of the earlier books, was revealed in *Brideshead* to be very bad indeed. But there is no irrelevancy. Every satirist in one way or another is a snob. And, for better or worse, the snobbery of Waugh's which is the outward mark of his English traditionalism is also essentially identifiable with his conception of Catholicism. We may decide that this is an outrageously false idea of religion, even, specifically, of Catholicism. But taking the book first on its own terms, as it is always the duty of the critic to do, its design reveals the snobbery and the religious experience, false or genuine, as entirely "relevant" to one another. Given the Charles Ryder of Book One, we can hardly imagine his conversion (covertly alluded to in the Epilogue) as having occurred in any other way than that described in Book Two, in any other environment than that of the Flyte world.

The snobbery does, of course, constitute a "problem" in the book. But it is a problem of which Charles Ryder (and beyond him, Waugh) is, at least at one level, acutely conscious. The principal fruit of his experience is the insight by which he makes finally the effort to put his nostalgia into perspective, and to dissociate what is mere snobbery (what Anthony Blanche refers to as the spiritual blight of English "charm") from the genuine and irreducible values of tradition, including the religious, represented by the Flytes. Not, I think, that Waugh entirely succeeds; but he is certainly aware that the problem, the need for the distinction, exists.

Let us examine more closely some of Ryder's attitudes. It is clear that he deplores "Hooper"—the new age of the war without ideals, of the substitution of a history of social movements for that of the glory of English and ancient arms in the education of the young, of the invasion of meadows and parklands by the builders of suburban housing developments. But, again, Hooper the man is in Ryder's eyes plainly as much the victim as the hero of the era he represents. And in the episode of the haircutting, when the old-line, career colonel attempts to impose the code of regimental tradition on the conscript subaltern, Ryder's sympathies are entirely with Hooper. The incident, he tells us, was the basis of a feeling he had for Hooper which "almost amounted to affection."

It is clear also that the "Et in Arcadia Ego" chapters represent "anti-Hooper," the values, the way of life, that command Ryder's deepest fondness and loyalty. But he is under no more entirely simpleminded illusions about Oxford, for example, than about the traditions of the army. Even there, and even in his day, "Arcadia" was a very small and secret place; the enchanted gate by which one entered it was extremely difficult to find. Oxford at large, he realizes, was Cousin Jasper's Oxford.

Nor should we miss his at least retrospective awareness of the unhealthiness that ruled even in Arcadia. For all the gentle melancholy, the downright sentimentality, the not too covert snobbery of name-dropping (titles of books and paintings, obscurely familiar allusions), there is much of the old Waugh still in these sketches. The satiric savagery is everywhere just under the surface. Even if we may feel ourselves expected, finally and wholeheartedly, to love Sebastian, with his teddy bear and elephant's foot wastebasket and borrowed ties and cars and ineffable responses to Clive Bell's rhetorical questions, the imperative certainly does not extend to Anthony Blanche. Ryder is expressing his honest judgment when he says to Cousin Jasper that he himself "doesn't care much" for Blanche either. And Tony, not Sebastian, is the ruling spirit of the little circle of enchantment. (See chap. v.) It is all too literally a fairyland, of which Anthony Blanche is the Oberon. And if we mistake it all simply for good, clean fun, the fault is ours not Waugh's. Blanche is very funny, shouting through his megaphone to the passing undergraduates. But funny in exactly the same way, finally, as another Tony in another novel of Waugh's that takes its cue from Eliot, as Tony Last, reading Dickens to the madman in the jungle. This is the height of satiric irony, at its most savage; at least here, momentarily, Waugh is fully aware that the fairyland *is* the waste land.

Similarly, there is at least an effort to discriminate between what constitutes the real nobility of the Flytes, their charm and liberality of mind, hospitality, tolerance, the wit and the charity that are the products of their privileged heritage—noblesse oblige—and the abuses, spiritual and otherwise, of their position. The vulgarization of taste, or of moral sensibility, whatever the reason for it, that can lead Julia into marriage with the soulless, "self-made" Mottram, is recognized as such. Plainly, we are meant to see this as a symptom of decadence of the aristocratic tradition. And about as plainly, I think, the attitudes of Brideshead are condemned as a corruption of the religious heritage. His stiff-necked warning to his sister that so long as she is living in sin Beryl could not "consent to be her guest," is not merely bad manners. It is an offense against charity. And it is only, we are meant to see, by the superior strength of her own, subsequent preoccupation of conscience that Julia (and ultimately, through his love for her, Charles) is able to ignore or transcend the insult, in a sense to forgive Brideshead, and say that he is "right."

It is only, I think, that the discriminations are not fine enough. Unfortunately, Julia's impassioned monologue, in which, following her brother's rebuke, she envisages the sufferings of Christ and her rejection of Him that marriage to Charles would constitute, is as vulgar in its way as Brideshead's own self-righteousness. The rank sentimentality of the reminiscences of "mummy" and "Nanny stitching by the hearth," combined with an evocation of the Crucifixion, carries vulgarity to the verge of blasphemy.

And where God is not involved, within the strictly "profane" sphere of "The Scared and Profane Memories of Captain Charles Ryder," the term is all too often applicable in a sense not intended by Waugh. There is a real profanation, too, of the image of Man. The scenes on shipboard, culminating in Ryder's seduction of Julia, furnish one of the best examples. Waugh, through Ryder, is merciless with the vulgarities of the setting and the character of the typical first-class passengers—with the decor of the ship, its blotting-paper colored carpets, its hallways "huge without splendor," with the ice swan filled with caviar for Celia's party, with Senator Oglander, and the "Episcopalian Bishop." Charles and Julia, we are given clearly to understand, are superior to all this. They suffer, withal good-humoredly, the champagne and the roses and the massage and the being shaved in bed, but cannot possibly be imagined to enjoy any of it. The Senator and the Bishop, Celia and her circle, are self-made caricatures of humanity; the ship a travesty on human civilization, and the voyage a mockery of the journey of human existence. Julia and Charles, and the storm, are the real thing. They do not hide from the awful face of Nature, but stand in proud humility before it, embracing on the open deck at the height of the gale. Actually to couple, they observe the minimal decencies of civilization and go to the cabin, but still performing their ecstasy in full responsiveness to the rhythms of the tempest: "now, while the waves still broke and thundered on the prow, the act of possession was a symbol, a rite of ancient origin and solemn meaning."

But, of course, it is not. The storm is no more real than Celia's swan. The writing here, with these ponderous and desperate abstractions—"symbol," "rite," "ancient," "solemn meaning"—is as pretentiously empty, as "huge without splendour" as the despised art of the ship's architect.

We get only now and then—as very briefly with the description of the great saloon doors swinging loose with the roll of the ship, before the fatuous intrusion again of Charles's reflections on the sure-footedness of brave little Julia—any barest sense of realism in the account of the storm: which, of course, is supposed to present itself as the prime symbol (along with the sexual act) of Reality and Nature. Perhaps most tellingly embarrassing is the scene on the deck:

*in a plunge deeper than the rest, I found myself flung across*
*her . . . against the rail . . . and we stood there embraced, in*
*the open, cheek against cheek, her hair blowing across my eyes;*
*the dark horizon of tumbled water, flashing now with gold,*
*stood still above us, then came sweeping down till I was staring*
*through Julia's dark hair into a wide and golden sky, and she was*
*thrown forward on my heart, held up by my hands on the rail,*
*her face still pressed to mine.*

*In that minute, with her lips to my ear and her breath warm*
*in the salt wind, Julia said, though I had not spoken, "Yes,*
*now," and as the ship righted herself and for the moment ran*
*into calmer waters, Julia led me below.*

All of this—the pathetic fallacies, of the "deep plunge"
enforcing the embrace, of the storm's conveniently abating long
enough, once the decision is made, to let them get below; the
lover "staring" through the woman's "dark hair" at the "wide
and golden sky"; her breath "warm in the salt wind"—is
Hollywood, *Saturday Evening Post,* and *Collier's,* at their worst.
Julia's "loins," finally, as we might have expected, are fashion-
ably "narrow." The feeling one gets is of having been to bed
with a shopwindow mannikin.

No other celebrated modern writer, himself an expert on
vulgarity in life and literature and a satirist of it, has been caught
in such shameless vulgarities of his own, except Aldous Huxley
in the book that is in some ways his *Brideshead*—Philip Quarles
his Charles Ryder—*Point-Counterpoint.* And I am not sure
but that Huxley has something even of the advantage over
Waugh, at least in the sense that his satires are always, more
honestly tainted with Kitsch romance.

We may also note the wine-tasting episode of Chapter IV,
Book One. Here, if anywhere, is the "real thing" of life among
ancestral splendors, in touch with the true profane, of aristocratic tradition. There can be no doubt of Ryder's utter
seriousness when it comes to wine, or of Waugh's complete
identity with his hero in this respect. And yet again, I feel, there
is a pervasive sense of unreality. Charles's and Sebastian's praises
for the vintages, if not clichés in quite the same way as those I
have quoted from the seduction scene, are pallid and quaint.

"Wilder and more exotic," Charles says, introducing a passage of their dialogue. But neither of these terms seems properly definitive of what follows, of the description of tastes: "little, shy . . . like a gazelle"; "dappled, in a tapestry meadow"; "like a flute by still water"; "like the last unicorn." Like Charles's landscape on the wall panel of the "office," the description of which immediately precedes the wine passage, it is all picturesque rather than painterly. Red or white, sweet or dry, light or full-bodied, old or new (we would, in fact, appreciate a little, more realistic *information* as to types, even labelings, failing more robustly evocative metaphors) all is uniformly ineffable. Charles tells us that they get drunk, that that is why they become confused after a time as to which bottle they are drinking from, or trying to describe; but from such airy potables as these, one must wonder how.

And then, much later, when Charles has dinner with Rex Mottram, the quality of his appreciation is finally revealed as merest "winesmanship." Half the pleasure of drinking, it appears, is in having the boor along to whose taste to prove the superiority of one's own . . . and only the more snobbishly exquisite, if he is too boorish even to realize that it *is* being proved.

But with none of these particular strictures, I feel, do we yet get at the central intent, and the causes of the essential failure, of the book. The novel is, first of all and most seriously, a "conversion" novel, a story that purports to show a man in the process of becoming a new man, of being "born again," and of learning to see the world and other men with the eyes of his new identity. More specifically, a fact too little acknowledged in previous criticism, that man, Charles Ryder, is a painter by profession. It is, then, a book about the artist, becoming the Catholic artist.

We have already touched on some of the problems under the first of these two headings: i.e., of the character of Charles Ryder as convert. And I have here and there suggested his partial identity with Waugh. "I am not I: thou art not he or she: they are not they," E. W. says in his prefatory author's note. But enough, nonetheless, that we can take C. R.'s views, on religion and art, quite seriously as representative of E. W.'s.

The book, we have noted, reveals the "positive" values behind the earlier Waugh satires to have been a Catholic-English traditionalism, an admiration of the recusant-aristocratic heritage, that at its worst degenerates into a snobbish sentimentalism. The question of how this debasement affects the theological problem of the book—of what is wrong with the "Christian" view of man in which the novel is conceived, and to preliminary understanding of which Ryder has come at the end—can best be considered first as a question of novelistic technique.

What Waugh has attempted is a mixture of the forms of satire and romance. This is particularly noticeable in the conception of character. Charles, Julia, Sebastian, Cordelia, for example, among the principal, sympathetic characters, and Brideshead among the less desirable, are characters of romance. Rex Mottram, Celia, Charles's father, Mr. Samgrass, Anthony Blanche at least part way through the story, on the other hand, are purely satiric creations—similar to the characters of Waugh's earlier fiction. That is, they merely represent more or less complex patterns of folly and depravity in modern society. They are two-dimensional, half-men. We neither admire nor despise them as persons; and feel no sympathetic emotions, either of delight or revulsion, in contemplation of their fates.

The difficulty arises when such as these are brought into the same fiction with the "real" characters, and in such a way as to influence the fates of the latter. It is a problem that becomes especially sticky when the fiction in question is a Christian one, i.e., that purports to represent men in their reality as souls, the object of the redemptive passion of Christ. Let us take as a first example Charles Ryder's relationship to Celia.

It is easy enough to see what Waugh is about here, or at any rate supposes himself to be about. Celia merely represents the unreality, unrealism, and irresponsibility, of Charles's own attitudes previous to his interest in Julia, his capitulation to the soullessness of modern civilization. His love for Julia, and proposal to marry her, divorcing Celia, is the first step toward self-realization and fulfillment. He mistakes the first step for the last, and comes only later to recognize the workings of Grace in the affair, that he is to be led to conversion by Julia, to divine love through the human, and is not to marry her. But insofar as the affair does serve in this way as an instrument of Grace, it is good, and we recognize throughout the thorough, God-informed humanity of the participants. (Julia's own marriage to Rex Mottram furnishes a parallel pattern in her spiritual history.)

But Celia is such a total fake, a caricature, that we must wonder how Charles, if we are to take *him* seriously, could ever have become involved with her. And if we are to write off their marrying, simply, as a youthful folly of his—though there is nothing of his directly revealed character that will satisfactorily explain it—then the biological consequences are rather harder to dispose of. The satiric humor of the description of Celia in her cabin on the ship during the storm, her creating "the atmosphere of a maternity ward" in the stateroom with the flowers and the nurse, making "a sacred, female rite even of seasickness," would have been the more effective if we did not know that she actually has enacted the rite in question, that they do have children. Waugh cheerfully lumps the children in with Celia, as cartoon characters. When Charles divorces her, he divorces them. But how is it possible that something of the father's humanity has not descended to them; how can he, as a matter of moral probability, quite so blithely dismiss them as "her [Celia's] children," and not at all his?

Further, Charles is himself the child of one of the half-men. Waugh's novel, of the convert-artist, is complete with its version, too, of the father search. Charles is, in effect, disowned by his father. He is, then, prospectively adopted by Lord Marchmain, apparently as a kind of surrogate for the lost Sebastian, and promised the estate as his inheritance if, as then supposed, he is to marry Julia. And, finally, giving up the inheritance along with Julia, he is ultimately inspired by old Marchmain's deathbed repentance to his own conversion— thus receiving the eternal inheritance, of course, instead of the temporal, and recognition as son of God the Father. Again, the pattern of development, from a new awareness of human values, and the search for happiness, for identity, at that level, all that is represented by the estate, to final recognition of the real object of the quest in the divine, is clear enough.

But, once more, the question is where the absolute minimum

of humanity, the smallest spark of soul necessary to kindle the desire and start the search, came from. The elder Ryder, with his absolute heartlessness, the cruel, knowing, and unerring wit which he hides under his mask of stodgy, provincial artlessness, is certainly one of Mr. Waugh's most exquisite creations. And, depending on how annoyed we are with Charles's absurdity, we may take a certain malicious pleasure in seeing his moral pretensions time after time neatly skewered by the guileful innocence of his father. It would be sheerest delight to have him left "pinned and wriggling on the wall." But, of course, that is impossible. The "romance" requires that we recognize Charles, for better or worse, as its hero. And with his identity in this role, the father has nothing to do. He is simply and totally indifferent to his son's humanity. Or, rather, Mr. Waugh, in his conception of the father's character, vis-à-vis Charles, is indifferent to it. The two are conceived on two entirely different planes, or in entirely different spheres, of the imagination. The elder Ryder is not merely *in*human in his attitude toward Charles; he is *un*human. And yet, here they are, in the same book; and with the assertion of a biological relationship between them; the one begotten by the other—*genitum non factum.* How is it possible?

It is quite impossible to imagine Ryder senior, or Celia, as subjects for conversion. They, like Rex Mottram (whom the priest has already despaired of in the religious instruction during his engagement to Julia, even before the specific impediment of his former marriage is revealed), are clearly beyond the pale of Grace. They are not, in the usual sense, merely so hardened in sin as to have put themselves beyond the possibility of redemption. Rather, they have no souls to save. And perhaps Mr. Waugh does see the process of man's self-debasement in modern civilization as having gone so far that some considerable portion (perhaps the majority) of the earth's population is in this condition. Perhaps he means to tell us by this book that the soulless ones, the characters of his satires, are real, or at any rate actual, people. But, if so, it is a queer version of Catholicism that can conceive of such a situation. And even queerer is the notion of God's economy that permits the two kinds, the whole and the half-men, the souled and the unsouled, to continue to breed together. Julia's child by Rex Mottram conveniently dies at birth, Nature properly rebelling at the idea of producing such a monster. But Charles himself is begotten, and begets, in such alliances.

But let us come back, finally, to Charles's development as artist. There is, of course, no strict parallel to be drawn between the history of Waugh's art as writer and that of Charles as painter. The differentiation of identities is more fundamental than what is enforced by the *Sons and Lovers* strategy of substituting the one artistic medium for the other. Still, we can hold Waugh responsible for the validity of the story's implicit theory of the relationship between art and religion and art and tradition—for the manner in which it "solves," or resolves, the problems it raises—and legitimately apply that theory in criticism of this book's own design.

At the time of Charles's exhibition in London following his return from Mexico and Central America, Anthony Blanche, momentarily half emerging from his satiric identity, reappears unexpectedly and gives Ryder a private lecture on his art in exposé of the falsity (already half-admitted by Charles himself) of his latest efforts. What Blanche says conveniently rehearses, *inter alia*, the stages of Charles's development:

"*I went to your first exhibition,*" *said Anthony;* "*I found it—charming. There was an interior of Marchmain House, very English, very correct, but quite delicious. 'Charles has done something,' I said; 'not all he will do, not all he can do, but something.'*

*Even then, my dear, I wondered a little. It seemed to me that there was something a little gentlemanly about your painting. You must remember I am not English; I cannot understand this keen zest to be well-bred. English snobbery is more macabre to me even than English morals. However, I said, 'Charles has done something delicious. What will he do next?'*

"*The next thing I saw was your very handsome volume—* '*Village and Provincial Architecture,*' *was it called. Quite a tome, my dear, and what did I find? Charm again . . . Then, to be frank, dear Charles, I despaired of you. 'I am a degenerate old d-d-dago,' I said, 'and Charles—I speak of your art, my dear—is a dean's daughter in flowered muslin.'*

*"Imagine then my excitement at luncheon today. Everyone . . . had been to your exhibition . . . it was you they talked of, how you had broken away, my dear, gone to the tropics, become a Gauguin, a Rimbaud. You can imagine how my old heart leaped.*

*. . . . . . . . . . . . . . . . . . . . . . . .*

*" 'Oh, the pictures,' they said; 'they're most peculiar.' 'Not at all what he usually does.' 'Very forceful.' 'Quite barbaric.' 'I call them downright unhealthy,' said Mrs. Stuyvesant Oglander.*

*"My dear, I could hardly keep still in my chair. I wanted to dash out of the house and leap in a taxi and say, 'Take me to Charles's unhealthy pictures' . . . And what did I find? I found, my dear, a very naughty and successful practical joke. It reminded me of dear Sebastian when he liked so much to dress up in false whiskers. It was charm again, my dear, simple, creamy, English charm, playing tigers.*

*. . . . . . . . . . . . . . . . . . . . . . . .*

*". . . My dear, . . . years ago . . . I warned you. I took you out to dinner to warn you of charm. I warned you expressly and in great detail of the Flyte family. Charm is the great English blight. It does not exist outside these damp islands. It spots and kills anything it touches. It kills love; it kills art; I greatly fear, my dear Charles, it has killed you."*

And Charles, without qualification, accepts Anthony's judgment. "You're quite right," he says.

But the question is, where do we go—where does Charles go—from here? Presumably, there are some qualifications to be made. When we are presented with a hero who is at once, we are repeatedly reminded, an artist and a prospective convert, we assume that the two aspects of the character have something meaningful to do with each other. And we can, in fact, retrospectively, fill in some of the arguments here that Charles himself is unable to supply.

We know, as Anthony by his intrinsic limitations of mind and Charles by his still incomplete experience are prevented from knowing, that Blanche is right only up to a certain point: that there is more essentially to the Flytes than mere charm; that Charles is soon to become involved with them in a real adventure of the spirit, through which he is to find the identity that he had tried to lose in the pseudo-adventure, "playing tigers," in Central America.

(In the previous chapter, Charles himself has spoken of how before the American journey he had, as artist, begun "to mourn the loss of something I had known in the drawing-room of Marchmain House [that is, at the time of his first visits there with Sebastian, and the painting of the landscape in the "office"] and once or twice since, the intensity and singleness and the belief that it was not all done by hand—in a word, the inspiration. In quest of this fading light I went abroad. . . ." He then goes on to tell us that the quest failed, that even at the time he was in America he knew it was failing, that he "remained unchanged, still a small part of myself pretending to be whole.")

But if the situation is what would seem to be indicated by all this—if Marchmain House, upon Charles's return there with Julia, is to be the scene of his once more, and finally, coming whole, of the hunt for *Christ*-the-Tiger—then there ought to be some proof of it in a reference to some further development of Charles's art. One more time in the book, somebody (Brideshead) asks "How's the painting, Charles?" And it is a legitimate question, certainly. It is likely to be, unfortunately, the question uppermost in the mind of the attentive reader throughout this last section of the novel. There ought to be, specifically, a reference to some new work of Charles's in which we can definitely see the connection, which I spoke of at the beginning of the essay, between the essential values of the aristocratic tradition (whatever these may be) that underlie the Flyte charm and the religious values. We ought to have something that at least begins to show the Tiger in the Park.

But Charles answers the question evasively, almost indifferently, with a vague reference to a new sketch of Julia. There is a hopeful, if shadowy, implication of development of an old theme, when Bridey says that he supposes such a subject (the human one) is more difficult than architecture. Does this mean that, as part of the unsuspected process of redemption going on in him, Charles is about to begin preferring people to buildings—contrary to his stated (chap. i, Book Two) previous

attitude? Or will he, perhaps, follow up Bridey's further suggestion about "action" subjects such as *Macbeth,* and become a
Shakespeare illustrator? But it all comes to nothing. Charles
drifts off into maundering reflections on Brideshead's character.
And this is the last we hear of him as painter.

It might be argued that he is in too agitated a state of mind,
or spirit, at this time to work at all, that the conversion is to
come later, and with it the new artistic insight and the new
paintings. But I am afraid nothing in the book points to such a
prospect.

What we do get, in the way of a final, implicit statement of
the connection between art and religion, is most discouraging.
This occurs in the Epilogue, simultaneously with the covert
allusion to Charles's either accomplished or about-to-be-
accomplished conversion, his reference to having "said a prayer,
an ancient, *newly-learned* form of words." (Italics mine.) And it
amounts, so far as I can see, to a complete and shameless
abandonment of the problem.

Ryder is in the art nouveau chapel of the estate. The lamp is
burning before the altar, and having indulged his reminiscences
and said his prayer, he takes note once more of the light in the
lamp as the light of Christian faith, shining through the
centuries:

*a small red flame . . . the flame which the old knights saw
from their tents, which they saw put out; that flame burns again
for other soldiers, far from home, farther in heart, than Acre or
Jerusalem. It could not have been lit but for the builders and the
tragedians, and there I found it this morning, burning anew
among the old stones*

(The Flytes, specifically, are the "builders and the tragedians";
for he has just spoken of "the fierce little human tragedy in
which [he] played" here at this house.) But the revealing phrase
is his passing reference to the lamp itself in which the light is
contained. It is, "a beaten copper lamp *of deplorable design.*"
(Italics mine.)

Deplorable, but apparently, from the very casualness of his
way of mentioning it, not terribly important in its deplorableness
for judgment of the essential truth which it contains. The

container of the flame, the design of it, he says in effect, is indifferent.

But that container, I must insist, is art. It is Christian art. And it is more than a little dismaying to discover this attitude as the outcome of Mr. Waugh's lengthiest, fictive statement of his religious experience.

It might seem to be implied that Charles has given up painting altogether, that religion is to take the place of art for him. From his refusing the suggestion that he take an artist's post in the army, and applying instead for a captaincy of infantry, needled by Lord Marchmain's slighting recollection of the staff artist his regiment in World War I had kept with them "until they went to the front," perhaps we are to infer that Christ's army, too, has no need of artists "at the front." And we might wonder, too, how Waugh could go on writing, once having backed himself into the statement of such a position.

But, however all that may be, the Epilogue scene, and the allegory of the lamp, does contain the secret of this one book's failure. Precisely because of its indifference to design, Waugh's inability here to grasp the unity of "form and content," the container-and-the-thing-contained, his effort to put the light of romance (or "tragedy") into the lamp of satire, and vice versa, the basic confusion of the traditional genres, the novel comes to grief. It is possible, of course, to accommodate elements of satire in the tragic romance as Fitzgerald, for example, has done in *The Great Gatsby*, where the "artificializing" of his world and himself by modern man is a fully conscious and consistently controlled theme, recognized as a part of the tragedy of his self-destructiveness. But in Waugh's novel there is no such control and recognition, and its absence is the more disastrous in the context of the novel's explicit Christian purpose.

Waugh may or may not have an ultimately right grasp of the values of tradition in other senses; we may or may not regard as permanent this implicit confession, through Ryder, that the tradition of English aristocratic life is dead for him, of no further use for the development of art, however attractive it may be as the pattern of a way of life. My own view is that the admission was, indeed, fatal—not least for his development as a Catholic artist—amply illustrated by the shallowness and confusion of his subsequent books. He has, in any event, demonstrated here a gross misunderstanding of the tradition of literary forms: which, after all, ought.to be the basic concern of the man of letters, Catholic, country gentleman, or whatever else. It is only a little more distressing when the misunderstanding seems to exclude the artist from the Kingdom of God.

# 10 *Delta Wedding:*

# Region and Symbol

The reputation of Eudora Welty continues to outrun criticism of her work.

In the eleven years since this essay was first published in the *Sewanee Review,* only one book-length study has appeared (Ruth M. Vande Kieft's *Eudora Welty*); and articles in the literary quarterlies still attempt, now and again, the tone of a *bon voyage.* Wherever it was she was going, I think it will be generally agreed that Miss Welty has by now arrived—perhaps for the second or third time—and it is no longer very discerning to treat the seasoned traveler as if she were the young Isabel Archer.

But, such is the nature of her work, itself, a study that is to be really comprehensive must be most particular. We will have to take one thing—or, anyway, one thing at a time. The Welty reader too should be lessoned with the characterizing refrain phrase of E. M. Forster's little essay on Virginia Woolf—"one thing—one." And the one thing I want to consider here is *Delta Wedding.* A great many critics seem to think that Miss Welty is at her best in the shorter forms; and perhaps she feels so too, to judge from the continued emphasis of her work. But this novel, it seems to me, is not only still the biggest thing, but still the most rigidly restricted, disciplined. It has most characteristically developed the sense of the symbolic particularity of things, of a place and a time and a people, that can make the good regionalist the most universal of artists—or of novelists, at any rate. It is the most "one," whole.

I mean to suggest, then, that the most important thing about the novel is its formal structure. But if the nature of its design has escaped many readers, the reasons are not hard to find. There is considerable prejudice against a serious novelist's treating material of this kind with such an attitude of sympathy as Miss Welty assumes. To a reader with any sensitivity at all, certainly it was obvious from the start that *Delta Wedding* was not simply another Mississippi plantation, historical novel, designed for a bosom-and-columns dust jacket. But, if the author's irony is felt from the first sentence, its essence is very subtle. And the patience of a good many of the liberal reviewers a few years ago was pretty short.

If Miss Welty wasn't starry-eyed in quite the usual way about the "South," she wasn't indignant either, or even decently tough and realistic now and again. She had distinctly her own version of what Wyndham Lewis called Faulkner's "whippoor-will tank"; but it might have seemed only unfortunately less manageable than his. The novel was, after all, historical. That its time was only about twenty and not seventy-five or a hundred years past was calculated to allay suspicion only slightly. Few eyebrows were raised over the treatment of the Negroes in the novel; but they might well have been. The darkies were sometimes just a little too charmingly typical. And where the attitude went beyond one of placid acceptance, it often became only half-heartedly apologetic, with a rather strong suggestion of the old "well, at least they had *status*" routine. What Miss Welty at her best could do with Negroes in some of the short stories seemed sadly absent here. And one could go only so far in justifying it on grounds of dramatic propriety, that the author was bound to the point of view of the white characters of the story; simply for purposes of realism, it might easily have been made a little more apparent how severely restricted that outlook was in this respect.

And yet the immediate inferences from all this are, clearly, not correct. And perhaps the best way of getting at why they are not correct is to allow the novel to establish for itself the perspective in which we are to look at its features.

One has first to see that Miss Welty is not taking any attitude toward the "South." The story is about the Delta, at the most—not the South, not even Mississippi. Yankees, of course, are unthinkable; but Ellen, the Virginian, is acutely conscious all her life of her own difference from the Delta family she mothers. And the circle is drawn even closer; Troy Flavin, who is largely responsible for the significance of the wedding as a symbol of threatened disruption, is alien by virtue of being a hill-country Mississippian. And (disregarding for the moment Laura McRaven, whose case is rather special), Robbie Reid, whom the family wisely regard as a far greater threat to the insularity of their world than Troy, is foreign as a native of the town of Fairchilds, as distinguished from the plantation.

The psychological basis of the relationship of the characters one to another here is simple enough. The barrier between Robbie Reid and the Fairchilds is greatest for several reasons— just that she is a woman, that she is the unworthy wife of the darling of the family, but most important of all, that she is a lifelong near-neighbor. In any society, of course, class distinctions are always, though ironically, most keenly appreciated by native members of the same community. Troy Flavin, not so much out of mere stupidity as simply because his origins are more remote, finds nothing so terribly formidable in the family he is "marrying into"—as he puts it with a confidence that at once dismays and amuses those who know the Fairchilds. And in the face of his naïve assurance, the family are fairly constrained to be gentle with him, though they make little effort to hide their feelings from Dabney. But the point I want to make now is that this narrowing of the circle is carried so far that it finally excludes emphasis upon the kind of typicality, the true provincialism, in character and situation, characteristic of the commonplace regional novel. The Fairchilds are finally most typical, if at all, in their very singularity. And it is at this point that the principle of exclusiveness almost ceases, or for the reader's purposes in understanding the novel ought almost to cease, to be a social principle at all. It becomes, rather, the formal principle, and the principle of sensibility, in a version of pastoral which has been before only vaguely hinted at in the Southern novel.

Miss Welty's awareness of the classic elements of pastoral in the situation is quite evident. One may take as an initial statement of the conventional paradox of pastoral, the familiar principle of inversion of values, one of Laura's early reflections:

"Jackson was a big town, with twenty-five thousand people, and Fairchilds was just a store and a gin and a bridge and one big house, yet she was the one who felt like a little country cousin when she arrived. . . ."

But it is the awareness revealed that is most important about a passage like this. What it says, the statement of the pastoral "formula" in these terms, is only a starting point. The tradition of the Southern novel has been all but exclusively pastoral from the start, of course—and in a great many different ways, both naturalistic and romantic. But there has been before no such fully conscious exploration of the implications of the mode as Miss Welty's, an insight that finally carries beyond the significance of the form for the mores of the society that produced it.

(Miss Welty's—with its wit, its merging of realism and magic, its delicacy, its formal and elegiac ironies, its universal mythiness, and basic to all the rest its struggle between anonymity and self-consciousness—is *late* pastoral. She derives, of course, much from her great fellow Mississippian, Faulkner. But there is no more instructive contrast than between his, earlier pastoralism—its naïve grandeur and richness, terror, pity, its depth of "humor and tragic intensity," in Warren's phrase—and her cool, witty, detached, exquisitely feminine sensibility.)

Miss Welty's depiction of the Delta society and its structure, of the family as the typical unit of that society, is studiedly accurate, right always in substance and, with the exception of a few distressing lapses into an overprecious style, nearly always in tone. The rightness of it meets the test of communication even to the reader unfamiliar with the actuality. And the structure of the society, in the pattern of the novel as well as in fact, clearly produces and supports the kind of hyperdeveloped individuality that the characters severally manifest. But it is one of the basic paradoxes of the novel—one of which several of the characters are keenly aware—that the strength of the society's ability to support is entirely the dynamic of the personality's constant and tireless struggle with it. And the center of interest, finally, is in the exercise of entirely private sensibilities; not so much in the relationships abstractly as such among the various people, as in the way in which each person privately sees those relationships.

Indeed, at the beginning of the novel, and again qualifiedly at the end, it is not even people and their relationships that are seen, but rather, things. Laura comes into the Delta country with the bemused aloneness of the adventurer into an enchanted forest. Other people, as people, are secondary realities; the signs of their existence, to the extent that she is aware of them at all, become talismans of a significance entirely private to her, the ticket she had stuck in her hat band, "in imitation of the drummer across the aisle." It is things that are most alive—the fields, the train itself becoming a creature of the fields. And then the train "seemed to be racing with a butterfly."

The vision is not quite ecstatic. The sun which in its sinking momentarily obliterates the most basic distinction—"all that had been bright or dark was now one color"—is a real sun. It sinks, and Laura arrives, and is met by the Fairchild cousins—real, other people. The last word on Laura before the conductor cries "Fairchilds!" is simply that she "felt what an arriver in a land feels." And though there has been fair warning that the land is to be much more than a land—"the clouds were large . . . larger than anything except the fields the Fairchilds planted"; "the Delta buzzards . . . seemed to wheel as high and as wide as the sun"; "the west was a milk-white edge, like the foam of the sea"—so far it is only a warning. There is no immediate plunge to that depth of the private consciousness in which the particular becomes the universal. If the reader constructs a cloud-cuckoo land here, it is his own doing. Miss Welty has no unrealistic intention of giving away her story in one lyric offering. Certain pertinent, practical facts stick in Laura's mind. She knows where she came from and where she is going and why. She is conscious of time and her reality in it; she has been here before. (The fact that the visit, to "nature," out of the life of the city, is a return, functions similarly, for example, to the same fact in Wordsworth's "Tintern Abbey." Even in her vision of the immensity of the clouds it is not just the fields they are compared to, but the fields "that the Fairchilds planted." The fields belong to them, and not simply as a matter of economics either, we are soon to discover. The myth is theirs too. The train was a legendary creature, it had its name of the Yellow Dog, in their consciousness before hers. Their baffling otherness, their exclusive possessiveness, threatens both to invade and to shut her out at every level of her sensibility.

But what we do get in this opening passage is enough of the ecstatic to reassure us that Laura's personal emotional problem doesn't really matter a great deal. (The reader is never permitted actually to "feel sorry" for Laura; the "poor Laura, little motherless girl" greeting that she anticipates has only a ritualistic solemnity, no real sadness.) And, conversely, we are assured that the personal "problems" of the others aren't going to matter a great deal either—which, in turn, is further assurance on Laura's account. We get, in other words, the symbolic sense; we begin to see things with a great, though not quite a whole, measure of aesthetic distance. (This, by the way, accounts I think for the time-setting of the novel. Aside from the fact that the early Twenties actually were a period of significant social and economic transition, the slight, but only slight, removal in time makes it easier for the author to put the emphasis where she wants it, upon probability rather than upon the kind of mere possibility that our generation demands not only of the immediately contemporary novel but of the usual historical one as well.) The action takes on from the beginning and never quite loses, even at the highest pitch of visual excitement, the somewhat cool, formal tone of the conscious pastoral.

One feels from the beginning that not actions, but reactions, are to count. A few things do manage to happen in the course of the novel: Dabney and Troy marry; Robbie comes back to George; it is decided that Laura will stay at Shellmound, at least for a time. But this is not a great deal, after all. And—the marriage is the most obvious example—it is perfectly clear that none of these things is of great moment in itself. The word "wedding" in the title is important. It is in a sense with the wedding, the ritual, not the marriage, that Miss Welty is concerned. The ritual sense is private, of course; the ceremony itself is passed over in a few words: "Mr. Rondo married Dabney and Troy." Mr. Rondo's status, the status of the church in the Fairchild world, perfectly defines the more than baronial self-sufficiency of the family, their superiority to any larger, public-institutional significance of their affairs. But, private both in the sense that the family has its peculiar rituals and even more in the sense that each individual has his own in which the others do not participate, it is ritual nonetheless. There are no raw emotions in the novel—and little of a structure of personal involvements, conflicts, as we have observed, about the center of a "problem" that is carried through to some solution in action. Nor is the story actionless simply in the sense of being introspective, with much private examination of motives, intentions, much logical self-analysis. No one has time for much introspection in this usual sense. There is, in fact, a great deal "going on" all the time. But the incidents are important mainly as points of refraction from which light is cast back upon various moments of symbolic perception in the minds of the several characters.

This is where Miss Welty is at her best and where one has to start looking for the "meaning" of the novel—in the whole particularity of the moment, the single, illuminating, still act of private perception. It is where one has to look for the truth about the characters, severally. They don't communicate much of themselves to one another, however much they are in a sense concerned with one another, and mutually dependent.

The thing is stated over and over again, this impregnable, at times reassuring, at times to one or another hopelessly baffling, privacy of the consciousness of every person, of the being of every thing that the consciousness entertains, even of every separate moment of consciousness. There are the various lights, with the obvious significance of light, especially of light inside something. The lamp that the aunts give to Dabney, a *night*-light, notably, itself an object of family tradition but, given to Dabney, becoming the prime symbol of her independence, her private rebellion of indifference when she carelessly breaks it, carrying out the theme of general disaster which the flame itself, the intended source of light and comfort, draws out upon the shade:

*The picture on it was a little town. Next, in the translucence, over the little town with trees, towers, people, windowed houses, and a bridge, over the clouds and stars and moon and sun, you*

*saw a redness glow and the little town was all on fire, even to the*
*motion of fire, which came from the candle flame drawing.*

The same lamp in India's perception, precious and cherished,
but in infinite secrecy, and so again a symbol of impenetrable
isolation, the magic circle of her privacy: "India made a circle
with her fingers, imagining she held the little lamp"—the vessel
of light, paradoxically, filled "with the mysterious and flowing
air of night." The light on the back porch, when Shelley comes
in alone for a moment away from the dancers, and "the moths
spread upon the screens, the hard beetles knocked upon the
radius of light like an adamant door," as she falls into musing;
the light in her room, as she sits wiriting in her diary, with the
beetle again clawing at the screen.

The various places of hiding and retreat. The seemingly
innumerable rooms of the house itself. The wood in which Ellen
walks, with its mysteriously ageless, directionless paths. The
privilege, if it is a privilege altogether, is denied not even to the
Negroes. Partheny, in the chinaberry-hidden fastness of her
house in Brunswicktown, retiring into the undisturbed, unques-
tioned and unanswerable, mystery of her "mindlessness." Aunt
Studney, with her jealously guarded sack that is to the children
perhaps the source of life itself, the place where babies come
from; her very existence hardly more, as the reader is permitted
to perceive it, than a legendary creation of the family's love of
the eternal secret, than the name which puns her one, uncommunicative phrase—"Ain't studyin' you."

Or simply the sudden, isolated moments of private illumination. Dabney's ride in the morning, when she sees Marmion,
sees it first reflected, in the river, "and then the house itself
reared delicate and vast, with a strict tower, up from its
reflection," sees it defiantly and exultantly alone, "while they
never guessed, she had seen Marmion . . . all had been before
her eyes when she was all by herself." The loneliness of Laura,
abandoned during the game of hide-and-seek, in which she
perceives the necessity of George's isolation:

*Then she saw Uncle George walk out of the house and stare out*
*into the late day. She wanted to call out to him, but . . .*
*something told her . . . that it was right for him to stand*

*apart, and that when he opened an envelope in a room no one should enter. Now she felt matter-of-factly intimate with it, with his stand and his predicament.*

Or, more definitive still, the sound of Mary Lamar Mackey's piano, the constant music which is a figure of the author's omnipresence, proceeding from an all but invisible source (we get only one brief close up of Mary Lamar), only now and again distinctly heard at some chance pause in the activity, but always there. At a moment of tense silence during the first hours of Robbie's visit, Mary Lamar

*was playing a nocturne—like the dropping of rain or the calling of a bird the notes came from another room, effortless and endless, isolated from them, yet near, and sweet like the guessed existence of mystery. It made the house like a nameless forest, wherein many little lives lived privately, each to its lyric pursuit and shy protection . . .*

The momentary perfection of the pastoral vision.

This sort of thing gives the novel its first appearance of disorder. The characters seem hopelessly unpredictable, their actions unmotivated and obscure, without intelligible issue; the transitions, from one scene to another, from the reflections of one character to another, appear entirely capricious. It would seem at first glance that Miss Welty has sacrificed an order of the whole entirely in the interest of an illusion of life in the details. But it ought to be apparent from the very symbols and symbolic instances of the privacy of consciousness given here, that there is order of a kind. The lives, the thoughts, of all the characters are intensely private; but because they are ritualistic too, and ritual is always inevitable, they fall into patterns that transcend the privacy, with or without the consciousness of the particular character. And, if the characters themselves are not often conscious of the pattern, the author is clearly conscious of it. It emerges, beyond its inevitability, as a principle of deliberate and controlled artistry, in an order of recurrence that informs the whole action of the novel. The order of the novel is a poetic order—of recurrent themes, symbols, and motifs of symbolic metaphor. And it must be close-read, as a poem.

Perhaps the thread nearest the center of the design is that of the story, told and retold, again and again reflected upon and alluded to, of George and Maureen on the railroad trestle. Certain reasons for the importance of the story to the Fairchilds are immediately apparent. It was just after the incident on the trestle that Troy and Dabney had "gone on up the railroad track and got engaged"; thus beginning the latest threat to the solidarity of the Fairchild world. It was then that Robbie Reid, providing the climax to the story with her accusation, "George Fairchild, you didn't do this for *me!*," brought into the open the whole complex of bitter feelings which the Fairchilds entertain for this earlier, and even more significant than Dabney's, "bad match"—their resentment at the love of poor, common little Robbie for George, George who is the universally acknowledged, living embodiment of their ideal of Fairchild man; their infuriated amusement at her daring to intrude the voice of her "rights" even against his defense of what is even more holy to the Fairchilds than George himself or any *living* thing, the memory of the dead Denis. Robbie's thinking of herself at that moment, her indignation at George's willingness to sacrifice himself for the semi-idiotic Maureen, defines perfectly for the Fairchild women, especially, her hopeless failure to understand their vision of themselves—and their investment of that vision in Denis, of whom nothing remains but his daughter Maureen, the crazy Virgie Lee, a few vague stories and a little pathetic "poetry," but who in their minds is the more dignified by the "tragedy" of indignities, and who finally is beyond reproach (as even George cannot be) simply by virtue of being dead, who as the symbol of the holy past is worthy of any sacrifice. Robbie's behavior at the trestle is all of a piece with the absurdity, the hopeless childishness, of her taunt that the Fairchilds are "not even rich!"—her failure to comprehend the myth of their aristocracy.

This much, then—beyond what is simply their love, aristocratically both pious and hilariously irreverent, for a story, any story, involving the family—all the Fairchilds understand, in one way or another. They understand also something of how important it is that the train was the familiar Yellow Dog, the train that is almost itself their property—so that it could not actually have killed George (thus the whole thing becomes absurd enough for amusement), and yet, faithful servitor, provides enough of the thrill of danger, of death, for the purposes of their ritual.

Ellen, who retains enough of the attitude of an outsider always to see (or to have to see, to figure out consciously) a little more than the others, understands also what it meant for Robbie. She is a little daunted, even, seeing that Robbie has had a vision, a vision of fact, that makes the Fairchilds' prattling over their legend a little ridiculous. She understands that a train on that track can kill, that it has in fact killed the astonishingly beautiful girl she met in the woods, and that if her daughters are spared it is only because they are not that beautiful, not beautiful enough to be heroines of a genuine tragedy. And she understands, finally, George's role in all of it. In a way that no one else can be, because no one else knows about the lost girl, she is at once grateful and ashamed at the implications of George's constant sacrifice. She comprehends the simple fact that George is a man, that he has reacted simply as a man to the beauty of the girl when he "took her over to the old Argyle gin and slept with her." She understands that it is with his possession and his knowledge of such facts, literally the facts of life, that he defends the Fairchilds against the intrusion of fact, against all that comes, like the train, bearing down upon them. She suspects, perhaps, that the Fairchild women are vaguely aware of the condescension in his nobility, aware that he can afford to indulge them in their disparagement and ignorance of fact, the fact of the outside world that begins at Memphis, simply because he does know it so well and because of the knowledge is supremely self-sufficient. She suspects that it is out of chagrin at this element of his attitude, at their own half-realized envy of his knowledge of life present and real, that they continue to shade his glory under the image of the dead Denis. She knows that he has worked the device of disparagement even on her, in telling her what he has done with the girl, protecting her from too sudden a vision of what beauty it is (not the garnet pin!) that is lost in the wood, that she has lost and the world knows; but she knows also that George's act has not degraded the girl's beauty, that if anything it has enhanced it. In short, she knows George—George the unknowable.

But beyond all of this even, beyond Ellen's or all the characters' conscious experience of it together, the legend serves as a unifying force. Basically, the train and the trestle (bridge) are communication symbols. In Ellen's case, the relationships she discovers in the light of the incident result in the one most nearly perfect personal communication of the story. The separate incidents of the trestle episode itself and of her meeting with the girl in the wood are brought together in her mind, after the photographer has told the wedding party of the girl his train has killed on the way down from Memphis, in a single, comprehensive vision which opens the way to her wordless communication with George at the dance. But the most important significance of her experience in the whole purposes of the novel is not for our interest in her, her effort to know George personally; her insight is important, rather, simply as an example of the kind of structural relationships that are to be seen. We have to go on to see that the Yellow Dog is also the train that has brought Laura—still another visitant from the outside world, and a permanent one, since she is heiress to Marmion—to Shellmound. It brings even the shepherd crooks, ironically, and other furnishings for the wedding, from Memphis. We have to see, further, that the symbols, characteristically, work both ways. That is, the legend for some means the failure of communication: for Robbie with the family, as we have seen, and for Shelley with Dabney, the engagement to Troy having closed a door upon Shelley's understanding of her sister, perhaps even upon her sympathy with the entire family.

Or, another way of putting it is that Ellen's "knowing" George is, after all, only a final understanding of the fact of his independence, the fact that he is unknowable. The legend makes George a symbol. Ellen specifically repudiates her "young girl's love of symbols" in her final attitude toward George; that is, the sort of thing that the Fairchilds make of him. Hers is a vision of the unmanageable fact of him. But Ellen's, perhaps, is a schoolgirl's understanding of the term. In the larger purposes of the novel he remains a symbol, not entirely the Fairchilds' symbol; but his very factuality itself becomes symbolic. It is notable that none of the men in the novel often admits the reader to his mind. Such is the Fairchild women's notion of their men, which the author accepts as a technical principle, that they are a kind of serviceable gods—infinitely capable, having access to wonderful powers of the outer world, and always decently keeping their own counsel. And if one uneasily suspects, with Ellen, that George is actually godlike in his manhood, that his stalwart impenetrability is not a matter of decency, but of having some counsel to keep, an unsearchable purpose—still this is only the excess of heroic typicality. As the reader has to know him, as he functions in the novel, the legend has made him—with the final qualification only that it has made all the Fairchilds too, and not, as they sometimes suppose, they the legend. (This is the point, of course, of Shelley's realization, when she runs the car across the tracks in front of the Yellow Dog, that it won't do to try "contriving" it.)

As an example of George's symbolic function, we may consider again Laura's experience. Ellen's, in fact, is not quite so exclusive an understanding of George as it might at first appear. At her childish level, Laura has entertained the same vision—of his necessary isolation, we will remember—and felt "matter-of-factly" intimate with the fact of the isolation, with him. And potentially this experience is a basis of sympathy between Laura and Ellen in the little girl's effort to make herself a part of the family. But George has "brought them together" without any conscious intention, without even any rational understanding of what is happening in the situation, either on his part or theirs. There is no willed, in the usual sense *personal* communication anywhere in the relationship. George functions here, then, precisely in the way that the various nonhuman, symbolic objects function to establish, and to illuminate, certain relationships. George is, in fact, the ultimate embodiment of the author's subtle conception of the subject-object relationship that is symbol—the object informed by, inseparable from, an always quickening, always manifest, but always inscrutable intelligence.

The people then, as well as things, are carried out of themselves by the legend. And, finally, the significance of the particular story carries outside itself to other stories; every legend is all legend. The way in which we have seen the thread of the trestle incident become involved with Ellen's reflections upon the fate of the girl she met wandering in the woods—the girl and the meeting figure in the statement of what might be followed out as a distinct, major theme in itself, the theme of loss—is but one illustration of the complexity of the structure. The symbols of the trestle story are actually parts of certain larger, extended motifs. The train is one of several means of transportation that have a symbolic function, more or less explicit, wherever they appear. The horses—Troy's horse, the horse that George gives to Dabney (having thought of it, significantly, when Robbie took his car to run away in), the horse that Dabney rides on her visit to her aunts (carrying a "wedding-present home on horseback"); the cars too—George's car which Robbie has wrecked, the new Pierce Arrow (all cars are still comparatively new), the darkened car in which Dabney and Troy ride away after the wedding, the lighted car in which the mayor and his family arrive for the reception. And so on. The trestle, over Dry Creek, is closely related to what may be loosely defined as the water motif—the bridge over the bayou "whose rackety rhythm Laura remembered," the old stories of the whirlpool, Laura's trip to Marmion with Roy when in a kind of baptismal ceremony she is pushed into the Yazoo and loses Ellen's garnet pin.

And any one of dozens of incidents, observations, unspoken perceptions, can become the central nexus in the whole complexity of interconnection. One need not start with the trestle episode or with any of the more obviously prominent incidents. One such observation as Shelley's at the reception—of the contrast between the darkened car of the newlyweds and the lighted car bringing the mayor, that "had come up alight like a *boat* in the night" (italics mine)—is enough. The simile has associations—we might assume at this level even somewhat consciously felt by Shelley—as remote as the comparison, early in the story, of a certain lamp in the living room at Shellmound to "a lighted shoe-box toy, a 'choo-choo boat' with its colored paper windows." Here, with the recollection of the dear and familiar object of their childhood play, the lamp itself having the radiance of its associations, too, already mingled with the light of the toy, is much of the pathos of Shelley's ironic realization that the public gaiety of the wedding party, the extraneous and trivial display of the "occasion" epitomized by the visit of so inconsequential and alien a personage as the mayor, is a mockery of the darkness of marriage that has closed between her and Dabney. (The darkness that is the inevitable privacy of any marriage, the darkness that for Shelley is especially associated with Troy Flavin, of his hateful "overseer's soul," of the blood of the Negroes on the floor of the office.) But beyond any possibility of Shelley's consciousness of the significance of her thought, the "boat" suggests all boats: the boat in which Laura rode with Roy when *she* saw Marmion, the house that is to be hers eventually, not Dabney's, and when she was admitted to the mystery of the Yazoo, the river that measures the time or the timelessness of the Fairchild world. (The prophecy of Shelley's fear for her sister's marriage is not, perhaps, altogether dark.) Or, reinforcing the first effect, the light, the lamp, is all the lamps—the heirloom night-light which Dabney broke.

One can follow a single object through the significance of its reappearances. The garnet pin—first as Battle's gift, and then through Ellen's use of her dream about it as a lullaby story to Bluet, associated with her motherhood—is the symbol both of loss and of gain; figuring in a restatement of the same theme in her meeting with the girl in the wood; in her effort to get Partheny's assistance in finding it, becoming the symbol of the old Negress' second sight; appearing finally as the central symbol in an incident which embraces all these themes, the womb-return descent of Laura into the waters of the Yazoo. "As though Aunt Studney's sack had opened after all, like a whale's mouth, Laura opening her eyes head down saw its insides all around her—dark water and fearful fishes." And the pin, lost in the water, becomes the image of a relationship between Laura and her new mother Ellen, between her and the Fairchilds a union in the untold secret of the loss, more enduring even that what she had hoped for as a reward for finding and returning the pin.

One could, and would, go on. Devious ways are open from any point. But perhaps with this much of detail, we can hazard a few conclusive generalizations.

To return to the question of Miss Welty's attitude toward the society she depicts, it should be apparent by now that in terms of approval or disapproval the evidence is mixed. In Ellen's vision of the hero, George, what appears to be a devastating criticism is implicit: the Fairchilds' "myth of happiness" would seem to be myth clearly in the worst sense, a childish retreat from reality. And it is possible to infer that the wedding of Dabney and Troy is a mockery of true marriage everywhere—even the marriage of Battle and Ellen; the marriage of the Fairchilds with the past or with the future, whichever way one wants to approach it; the marriage of minds among all the characters.

But perhaps the crucial point of the problem is the status of the Negroes. If Miss Welty does, as I have suggested, "accept" the Fairchilds' typical attitude here, I think that acceptance is finally, though not perhaps quite so clearly, like her acceptance of the women's attitude toward the men. It is an acceptance as a technical principle only, and one that comes in at a deeper level for some very heavy qualification. For the purposes of that double attitude of pastoral that William Empson has defined, as well as in a more practical sense for people like the Fairchilds, the Negroes are a great convenience. It is at the expense of these "*rude* swains" that the Fairchilds can be the "*gentle* swains" (to use Milton's pair of terms for it) that they are—so that we can simultaneously look down upon the narrow complacency, and envy the imaginative and moral richness, of their country simplicity. But Miss Welty implicitly recognizes the "convenience" for what it is. And the recognition is, in fact, very closely tied in with that problem of the women's attitude toward the men.

Dabney's preparations for her marriage are, significantly, associated with her riding forth into the fields. Troy Flavin emerges partially as a kind of "field god," similar to Floyd in "At the Landing," or Cash in "Livvie." And the mystery of his virility is in the present situation very closely connected, of course, with his intimate knowledge of the Negroes. It is this of which Shelley is at once so afraid and so contemptuous when she finds Troy settling a fight among the Negroes in the overseer's office. And the phrase of her reflection on her way back to the house, her wondering if "all *men*" are like him, makes the connection with George's role. George too, about whom Dabney is thinking on her ride to visit her aunts, is marked with the blood of the Negroes—he with the blood of compassion when he caught the knife and bound up the wounds of the little Negro boy, Troy with the blood of his knowledge of the Negroes in their labor. But, the significance of such distinctions as the latter aside, they are *men*: George coming naked from the water to catch the knife, Troy the dark figure on a horse that Dabney catches sight of on her way to her aunts' house; and their tolerance for the blood of Negroes is an essential part of their maleness. And Dabney senses something of this, the part that a new knowledge of the lives of the Negroes, of their intimacy with the earth, must play in the rebellion from her family that her marriage represents.

But this is the crucial point also in the sense that Dabney's discovery of the male mystery is clearly hopeful for the society as well as critical of it. Troy is the "field god," and as such he is a principle of rejuvenation. The marriage promises ultimately, perhaps, not disruption but renewal, or renewal out of the disruption. And while Troy's is in a sense an influence from outside, it is defined, as we have seen, and complemented, partially by the role of George—and that, paradoxically, as an essential part of his status as the family hero. It can hardly be denied that Miss Welty does see the strength for rejuvenation as in part the family's own strength, the strength of their own myth as they themselves understand it, though she sees with equal clarity the limitations of that understanding.

Or, if the argument requires further elaboration, one must not forget that central to the old aunts' family sense is the reverence for disaster. Primrose insisted that people keep "their kinfolks and their tragedies straight." And there is reason to believe that they can accommodate Dabney's breaking the lamp too, that her breaking it is one with her keeping it ultimately; the "present" is given and must be kept whether she will or no, whether the "little old piece of glass" is kept intact or not. The themes of protection and disaster are inextricably bound up together from the first, in the family legend as in the design of the lamp and its shade, and their unity is unbreakable. Accepting the implicit pun on *present*—perhaps the marriage of past and present is not broken; perhaps that quality of the Fairchilds, at first so baffling to Laura, their being so intensely "of the moment," is simply the result of their supreme confidence of their footing in the past. And, finally, Laura herself—who comes closer than anyone to being Miss Welty's stand-in in the novel—remains to live with the family on terms that are, though again qualifiedly, both sympathetic and hopeful.

And yet I would insist that the question of approval or disapproval, of a prophecy of hope or disaster, is still not the key to Miss Welty's final attitude. Her principal interest in the society, her sympathy with it, is for the *vision* it supports. We need not trouble ourselves ultimately over the fate of the society as such, or its worth in itself, or even the problem of whether it ever existed or could exist, actually, quite as it is pictured. The picture is right enough, in every sense, to provide the vision. And that is unquestionable; the novel itself, its living form, the constant order and quickness of its sensibility, is the essential proof of the vision. In fact, the novel is the vision. And I do not see, from the evidence of the novel itself, that Miss Welty is especially either disturbed or elated by the prospects of the actual Fairchild world. She is simply, like Laura with George, for the all-important moment "matter-of-factly intimate" with the dual paradox of the pastoral outlook: all human society being ultimately suspect, the vision must to some extent condemn the society that produces it; and yet the particular society that makes this truth most apparent is the "best" society.

This is the essential realism of Miss Welty's art. This is how her intensely narrow view—the concentration of her narrative requiring more than two hundred pages for the treatment of the events of a few days in the life of a hopelessly provincial family—becomes precisely at its most restricted a world view.

But the last scene of the novel sums up the situation. We come back to the mind with which we began—Laura McRaven's mind. And Laura achieves her sense of belonging at last. She has been told that she is to stay, that Marmion is to be hers some-day. The picnic, for her, is a celebration of her reception as a member of the family. But she accepts the decisions from the first with the secret thought that sometime she may go back to Jackson, to her father. The reservation—exactly equivalent to the author's final detachment, the keeping her counsel with re-spect to the values of the Fairchild world, the worth of the "in-heritance"—does not diminish her present joy. But it is there. And the moment at which she feels most overwhelmingly at one with the family is when she can scarcely see any of them, but sees with them the falling star. The "star" is a star—single, remote, and inaccessible, indifferent. And if it is not quite in-different, if it does belong to the family in their common seeing, then it is falling. And yet, for the moment of its falling, it brings them together. Laura, and the Fairchilds, and the star, are one in the light of the star—and turning again with a gesture of em-bracing them, she embraces the firmament, "both arms held out to the radiant night." That one moment of pure vision, the people themselves in darkness, unseen, the star unseeing, be-comes the sufficient thing in itself—the one thing.

# 11  *Robert Penn Warren:*

# The Dialectic of Self

More than ten years ago, Robert Penn Warren defined the pre-eminent position of William Faulkner among modern American novelists. His judgment—that Faulkner's books, "for range of effect, philosophical weight, originality of style, variety of characterization, humor, and tragic intensity are without equal in our time and country"—remains unchallengeable. Almost all the Faulkner criticism that has been written in the meantime, a near surfeit of it, indeed, has been purely appreciative, something as if called forth by Warren's essay simply to confirm and strengthen his insights. And the work of no other novelist, new or of Faulkner's own generation, has been put forward by any critic of importance to rival his claims to such attention.

But if any American novelist of the generation just younger than that of Faulkner and Hemingway has seemed likely to attain a stature sufficient to make him the successor, if not the rival, of Faulkner, it is Warren himself. And it is precisely in the essay on Faulkner, moreover, that we find one of the best commentaries on his own vision and purposes as novelist.

One must hesitate yet to predict the final direction of Warren's development, and the chances of his producing other novels of the scope and strength of *All the King's Men* and *World Enough and Time. Band of Angels, The Cave,* and *Wilderness* are certainly weaker performances. It is quite possible that his final reputation as novelist will have to depend on the earlier work. But however this may be, it seems to me sufficiently interesting for the moment to try defining something of what he has accomplished in his art, and what his critical work —for our specific example, again, the essay on Faulkner—has to do with both the scope and the kind of that accomplishment.

For it has been at once his strength and his weakness that Warren is a critic (and professor and poet) as well as a novelist. One must think of him, perhaps, primarily as novelist, of the novel as the single form, or medium, in which he is most effective. But the effects of his other activities are everywhere apparent in the fiction, and ultimately inseparable from whatever total effect any one of the novels, as such, may achieve. In opposition to the recurrently fashionable, simplistic theory that the practice of criticism, especially academic criticism, is necessarily a hindrance to the novelist or poet, I would insist first on the strength that Warren as artist has derived from his critical awareness. If anything, the comparative shallowness and failure of control in the three latest novels would seem to have gone hand-in-hand with his slackening interest in strictly literary criticism and his temporary retirement from teaching. But the principal point to be established is that, for better or worse, the novels are not fully understandable without reference to the criticism—that the two minds, of the poet-novelist and the critic, are identical.

Warren, in short, is first of all the artist of intellectual self-awareness and sophistication. This is his essential difference from Faulkner.

What the essay on Faulkner amounts to is a definition and defense of regionalism. It was inevitable that Faulkner's work be discovered, sooner or later, as the supreme embodiment of the virtues of the Southern regionalism for which Warren has long been one of the principal theoretical spokesmen. But it is also important to realize that he was, in fact, "discovered," and that it was, not sooner, but later; that Faulkner developed his art quite independently of the Fugitive and Agrarian movements, and in an entirely different intellectual atmosphere. Faulkner, back home in Oxford after the war and the brief flings at the expatriate artist's life in New York, New Orleans, and Paris, simply was—became, as it were, without thinking about it— what the Vanderbilt intellectuals were theorizing about.

It is not that Faulkner is any sort of "unconscious" artist, neither the rude, unlettered bard, nor the divine madman, that some commentators have made him out. He has, obviously, a better education than many, even quite recent and sympathetic, critics have given him credit for; and he is the most intensely careful of craftsmen in his writing. But (there is a difference between "unconsciousness" and "unselfconsciousness") he is intellectually naïve, naïve, specifically, as regionalist, in a way that probably no novelist, no Southern novelist, beginning his career as Warren did even one decade later, and certainly no one of Warren's intelligence, could be again.

Faulkner is not simply regionalist, but thoroughgoing pastoralist. For him (at least in the novels of his great period—the later things, from *Intruder in the Dust* on, are another matter) the region is pure myth, fable, a world whole and entire in itself, in which as artist he can live without ever the remotest desire to inquire into other, possible modes of existence, the order of other, different societies in other places. His novels achieve their universality of significance precisely, if paradoxically, by virtue of their intense and exclusive concentration on the regional society. There is only Yoknapatawpha County—and, vaguely of a piece, the world outside. The region of the myth is threatened by history, by intrusive influences from the outside world, but there is no real sense of its being itself part and product of that history.

But Faulkner's is very probably the last such regional synthesis that we shall see in American literature, the last in any way realistic and believable representation of the Southerner as "a different kind of American," of the South as actually constituting a "region" in the sense of distinct cultural community. To the regional theorists of the Twenties and Thirties—for only a cause already consciously "lost" could have produced such a movement as Fugitivism, and the clear cogency as well as the eloquence of the essays of *I'll Take My Stand*—the South was all too obviously back in the current of history. And this historical awareness, the awareness that regionalism could be adhered to now only as idea, is apparent from the first in Warren's development as novelist.

The essay on Faulkner does, as I have said, furnish a commentary on Warren himself. The critical study probably represents a background of interest and acceptance of influence that goes back farther than the writing of *All the King's Men*. And he could derive from his appreciation of two essential truths of Faulkner's art—that of the relationship between the realism and the legend in Faulkner's treatment of the "South," the way in which Yoknapatawpha County functions as the world's stage, and that of his handling of time relationships, the fact that for Faulkner "the 'truth' is neither of the past nor of the future . . . [but] of both"—principles of order for his own fiction. But they were principles that had to be readapted, to the purposes of the new historical consciousness.

Several aspects of Warren's practice might be explicated in these terms, each one of which probably calls for a separate essay. For one thing, there is the characteristic grounding of the fiction in some matter of more or less public, historic record, whether of past or near-present. The whole problem of the relationship between historical and fictive (or poetic) truth is one that has a kind of direct and immediately conscious fascination for Warren that it never has for Faulkner. There is the generally more cosmopolitan variety of types among his characters, and, related to this, even in the fictions that recreate the more remote past of the South, a sense of the comparatively easy accessibility of other regions. There is the distinctly un-Faulknerian manner in which he, the author—whether in the mask of a Jack Burden or more openly in the commentaries counterpointing Jeremiah Beaumont's diary entries—puts himself directly "on stage." There are various features of the stylistic practice—in which, of course, the structure of attitudes is necessarily involved—including, in addition to what he accepts from the great regionalist, certain influences from the writer who with his expatriate, journalistic internationalism and deliberate poverty of language is Faulkner's most direct opposite among the novelists of the post-World-War-I generation, Ernest Hemingway. There is the conscious and deliberate, almost scholarly adherence to traditional principles of structure, as for example in the striving for an authentic tragic form in *All the King's Men* that Robert Heilman has pointed out. There is—related, obviously, both to the tragic sense and to the historical awareness, the heightened, post-Faulknerian consciousness of the breakup of the regional culture—his central concern with what might be called the public dimension of human affairs, and with the relationship between the public and private selves of man. This concern is most apparent, most at the surface, in *All the King's Men;* but it is actually of no lesser importance in any of the other novels.

But the problem I want specifically to take up here, with a brief reconsideration of the structure of *All the King's Men,* illustrates perhaps better than any other that self-conscious intellectuality of which I have spoken as distinguishing Warren from the naïve fabulist, Faulkner. This is the problem of his dialectic sense.

The theme that has principally exercised his imagination is that of the incompleteness of man, the struggle to reconcile the idea and the need of unity with the facts of multiplicity in human experience. He has, on the one hand, an immense fascination with the varieties of human possibility, with man becoming. But, opposed to this—Warren's formulation of the problem is, I think, basically a moral one—there is the old Hawthornean, post-Puritan hatred of hypocrisy, the profound feeling that man, a man, should *be* what he seems. And it is from this opposition that the peculiar tension of his fiction derives—the conflict between the psychological and merely sensual, human richness of the story, with its endless complications of mere plot, that threatens continually to get out of hand, and the continually and rather desperately reimposed philosophical order, the precarious balancing of antinomies.

If *All the King's Men* must share honors with *World Enough and Time* as Warren's finest work, the earlier novel still remains the better known; and I have chosen to discuss it for this reason, that being so it is the more readily available for treatment in a short essay. But we might well begin consideration of the theme of the dialectic with some reference to that element of the work which was the principal ground of its great popular success—what Warren himself called its "journalistic relevance"—and to the ultimate exploitation of this in the film based on the novel.

The most significant thing Hollywood "did to" the book in preparing a movie script was to subordinate the role of Jack Burden. Burden is all but a supernumerary character in the film, largely the ghostly voice of the narrator offstage, now and again fitted with a form and face to appear briefly as one of the crowd around Willie Stark.

In short, the moviemakers cut the design of the work neatly in half, reducing it to a straightforward story of Willie Stark as man of action, indeed to what the cover blurb of one paperback edition calls it: "the world-famous American novel of power and corruption, and the meteoric rise and fall of Willie Stark—politician."

But in so doing, they accomplished something really impossible. For without Jack Burden, Willie is not the same man. Somewhat consciously after the example of Conrad, say, in *Heart of Darkness*, and of Fitzgerald in *The Great Gatsby*, Warren created in the two of them, Willie and Jack, a composite hero—the man of action *and* the man of reflection—neither side of whom is intelligible apart from the other. It is precisely the occasion of the tragedy, the tragic aspect of the age which the book represents, that the hero should have to be divided into the two persons.

This, if anything, is the large, central theme of the novel: the familiar theme of the dissociation of sensibility, the split of consciousness, in modern man. It is stated, of course, succinctly, in the allusive title. "Humpty-Dumpty sat on a wall / Humpty-Dumpty had a great fall / And all the King's horses and all the King's men / Couldn't put Humpty together again." And with reference to this miniature of the classic situation of tragedy— the hero raised to a height of success and honor, and then falling, from the "wall" of some precarious balance between opposed purposes or motives in his career—it is both Willie and Jack, we must realize, who are Humpty.

And, indeed, the hero, this Humpty-Dumpty, Shem-and-Shaun, is not simply doubled, but doubled and redoubled. Behind the two principals are other, more or less two-dimensional characters whose oppositions shadow the primary antithesis.

There is Tiny Duffy, the lieutenant governor, whom Willie keeps with him as a reminder of what he himself could become if he loses the direction of his purpose. Jack at one point speaks directly of Duffy as Willie's "other self . . ." and of how

". . . all the contempt and insult which Willie Stark was to heap on Tiny Duffy was nothing but what one self of Willie Stark did to the other self because of a blind, inward necessity." And again, in a variation on the nursery-rhyme imagery:

*The Boss had busted Tiny Duffy and then he had picked up the pieces and put him back together again as his own creation. He must have taken a lot of pleasure in looking at Tiny's glittering rig and diamond ring, and thinking that it was all hollow, that it was a sham, that if he should crook his little finger Tiny Duffy would disappear like a whiff of smoke. . . . In a way, Tiny's success was a final index of the Boss's own success.*

And, earlier, in the description of the first election campaign— when Willie has finally discovered that he is being used by one political faction as a decoy candidate, to split the opposition— there is an hilariously pathetic episode in which the fat Duffy, pushed off the speaker's platform by the drunk and revengeful Willie, teeters precariously for an instant on the edge of the stand before crashing to the ground—enacting here, obviously, a slapstick comic version of the Humpty role.

Behind Jack, on the other hand, is the idealistic doctor, Willie's assassin, Adam Stanton. Adam represents, in extreme and ultimately impossible purity, the ideals of personal integrity and selfless humanitarianism which Jack has held onto under his mask of breezy cynicism, and which he risks in his association with Stark. It is Adam whom Jack himself sees as the antagonist of Willie. Speaking of himself in the third person, Jack records, toward the end of the narrative, how

*he had seen his two friends, Willie Stark and Adam Stanton, live and die. Each had killed the other. Each had been the doom of the other. . . . Adam Stanton, whom he came to call the man of idea, and Willie Stark, whom he came to call the man of fact, were doomed to destroy each other, just as each was doomed to use the other and to yearn toward and try to become the other, because each was incomplete with the terrible division of the age.*

But the narrative, so to speak, needs these secondary characters, Jack Burden needs them, in order to project, in an abstractly simplified form for analysis, the problems of his own relationship with Willie. The situation he describes, of Adam's and Willie's doomed opposition, their mutual attraction and repulsion, their complementary incompletenesses, is simply a condensed, as it were disinterested, view of the way Jack and Willie stand toward each other.

There are certain complications of the scheme that need to be taken into account. In order, for example, to keep the composite, Humpty-Dumpty identity of Willie and Jack intact, Jack must be made finally to identify, in some sense, with Tiny Duffy. He must see, as he does when he has first been tempted to put the finger on Duffy as Willie's betrayer, or later, to take a more subtle pleasure of vengeance in withholding the information he has, that in condemning Duffy he inevitably condemns himself, that they are "twins . . . bound together forever." And in the first passage I have quoted concerning the relationship of the Boss and Tiny, how Willie had "busted him . . . and then picked up the pieces and put him back together again as his own creation," there is a prophetic, moral irony at Willie's expense. We are to see that it is not Warren, but Willie, with his distortion of Puritan morality, who has made a two-dimensional character of Duffy; and that in so doing, in assuming the godlike role of destroyer and creator, in failing to recognize Duffy's fellow-humanity, he projects his own doom. But, although this point is enforced again and again—in Burden's later reflections on Tiny, his several times renewed surprise in discovering that "the Boss's poodle . . . the funny fat man . . . the cartoon character" is human—the reinforcement is a little too insistent to be dramatically convincing, and the fact remains that Duffy (as well, I think, as Adam Stanton) never emerges as a full, fictive personality, but only as a more or less variable "term" in the "argument" of the book.

In the representation of the two main characters, of course, psychological realism, probability, requires a complexity of personality that necessarily obscures the philosophical dialectic, so that the latter must be shadowed forth on the screen of the action of the minor figures. There is something, consciously, of the man of reflection in Willie himself, certainly, as in the comparable figure of *Heart of Darkness*, Kurtz, something of the man of eloquence, as well as the man of action. Thus it is not altogether by "blind necessity" here, but by a more deliberate and knowing sympathy, that he is attracted to Jack. And in Burden there is a similar, conscious yearning for participation in the world of action—evidenced in the first place by his having turned his power of language to the uses of journalism instead of going on with his career as historian. Further, since the story is told throughout in the first person by Jack, he is too directly and self-interestedly involved to be represented convincingly as able to analyze his relationship to Stark without some means of objectifying, mirroring it, in other relationships.

(One might legitimately be tempted at this point to undertake some reflections on the relationship between narrator and author, and the character of Burden as "mask" for Warren. And I offer, incidentally, for whatever it may be worth, the suggestion that in the career of Jack—the historian turned journalist-political aide whose earlier academic research can be, ironically, completed only in and through his work in the latter role—there is an image, and effort at justification, of Warren's own history of the professor turned novelist. But that, as I have said, is the subject of another essay. We have here, meanwhile, to pursue the pattern of characterization into other elements of the book's structure.)

Corresponding to the two parts of the hero are the two worlds of the novel. There is the world of the gullied red-clay hills, the cut-over pine country, of Mason City and its tin-roofed little houses "with the sad valentine lace of gingerbread work around the eaves of the veranda," the world of the red-neck farmers, the "hick" world of Willie Stark.

And there is the world of Jack Burden's origin: the quiet and mannerly world of the low country, of Burden's Landing; the aristocratic world of the Stantons and the Irwins, where people dress for dinner, and belong to tennis clubs, where Judge Irwin sits in the leather-upholstered armchair in his library and makes miniatures of medieval siege weapons, and has his whisky brought to him on a silver tray.

The "burden" of Jack Burden is to find the means of access between the two worlds—with and through, of course, Willie Stark. And the action of the story is suspended, as it were, between the two worlds, on the soft-sprung wheels of Willie's Cadillac. The novel opens—as someone has pointed out, in what is by now a convention of modern Southern fiction (actually, it is a convention of modern American fiction)—upon the road, with the episode of a visit by Stark, comparatively late in his public career, to his father's home outside Mason City.

The recurrent emphasis of the imagery is upon the automobile, which operates here with an extension of approximately the same symbolic values, sexual and sociological, that it has in Fitzgerald, say, or again in Faulkner.

*For this is the country where the age of the internal combustion engine has come into its own . . . where the eight-cylinder jobs come roaring around the curves in the red hills and scatter the gravel like spray, and when they ever get down in the flat country and hit the new slab, God have mercy on the mariner.*

And the mood established in this first section—the account of the trip first to Stark's father's home and then, during the night, to Burden's Landing, for Willie to pay his call on Judge Irwin—symbolically defines the psychological and intellectual situation of the narrator throughout the action. (We may observe how certain details of imagery are carried over from one episode to the next to enforce the ironic connection of the two worlds, and the continuity of Burden's consciousness, as for example in his mental picture first of an hypothetical farm woman lying in the bedroom of one of the country houses of the Mason City area, and then of his mother asleep behind the jalousied windows of her elegant big house as they roll past along the bay road.)

Burden's story is a story of search, the quest for identity, again. He is always on the road, always reliving the journey. He is the Ancient Mariner. (Warren has not been content to present the automobile merely as automobile, but points up the implicit symbolism with a recurrent, nautical metaphor—the cars that "scatter the gravel like spray . . . and . . . God have mercy on the mariner," and Willie's limousine that is "a cross between a hearse and an ocean liner.") Even at the end, married to Anne Stanton and living again in Burden's Landing—but not with any prospect of permanence, Jack is careful to make it clear—he is "back home," has "landed his burden," only about as decisively, let us say, as Odysseus returned to his true Penelope, lying awake all night to tell his tales.

For the end, of course—observe the Faulknerian, Fitzgeraldian, Conradian, Coleridgean, the Homeric, time-scheme of the narration—is the beginning. Jack Burden, within the rather obvious father-search pattern of his career, is in his relationship to Willie both Odysseus and Telemachus by turns. (One can hardly miss the significance of the transformation of Stark from "Cousin Willie," the "plowboy" and "teacher's pet," who was glad to meet "*Mr.* Burden" to "the Boss" who, when some years later they reminisce about the occasion of their first encounter, specifically addresses Jack as "boy.") And the traditionally opposed, symbolic values of the two worlds—the innocence, simplicity, purity, and potency ordinarily associated with the high country, and the perverse decadence and guile, the sterility of the low country (compare the relatively straightforward acceptance of the convention in Hemingway's A *Farewell to Arms*)—are exchanged and re-exchanged four or five times in the course of Burden's readjustment of his moral perspectives.

But mention of the time-structure of the novel brings us to one final set of correspondences. The two worlds of Stanton and Stark represent, respectively, the past and the present. And these in turn (to use the pair of terms that Jack chooses for defining the dialectic opposition of Adam and Willie) correspond roughly to idea and fact.

Before turning reporter, i.e., before entering the world of the present and factuality, Jack had been an aspiring historian, working on a doctoral dissertation, never completed, to be based on the private papers of his Civil Wartime "ancestor," Cass Mastern. And it is in an ironic version of this role that he undertakes, for Willie Stark, the research into the past life of Judge Irwin and the Stantons that leads him, first, to the dirt on the Judge that Willie wanted—the evidence of corruption in the politics of the old, aristocratic order that Jack had once so desperately supposed to be entirely pure and noble—and, finally, to the discovery that he himself is the bastard son of

Irwin, not, as he had supposed, of that one of his mother's many husbands whom he calls the Scholarly Attorney.

This, of course, is an essential part of the novel's plot. It is the means by which Jack comes to his final understanding of the relationship between the two worlds, of how "this time came out of that time," and of what has been wrong with his relationship to his mother, and so, in turn, to Anne Stanton. It is the basis of his final acceptance of "the awful responsibility of Time," and so of the completion of the traditional, tragic design in the novel, with the postclimactic, hopeful look to the future at the end. It also provides one of the essential springs to the double catastrophe—the death (with his assassin) of Willie Stark, and the suicide of Judge Irwin—in which Jack has, not once but twice, found his "father" only by killing him. If Jack had not dug up the dirt, found the blotch on the Irwin and Stanton scutcheon, then Adam would never have been provided the immediate motivation for the shooting, nor Judge Irwin that for his suicide.

But back of all this is the question of the significance, for Jack, and for Warren's total design in the novel, of the Cass Mastern story itself. The problem is extremely complex, and we can make no pretense to a treatment of it in all aspects. One thing that seems to me very important, however, and that has not been noted, so far as I know, in the published commentaries on the novel, is that this is about the only place, in this eminently Southern work, that the racial problem, as such, is touched upon.

Between the main action of the novel and the Mastern story—of the conflict of idealism and passion, of a man's betrayal of his friend to his death, of the punishment of the innocent by the guilty for their own projected guilt, of the ironic selfishness of remorse, of the hero's final self-immolation and death in the service of a public cause whose principles he cannot support—there are a number of obvious, and very interesting, parallels. But the one point I want to make here is a negative one: that, for the function of the episode in the total structure of the book, it is not a matter of first importance that the story involves the problems of the injustice of slavery.

The view of the sociologically minded critic would be that any novel about the "South" which pretends to "realism" and "seriousness," any Southern novel of "conscience," must take into central account the question of race relations. But Warren's kind of regionalism, his kind of realism, makes him no more concerned to satisfy this demand than he was to be true to the "facts" of Huey Long's career, and as a right-thinking citizen of the democracy accurately to portray the evils of demagoguery— his supposed failure in which raised such howls of dismay from the liberal, Eastern critics at the time of the book's appearance.

What we get through Jack Burden's handling of the Cass Mastern story is a kind of final synthesis of idea and fact, an alteration of the formula to something like the idea *of* fact. Or, to put the matter another way, the story provides Burden with the essential metaphor for his grasp of the truth of human dependency and the moral universe, specifically, his metaphor of the world as the great web, about which he tells us Mastern learned through his sin and its consequences, that "if you touch it, however lightly, at any point, the vibration ripples to the remotest perimeter." But the whole story, actually, is metaphor, or parable—which is the precise kind of story it is, about that time and place and the circumstances of that society, in order to give Jack the farthest possible, but still personal, reach into the past, a past even beyond the time of Judge Irwin and Governor Stanton, to learn that the human condition was always the same, that "any this time came out of any that." The fact that the innocent victims of Mrs. Duncan's and Mastern's sin (and of his misdirected remorse) were Negro slaves, has neither more nor less significance than that, for example, Christ's parable of the Good Samaritan is based on a then-current and familiar situation of social prejudice among the Jews.

Rich though the novel is in its representation of the particularities of time and place, Warren is concerned primarily to present the relationship of two men, Jack and Willie, in a tragic situation of incomplete and belated understanding, a failure of communication, which is the universal situation of modern man. The fatal incompleteness of the human relationship in the white-Negro, master-slave situation, with which Jack in the parable identity of Cass Mastern is momentarily concerned, is only one, not necessarily even the most important, historical manifestation of the permanent failure.

At the end of the book, Jack Burden has "adopted" old Ellis Burden—his "notfather," as we might in Faulknerian phrase call him—as the only one of his "million fathers" with whom he can live. And I suppose the final, retrospective irony is that, through his discovery that he is Judge Irwin's bastard, not the son of the Scholarly Attorney, Jack learns that Cass Mastern was not even, as he had supposed, his ancestor.

The central, regionalist preoccupation of Faulkner is with blood, with the bloodline, with the themes of incest and miscegenation. For Warren, these are characteristically only instrumental concerns, toward the final expression of an almost terrifyingly abstract moral vision, whereby the ultimate significance of the human drama is discoverable only within the shadow play of the dialectic. Whatever the affinity he felt for the man of the papers and the photograph, Jack Burden must learn, it was something at once thinner and stronger than blood.

# *Afterword*

In the final paragraphs of the Introduction, I issued a warning to the reader, that he was not to expect in the volume as a whole any systematic approach to the problem indicated by the title. The book, I said, is a book of "responses, of appreciations . . . , and of judgments—not a book of demonstrations." If anyone thought that this warning was something in the nature of Mark Twain's "Notice" to readers of *Huckleberry Finn*, a come-on by way of prohibition, I trust he is by now disabused.

I have undertaken to present a collection of essays, in the sense of an inquiry, or series of inquiries, as loosely organized, as tentative and open-minded, albeit as earnestly probing, as the term "essay" will permit. And I come now, in the same spirit, to nothing like a formal conclusion, but only to a kind of recapitulation which even in itself is meant to reveal more what might have been done than what has been done, which is more about the ten or twelve books I might have written (might have wanted to write) than the one I have written. I want, in brief, to leave the reader with the whole subject of the book once more entirely opened up, rather than closed.

The tentative character of the approach is somewhat imposed, as I have already suggested, by the nature of the theme itself. In modern man—that, in Marcel's phrase again, "assemblage of functions"—the very sense of selfhood has been so far obscured that in setting out upon the quest for identity we can have only the vaguest intimation of what it is we are seeking. We are all in the situation of the first of our heroes here, Charles Marlow, having only the fact that we find ourselves searching to assure us that the search has an object, and no means whatever of determining whether we are looking in the right direction. This panther we have pursued through the foregoing pages is of so subtle an essence as to have left over wide tracts of the fictive landscape no spoor at all distinguishable as hers alone. It is inevitable that, in nosing about to pick up the trail, we should have scared out of hiding all manner of other, formidable thematic quarry which could be either subdued or eluded only by the most elaborate and exhausting maneuvers.

But I believe every one of the other themes we have dealt with (or failed to deal with) is, essentially, comprehended by the title theme. Or, if "comprehended by" seems still to claim too much, I may say that they are all comprehensible *in terms of* this central concern with the discovery of self.

There is, first of all, the theme of loneliness. It is more, for every one of the heroes of the novels we have read, than a simple matter of being or feeling companionless in the world. I am speaking rather of that, it seems to me, peculiarly and incomparably modern terror, the loneliness of self-estrangement. Every one of our heroes (and heroines) undergoes at one point or another the experience, in attempting directly to contemplate himself, of facing the stranger, the mask, or the simple nothingness—"panic and emptiness."

Or the one man (Stephen Dedalus, Jack Burden, Paul Morel) may sense within himself the potential presence of many men, all as it were pleading for recognition and acceptance; and be driven to the task of choosing his identity from among the several suppliants—no one of whom can be rejected without intolerable anguish. Or again, he may have many different identities in the eyes of different observers. In the case of characters like Kurtz and Gatsby, this is a fairly simple device of suspense—i.e., for keeping the *reader* in suspense, while the alter-hero narrator makes his way through the deceptions to a final confrontation with the "real" man. But in the characterization of Willie Stark, for example, we have the sense of the man's own, confused groping among these various selves, images of himself, proffered from the outside by other people, and attempting to make a choice.

In several of the novels, we have encountered the problem of the divided hero. *Heart of Darkness, The Great Gatsby, All the King's Men.* These are novels in which the "I" of the narrative attempts primarily to define himself in relationship to the "him," the "other," who has an actual, separate, physical identity. And yet, in the latter two books, if not the first, there is considerable evidence that the two different, fictive persons of the composite hero are created from different aspects of the author's personality. The dramatically explicit fact of Burden's strange affinity for Stark, Carraway's for Gatsby, can be tested with reference to an implicit purpose of self-examination, self-justification, on the part of their creators.

And if this should seem too deliberately to risk the dangers of the "biographical heresy," in other instances there is really no avoiding the obligation to include that of the author among the selves with which we are concerned. "Heresies" notwithstanding, the problem of the relationship between author and hero is, I think, a fundamental question of form in any novel. (The strictly formalist critic's very refusal to deal with it is a way of acknowledging its importance.) But it demands special attention in such books as Lawrence's *Sons and Lovers* and Joyce's *Portrait*, which we recognize as fictive accounts of some considerable portion of the authors' lives—in which each seems to have attempted to define the essential continuity of himself among the accidental circumstances of his existence.

But even where these particular problems do not present themselves—and we are concerned with questions, for example, of the influence of one novelist on another, or of the place of a certain work in the author's career as a whole, or of its relation to the character of the society in which he lived—in no instance have we necessarily departed from the guiding theme. For all of these interests are directly related to the task of defining the artistic self of the writer that is presented in his works—the self that is identical with his total vision. In *Light in August*, unlike some of his other books, there is no character who very closely resembles the "real-life" Faulkner. But the town and the countryside, the entire citizenry, the entire atmosphere of a region and an era, the idiom of a people's prejudice and humor—all those, besides the rhythms of the prose, the fictive method, are all "Faulkner." They are "Faulkner," as distinguishable from "Warren," or from "Hemingway." They are earlier Faulkner, as opposed to later Faulkner.

The theme of the father search is obviously involved. More or less prominently, it is present in nearly every one of the novels represented. It easily could have become, if I had permitted it, the central theme of the study. But I shall allow the essay on *A Portrait of the Artist as a Young Man* to carry the burden of my conviction that this is, in fact, only one aspect of the major quest, and not simply another and as good a name for the whole, same thing; that, in effect, one's father is truly not the same person as one's self, and that much mischief has been done in modern criticism (and the modern world in general) by our wanting to think that he is.

I have included only one, outright "conversion" novel, *Brideshead Revisited*. But, metaphorically at least, the Christian idea of rebirth, the taking on of a totally new identity through an experience of spiritual enlightenment, informs the careers of several of the heroes—Marlow, and Jack Burden, for example. It is by no means only in the novels of Faulkner, with their Christ figures and specific, Biblical analogues, that the outline of the Christian myth is dimly discernible in the formal conception.

We have several times engaged the theme of the alteration, loss, exchange, and merging of identities in the love relationship. I mean now, in distinction from the central concern in such novels as *Heart of Darkness*, particularly the love of man and woman: in *Sons and Lovers*, *A Farewell to Arms*, *Howards End*, *To the Lighthouse*, and others. Related to this is the theme of the ambivalence of sexual identity—of the woman-in-the-man and the man-in-the-woman—not only in the obvious forms of the homosexual yearnings of Rinaldi and the desire of Catherine to take on the male characteristics of Frederick in *A Farewell to Arms*, but in such more subtle statements as the opposition of the male and female principles, the active and the passive, in the personality of Paul Morel, or Stephen Dedalus' use of the gestation metaphor for the process of artistic creation. The final rejection of sexuality as an essential determinant of self, in the characterization of Lily Briscoe, is a negative statement of the same theme.

There is Mr. Sean O'Faolain's theme of the vanishing hero. I have taken leave here to use precisely the author to whom O'Faolain attributes the most nearly intact, modern vision of the tragic hero, Ernest Hemingway, as my principal example of the loss of that vision. I suggest that the reason for this particular mistake of O'Faolain's is that his book was conceived in the initial error of an attempt to isolate the problem of the disappearance of the hero from the context of the general loss in our time of a reliable concept of the person. It is easier to detect the unheroic character of Hemingway's stand-ins, if one first sees that they are not people. But, apart from this specific problem, and example, the *rhetoric* of the antiheroic in modern literature in general, as device of self-effacement toward self-discovery, is clearly our concern.

I think further, in relation to heroics and antiheroics, of the whole theme-complex of the waste land in modern literature: but specifically, of the identification of the modern Noman, in his Noman's Land, with traditional heroes. (Joyce, and Faulkner, and Fitzgerald.) It is safe to say, perhaps, although there are certain notable exceptions, that traditional references of this kind in the older novel tended to be "merely" metaphoric. The modern is satisfied with nothing less than complete, if oftentimes multiple, identification—that is, with establishing the truly *mythic* identity of the hero.

Closely related to this new mythography, if not simply another aspect of the same thing, is the new symbolism. It is, of course, most strikingly characteristic of all modern art that, in revolt against the "official" materialistic philosophies, it has rediscovered the world as symbol. Literally every object of sense-experience, as never before, signifies, is something more than itself, is imbued with awe. Any scarecrow a Christ; any paddler the holy swan. But specifically for our purposes, any landscape the "terrible paysage" of the mind, without benefit of opium; any journey the voyage into self, and not necessarily with the guidance of Freud. We begin, again, with Charles Marlow.

But perhaps the very philosophical center of the book is the essay on *To the Lighthouse*, with the consideration there of the problems of self and time. Sartre too, like Sean O'Faolain, is wrong in his choice of authors, when he writes about Faulkner's "decapitation of Time." What he attributes to Faulkner, the denial of the future, the dimension of moral choice, is much more true of Virginia Woolf. But, regardless of her particular shortcomings—or, if "shortcomings" is too hedging a term, regardless of the essential and final failure of vision which I have condemned in her novel—Mrs. Woolf's preoccupation with the Bergsonian idea of self-experience as identical with time-experience, consciousness in or of the *durée réelle*, is the central preoccupation of modern fiction.

The time-identity theme is complex, many-faceted, it assumes widely varied configurations in the works of different writers. But the essential unity is, although not always without difficulty, discoverable. In an extra-Bergsonian sense of the latter term, we have several times touched upon the problem of identity as duration. Many of our heroes—Marlow-Kurtz, Jack-Willie, Carraway-Gatsby, Stephen, Laura McRaven—are haunted, as Wordsworth only dreamed of being, by the simple question "Am I, now, what I was?" . . . twenty years ago, or whenever. The obsession is such, in the mind of a character like Faulkner's Quentin Compson, to amount to an identification of time with evil itself, with the Fall. Everywhere, there is the burden of T. S. Eliot's realization of the terrible trap between the intention and the act—how in a moment the conditions of choice are altered so as to render the decision meaningless before it is made—and of the corresponding, or identical, inadequacy of language, the poet's predicament of having "only learnt to get the better of words / For the thing one no longer has to say, or the way in which / One is no longer disposed to say it." The entire development of the so-called stream-of-consciousness technique in the modern novel, however varied its adaptations and various its philosophical sources, is a strategy of that time-war, a series of "raids on the inarticulate." And so is the technique of motif-structure, whereby the novel seeks to achieve something of the static, or nonprogressive, time-form of the lyric poem. In the older novel, the time-structure was usually conceived on the pattern of more or less *willed* action of the characters, action flowing in consequential form from thought and decision. With the breakdown in our times of the concept of the person as a responsible moral agent, such a form, plot in the standard sense, is inevitably and radically altered—or must be employed as conscious anachronism, and supported by some structure (such as motif) of extramoral significance.

We do, of course, still get a good deal of plot in serious novels. Not only the comparatively early *Howards End* but the works also of Robert Penn Warren, much later, furnish good examples. And these writers are fond too of reviving particular plot contrivances of the eighteenth- and nineteenth-century novel, the conventions of the "fatal chance." But the essential difference between, let us say, Warren's and the typical Victorian use of the bastardy theme, is that Warren's hero in some sense *never* finds out who he is. Or, if he does, the discovery is by no means identical with the discovery of his parentage.

Forster and Warren, and Fitzgerald, and Faulkner, are also much preoccupied with the problem of will—i.e., specifically, with the question of moral responsibility. For the three Americans, this concern is more or less co-extensive with their treatment of the "American dream," the notion, as I have previously defined it, of a man's capacity to *be* what he can *make* himself. But, although of course with considerable variation of statement, the handling of the idea in all of them is consistently ironic, with the emphasis on "dream"; and the hero's most definitive experience is much more likely to be one in which he is caught up in a pattern of all but totally inexplicable forces, operating from outside the sphere of calculable and controllable time, and with no final insight into the outcome, the catastrophe, as product of his own or anyone else's particular act of will, either reasoned or capricious.

The vulgar complaint is that the modern novel is one in which "nothing happens." And it is true that in all the novels we have dealt with the heroes are, in one way or another, like Charles Marlow of *Heart of Darkness*—not choosing but compelled to the "chance" encounter in which they find themselves committed to their destiny, and all the external actions, including their own, which they witness seeming significant only as "hints for nightmares," life to be resolved, if at all, only in the *bad* dream.

But, still, there are legitimate and necessary discriminations to be made. Marlow had at least his "choice of nightmares."

The implications for the view of man's moral nature are not the same in the works of all the different authors. The revolt against the tyrannical philosophies of materialism, of spatialized time, need not end in the desiccant aestheticism of Virginia Woolf, nor on the other hand in the stronger and more dignified, but yet more terrifying, abstract ethical passion of a Robert Penn Warren. We have witnessed the possibility of other, more humane choices. And to the extent that it is, still, all within the realm of nightmare, how can we, after all, pretend to be so sure that anything does, in our own "real," clock-timed lives, responsibly "happen"?

If what we are interested in is not self-appeasement but self-knowledge, we shall recognize the profound responsibility of these novelists, who refuse to tell us stories, at least to the present reality of man's predicament. In the very interest of recovering the place of man within the realm of chronological time—where the usurpations of scientism and industrialization have denied him an effective self, reduced him to an "assemblage of functions"—we shall welcome the nightmare. For there is no other way but that dark way, without clock, without compass, even to the certain knowledge that we have, indeed, lost something—which may be ourselves.

# *Notes*

### Introduction

*Page 6*: Marshall McLuhan, *The Gutenberg Galaxy* (Toronto: University of Toronto Press, 1962).

*Page 13*: Gabriel Marcel, "On the Ontological Mystery," *The Philosophy of Existentialism* (New York: Citadel Press, 1962).

*Page 14*: Gabriel Marcel, "The Need for Transcendence," *The Mystery of Being* ("Gateway Editions," Vol. I, chap. iii [Chicago: Henry Regnery Co., 1960]).

*Page 14*: John Edward Hardy, *The Curious Frame: Seven Poems in Text and Context* (Notre Dame, Indiana: University of Notre Dame Press, 1962).

*Page 14*: Marcel, "Truth as a Value: The Intelligible Background," *The Mystery of Being* (Vol. I, chap. iv).

### *Heart of Darkness*: The Russian in Motley

*Page 33*: F. R. Leavis, *The Great Tradition* (London: Chatto and and Windus, 1948).

*Page 33*: E. M. Forster, remarks on Conrad quoted by F. R. Leavis in *The Great Tradition*.

### *Howards End*: The Sacred Center

*Page 35*: Lionel Trilling, *E. M. Forster* (Norfolk, Conn.: New Directions Books, 1943).

*Page 43*: K. W. Gransden, *E. M. Forster* (Edinburgh: Oliver and Boyd, 1962).

*Page 48*: *Ibid.*, p. 55.

*Page 49*: Trilling, *E. M. Forster*, p. 135.

### *Sons and Lovers*: The Artist as Savior

*Page 53*: Mark Spilka, *The Love Ethic of D. H. Lawrence* (Bloomington: Indiana University Press, 1955).

*Page 60*: *Ibid.*

*Page 64*: Harry Moore, remark on "quickly" quoted by Spilka, *The Love Ethic of D. H. Lawrence.*

*Page 64*: Spilka, *The Love Ethic of D. H. Lawrence.*

*Page 65*: Aldous Huxley (ed.), *The Letters of D. H. Lawrence* (London: William Heinemann, Ltd., 1932), p. 46.

*Page 66*: F. R. Leavis, *D. H. Lawrence, Novelist* (London: Chatto and Windus, 1955).

*Joyce's Portrait*: The Flight of the Serpent

*Page 71*: John Nims, "Dedalus on Crete," *Dedalus on Crete* (Los Angeles: St. Thomas More Guild, 1956).

*Page 71*: Hugh Kenner, *Dublin's Joyce* (Bloomington: Indiana University Press, 1956). My indebtedness to Kenner throughout this study of the *Portrait* is, I trust, apparent.

*Page 77*: *Ibid.*

*Page 80*: Nims, "Dedalus on Crete."

*Page 80*: I believe that the first reader to follow out the meanderings of the moocow's trail through the novel was my friend Mrs. Jean Kyle, in a paper written for my Joyce seminar some thirteen or fourteen years ago at the University of Oklahoma.

*The Great Gatsby*: One in Two

*Page 82*: James E. Miller, *The Fictional Technique of F. Scott Fitzgerald* (The Hague: M. Nijhoff, 1957).

*Page 93*: R. W. Stallman, "Gatsby and the Hole in Time," *Modern Fiction Studies*, I.

*To the Lighthouse*: Vision Without Promise

*Page 97*: Glenn Pedersen, "Vision in *To the Lighthouse*," *Publications of the Modern Language Association*, LXII.

*Page 100*: Bernard Blackstone, *Virginia Woolf* (New York: Harcourt, Brace and Co., 1949).

*Page 103*: James Hafley, *The Glass Roof* ("University of California Publications: English Studies" [Berkeley and Los Angeles: University of California Press, 1954]).

*Page 109*: Pedersen, "Vision in *To the Lighthouse*."

*Page 117*: *Ibid.*

*Page 118*: *Ibid.*

*Page 118*: Hafley, *The Glass Roof.*

A *Farewell to Arms*: The Death of Tragedy

*Page 130*: John Peale Bishop, "Homage to Hemingway," *Collected Essays of John Peale Bishop* (New York: Charles Scribner's Sons, 1948).

*Page 130*: Sean O'Faolain, *The Vanishing Hero* (London: Eyre and Spottiswoode, 1956).

*Page 132*: Carlos Baker, *Hemingway: The Writer as Artist* (Princeton, New Jersey: Princeton University Press, 1956).

*William Faulkner*: The Legend Behind the Legend

*Page 142*: Malcolm Cowley, "William Faulkner's Legend of the South," *Sewanee Review*, LIII.

*Page 142*: George Marion O'Donnell, "Faulkner's Mythology," *Kenyon Review*, I.

*Page 144*: Cleanth Brooks, "*Absalom, Absalom!*": The Definition of Innocence," *Sewanee Review*, LIX.

*Page 146*: Hyatt H. Waggoner, *William Faulkner* (Lexington: University of Kentucky Press, 1959).

*Page 146*: Irene Edmonds, "Faulkner and the Black Shadow," in *Southern Renascence: The Literature of the Modern South*, edited by Louis D. Rubin and Robert Jacobs (Baltimore, Maryland: The Johns Hopkins Press, 1953).

*Page 146*: There have been, of course, efforts to prove Faulkner a fumbling and tentative artist. This is the burden, for example, of Sean O'Faolain's Faulkner chapter in *The Vanishing Hero*. But O'Faolain's strictures, coupled as they are with his weird and snobbish fancy in the tale of the unidentified little old Southern lady who explained to him that Faulkner could not write very well because he knew the life only of the "poor white trash" of the region, will hardly suffice as the "demonstration" I require.

*Page 147*: Robert Jacobs, "Faulkner's Tragedy of Isolation," in *Southern Renascence*. In his essay "William Faulkner: The Passion and the Penance," in *South: Modern Southern Literature in Its Cultural Setting*, edited by Louis D. Rubin and Robert Jacobs (Doubleday Dolphin Books, 1961), Jacobs somewhat modified his views on the importance of religious symbolism in Faulkner, apparently in response to Waggoner's book.

*Page 147*: William Van O'Connor, "Protestantism in Yoknapatawpha County," in *Southern Renascence*. Within a year—in *The Tangled Fire of William Faulkner* (Minneapolis: University of Minnesota Press, 1954)—O'Connor too had partly changed his mind, and was willing to recognize the importance of Faulkner's religious references. But in neither O'Connor's nor Jacobs' thinking was there any basic shift of emphasis.

*Page 155:* John Edward Hardy, "An Antic Disposition" [On T. S. Eliot's *The Cocktail Party*], *Sewanee Review*, LXV.

*Page 156:* On Faulkner's use of the Christian myth, see also Claude-Edmonde Magny's argument that Faulkner's world is pre-Incarnational: *L'age du roman américain* (Paris: Editions du Seuil, 1948).

*Brideshead Revisited: God, Man, and Others*

*Page 166:* I use the term "romance" first in the sense simply of *roman*, novel—the kind of fiction that purports to represent the doings of real people in real places, in historical time—and only secondarily in the sense that Waugh's book is also a love story, or that it has certain elements of the "romantic," or exotic, such as the adventures of Sebastian with Kurt, the reminiscences of Oxford, the account of Lord Marchmain's life with his Italian mistress. My usage has nothing at all to do, of course, with the kind of distinction between "romance" and "novel" made by Richard Chase in *The American Novel and Its Tradition*.

*Delta Wedding: Region and Symbol*

*Page 175:* John Edward Hardy, "*Delta Wedding* as Region and Symbol," *Sewanee Review*, LX.

*Page 175:* Ruth M. Vande Kieft, *Eudora Welty* (New York: Twayne Publishers, 1962).

*Robert Penn Warren: The Dialectic of Self*

*Page 194:* This essay, in a slightly different form, appeared in the Autumn, 1960, issue of *Virginia Quarterly Review*.

*Page 194:* Robert Penn Warren, "William Faulkner," final version in Warren's *Selected Essays* (New York: Random House, 1958). This is considerably revised from the 1946 original in *The New Republic*, and various reprintings.

*Page 197:* Robert Heilman, "Melpomene as Wallflower: Or, The Reading of Tragedy," *Sewanee Review*, LV. Throughout the study of *All the King's Men* here, I have borrowed freely from Heilman's interpretation.

## Afterword

*Page 211:* Sean O'Faolain, *The Vanishing Hero* (London: Eyre and Spottiswoode, 1956).

*Page 212:* Jean-Paul Sartre, "Time in Faulkner: *The Sound and the Fury,*" in *William Faulkner: Two Decades of Criticism,* edited by Frederick J. Hoffman and Olga W. Vickery (East Lansing: Michigan State College Press, 1954).

# Index